'*Out of Place* is an intensely moving act of reclamation and understanding, a portrait of a transcultural and often painful upbringing written with wonderful vividness and unsparing honesty. To read it is to come to know [Said's] family and his younger self as closely as we know characters in literature, to be shown, intimately and unforgettably, what it has meant in the last half-century to be a Palestinian.' Salman Rushdie

'This is a fascinating book, written by a brave and gifted man.' Geoffrey Wheatcroft, *Sunday Telegraph*

'An intense and powerful evocation of childhood, a very personal search for identity in a disappearing Levantine world.' David Gilmour, Books of the Year, *Spectator*

'This delicate and candid memoir by a very private man moved me enormously. Written in 'counterpoint' to his illness (leukaemia) at times when he was recovering from chemotherapy, its importance may be measured by the ferocity of the public attempt which preceded and accompanied publication to discredit him as an authentic Palestinian voice.' Ahdaf Soueif, Books of the Year, *Independent*

'One of the most instructive features of this fine and beautifully written autobiography is the way Said stresses the essentially tolerant cosmopolitan nature of the "Levantine" outlook, always discernible underneath the tyrannies of colonial divide-and-rule or nationalistic hatreds . . . Said, whose mature metaphysics seems to me to be very close to Buddhism, states his admirable recipe for sanity in his very last sentence: "With so many dissonances in my life I have learned actually to prefer being not quite right and out of place." John Murray, *Independent on Sunday*

'It is a powerful and, at the most fundamental level, a thoroughly convincing statement about a man who has helped to illuminate our crisis-ridden world with its contradictions and complexities.' Malise Ruthven, *Times Literary Supplement*

OUT OF PLACE

Edward W. Said is one of the world's most influential literary and cultural critics. Professor of English and Comparative Literature at Columbia University, he is the author of eighteen books, including *Orientalism* (which was nominated for the National Book Critics' Circle Award), *Culture and Imperialism*, and *Beginnings*. He is also a music critic, opera scholar, pianist and the most eloquent spokesman for the Palestinian cause in the West.

Out of Place

A MEMOIR

EDWARD W. SAID

Granta Books
London

Granta Publications, 2/3 Hanover Yard, London N1 8BE

First published in Great Britain by Granta Books 1999
This edition published by Granta Books 2000

A CIP catalogue record for this book
is available from the British Library.

1 3 5 7 9 10 8 6 4 2

ISBN 1 86207 370 8

Typeset by M Rules

Printed and bound in Great Britain by Mackays of Chatham plc

To Dr. Kanti Rai and Mariam C. Said

CONTENTS

ACKNOWLEDGMENTS

THIS BOOK WAS WRITTEN MOSTLY DURING PERIODS OF ILL-
ness or treatment, sometimes at home in New York, sometimes while
enjoying the hospitality of friends or institutions in France and Egypt. I
began to work on *Out of Place* in May 1994 while I was recovering from
three early rounds of chemotherapy for leukemia. With unstinting
kindness and patience Dale Janson and the superb nurses of the Ambu-
latory Chemotherapy and Transfusion Unit at Long Island Jewish Hospital took care of me for the days, weeks, and months I spent in their
charge until I finished writing.

My family—Mariam, Wadie, Najla—bore with me throughout the
five years of work on my manuscript, plus of course my illnesses,
absences, treatments, and my generally all-round state of being hard to
put up with. Their humor, unconditional support, and strength made
the whole thing easier to live through, for me if not always for them,
and I am profoundly thankful.

My dear friend Richard Poirier, surely America's finest literary
critic, gave me early encouragement and read through various drafts, as
did Deirdre and Allen Bergson. To them I am genuinely indebted. To
Zaineb Istrabadi, my excellent assistant at Columbia, must go a prize for
deciphering my handwriting, reproducing it for me in readable form,
helping with numerous drafts, and always without impatience or a

disagreeable word. Sonny Mehta gave me his friendship and support, a rare publisher and comrade. Once again I would like to thank Andrew Wylie for seeing this work through from start to finish.

It is customary, even routine, to thank one's editors. In my case there is nothing pro forma about the feelings of affection, admiration, and gratitude I have for my friends Frances Coady of Granta and Shelley Wanger of Knopf. Frances helped me to see what I was trying to do, then made the most acute suggestions for sculpting a bulky, disorderly manuscript into a semblance of form. Always patiently and humorously, Shelley sat with and guided me as we went through hundreds of pages of often overwritten and inchoate prose.

Dr. Kanti Rai's redoubtable medical expertise and remarkable humanity kept me going while I wrote and eventually finished this book. From the beginning of my illness, he and Mariam Said cooperated benignly, and literally kept me from sinking. I gratefully dedicate this book to Mariam for her loving support and to Kanti for his humane skill and friendship.

E.W.S.

New York, May 1999

PREFACE

Out of Place IS A RECORD OF AN ESSENTIALLY LOST OR FOR-gotten world. Several years ago I received what seemed to be a fatal medical diagnosis, and it therefore struck me as important to leave behind a subjective account of the life I lived in the Arab world, where I was born and spent my formative years, and in the United States, where I went to school, college, and university. Many of the places and people I recall here no longer exist, though I found myself frequently amazed at how much I carried of them inside me in often minute, even startlingly concrete, detail.

My memory proved crucial to my being able to function at all during periods of debilitating sickness, treatment, and anxiety. Almost daily, and while also writing other things, my rendezvous with this manuscript supplied me with a structure and a discipline at once pleasurable and demanding. My other writing and my teaching seemed to take me far away from the various worlds and experiences of this book: clearly one's memory operates better and more freely when it isn't goaded into service by devices or activities deigned for that purpose. Yet my political writings about the Palestinian situation, my studies of the relationship of politics and aesthetics, specifically opera and prose fiction, and my fascination with the subject of a book I have been writing on late style (beginning with Beethoven and Adorno) must surely have fed into this memoir surreptitiously.

After I finished the manuscript, I made a trip to Jerusalem and then to Cairo in November 1998: I stayed in the former while I attended a conference on Palestinian landscape held at Bir Zeit, and I journeyed to Egypt to participate in the doctoral thesis defense of a gifted student of mine who teaches at Tanta University, fifty miles north of Cairo. I discovered anew that what had been a network of towns and villages in which all the members of my extended family had once lived was now a series of Israeli locales—Jerusalem, Haifa, Tiberias, Nazareth, and Acre—where the Palestinian minority lives under Israeli sovereignty. In parts of the West Bank and Gaza, Palestinians had self-rule or autonomy, but the Israeli army retained overall security control, nowhere more starkly than at borders, checkpoints, and airports. One of the routine questions I was asked by Israeli officials (since my U.S. passport indicated that I was born in Jerusalem) was exactly when after birth I had left Israel. I responded by saying that I left *Palestine* in December 1947, accenting the word "Palestine." "Do you have any relatives here?" was the next question, to which I answered, "No one," and this triggered a sensation of such sadness and loss as I had not expected. For by the early spring of 1948 my entire extended family had been swept out of the place, and has remained in exile ever since. In 1992, however, I was able for the first time since our departure in 1947 to visit the family-owned house where I was born in West Jerusalem, as well as the house in Nazareth that my mother grew up in, and my uncle's house in Safad, and so on. All of them had new occupants now, which for tremendously inhibiting and unspecifiable emotional reasons made it very hard and actually impossible for me to enter them once again, even for a cursory look.

While in Cairo during my November 1998 trip, I went to pay a call on our old neighbors Nadia and Huda, and their mother, Mrs. Gindy, who for many years lived three floors below us, on the second floor at 1 Sharia Aziz Osman. They told me that number 20, our old apartment, was empty and up for sale, but, having thought about it for a moment after they suggested buying it back, I felt no enthusiasm for reacquiring a place we had vacated almost forty years ago. A moment later Nadia and Huda said that before we had lunch, there was somebody waiting for me in the kitchen. Would I like to see him? A small, wiry man in the dark robe and turban of a formally dressed Upper Egyptian peasant came into the room. When told by the two women that this was the Edward he had patiently been waiting to see, he drew back, shaking his head. "No, Edward was tall, and he wore glasses. This isn't Edward." I had quickly recognized Ahmad Hamed, our *suffragi* (butler) for almost three decades, an ironic, fanatically honest and loyal man whom we had all considered a member of the family. I then tried to persuade him that it was indeed me, changed by illness and age, after thirty-eight years of absence. Suddenly we fell into each other's arms, sobbing with the tears of happy reunion and a mourned, irrecoverable time. He talked about how he had carried me on his shoulders, how we had chatted in the kitchen, how the family celebrated Christmas and New Year's, and so on. I was astounded that Ahmad minutely remembered not only the seven of us—parents and five children—but also each of my aunts, uncles, and cousins, and my grandmother, in addition to a few family friends. And then, as the past poured out of him, an old man retired to the distant town of Edfu near Aswan, I knew again how fragile, precious, and fleeting were the history and circumstances not only gone forever, but basically unrecalled and unrecorded except as occasional reminiscence or intermittent conversation.

This chance encounter made me feel even more strongly that this book, which revealed as much as I could of life lived in those days, mostly between 1935, the year of my birth, and 1962, when I had about completed my doctorate, had some validity as an unofficial personal record of those tumultuous years in the Middle East. I found myself telling the story of my life against the background of World War II, the loss of Palestine and the establishment of Israel, the end of the Egyptian monarchy, the Nasser years, the 1967 War, the emergence of the Palestinian movement, the Lebanese Civil War, and the Oslo peace process. These are in my memoir only allusively, even though their fugitive presence can be seen here and there.

More interesting for me as author was the sense I had of trying always to translate experiences that I had not only in a remote environment but also in a different language. Everyone lives life in a given language; everyone's experiences therefore are had, absorbed, and recalled in that language. The basic split in my life was the one between Arabic, my native language, and English, the language of my education and subsequent expression as a scholar and teacher, and so trying to produce a narrative of one in the language of the other—to say nothing of the numerous ways in which the languages were mixed up for me and crossed over from one realm to the other—has been a complicated task. Thus it has been difficult to explain in English the actual verbal distinctions (as well as the rich associations) that Arabic uses to differentiate between, for example, maternal and paternal uncles; but since such nuances played a definite role in my early life I had to try to render them here.

Along with language, it is geography—especially in the displaced form of departures, arrivals, farewells, exile, nostalgia, homesickness, belonging, and travel itself—that is at the core of my memories of those early years. Each of the places I lived in—Jerusalem, Cairo, Lebanon, the United States—has a complicated, dense web of valences that was very much a part of growing up, gaining an identity, forming my consciousness of myself and of others. And in each place schools have a privileged place in the story, microcosms of the cities or towns where my parents found these schools and put me. Since I am myself an educator it was natural that I should have found the school environment particularly worth describing and telling about, although what I was not prepared for was how well I remembered the earlier institutions I attended, and how comparatively more the friends and acquaintances I had there have been a part of my life than those from university days, or my boarding school years in the United States. One of the things I tried to explore implicitly is the hold those very early school experiences had on me, why their hold persists, and why I still find them fascinating and interesting enough to write about for readers fifty years later.

The main reason, however, for this memoir is of course the need to bridge the sheer distance in time and place between my life today and my life then. I want only to mention this as an obvious fact, not to treat or discuss it, except to say that one of its results is a certain detachment and irony of attitude and tone, as I have set about reconstructing a remote time and experience. Several people described here are still alive and will likely disagree with or dislike my portrayals of them and others. Much as I have no wish to hurt anyone's feelings my first obligation has not been to be nice but to be true to my perhaps peculiar memories, experiences, and feelings. I, and only I, am responsible for what I recall and see, not individuals in the past who could not have known what effect they might have on me. I hope it is also clear that, both as narrator and as character, I have consciously not spared myself the same ironies or embarrassing recitals.

OUT OF PLACE

I

ALL FAMILIES INVENT THEIR PARENTS AND CHILDREN, GIVE each of them a story, character, fate, and even a language. There was always something wrong with how I was invented and meant to fit in with the world of my parents and four sisters. Whether this was because I constantly misread my part or because of some deep flaw in my being I could not tell for most of my early life. Sometimes I was intransigent, and proud of it. At other times I seemed to myself to be nearly devoid of any character at all, timid, uncertain, without will. Yet the over-riding sensation I had was of always being out of place. Thus it took me about fifty years to become accustomed to, or, more exactly, to feel less uncomfortable with, "Edward," a foolishly English name yoked forcibly to the unmistakably Arabic family name Said. True my mother told me that I had been named Edward after the Prince of Wales, who cut so fine a figure in 1935, the year of my birth, and Said was the name of various uncles and cousins. But the rationale of my name broke down both when I discovered no grandparents called Said and when I tried to connect my fancy English name with its Arabic partner. For years, and depending on the exact circumstances, I would rush past "Edward" and emphasize "Said"; at other times I would do the reverse, or connect these two to each other so quickly that neither would be clear. The one thing I could not tolerate, but very often would have to endure, was the disbelieving, and hence undermining, reaction: Edward? Said?

The travails of bearing such a name were compounded by an equally unsettling quandary when it came to language. I have never known what language I spoke first, Arabic or English, or which one was really mine beyond any doubt. What I do know, however, is that the two have always been together in my life, one resonating in the other, sometimes ironically, sometimes nostalgically, most often each correcting, and commenting on, the other. Each *can* seem like my absolutely first language, but neither is. I trace this primal instability back to my mother, whom I remember speaking to me in both English and Arabic, although she always wrote to me in English—once a week, all her life, as did I, all of hers. Certain spoken phrases of hers like *tislamli* or *mish ᶜarfa shu biddi ᶜamal?* or *rouhᶜ ha*—dozens of them—were Arabic, and I was never conscious of having to translate them or, even in cases like *tislamli,* knowing exactly what they meant. They were a part of her infinitely maternal atmosphere, which in moments of great stress I found myself yearning for in the softly uttered phrase *"ya mama,"* an atmosphere dreamily seductive then suddenly snatched away, promising something in the end never given.

But woven into her Arabic speech were English words like "naughty boy" and of course my name, pronounced "Edwaad." I am still haunted by the memory of the sound, at exactly the same time and place, of her voice calling me "Edwaad," the word wafting through the dusk air at closing time of the Fish Garden (a small Zamalek park with aquarium) and of myself, undecided whether to answer her back or to remain in hiding for just awhile longer, enjoying the pleasure of being called, being wanted, the non-Edward part of myself taking luxurious respite by not answering until the silence of my being became unendurable. Her English deployed a rhetoric of statement and norms that has never left me. Once my mother left Arabic and spoke English there was a more objective and serious tone that mostly banished the forgiving and musical intimacy of *her* first language, Arabic. At age five or six I knew that I was irremediably "naughty" and at school was all manner of comparably disapproved-of things like "fibber" and "loiterer." By the time I was fully conscious of speaking English fluently, if not always correctly, I regularly referred to myself not as "me" but as "you." "Mummy doesn't love you, naughty boy," she would say, and I would respond, in half-plaintive echoing, half-defiant assertion, "Mummy doesn't love you, but Auntie Melia loves you." Auntie Melia was her elderly maiden aunt, who doted on me when I was a very young child. "No she doesn't," my mother persisted. "All right. Saleh [Auntie Melia's Sudanese driver] loves you," I would conclude, rescuing something from the enveloping gloom.

I hadn't then any idea where my mother's English came from or who, in the national sense of the phrase, she was: this strange state of ignorance continued until relatively late in my life, when I was in graduate school. In Cairo, one of the places where I grew up, her spoken Arabic was fluent Egyptian, but to my keener ears, and to those of the many Egyptians she knew, it was if not outright Shami, then perceptibly inflected by it. "Shami" (Damascene) is the collective adjective and noun used by Egyptians to describe both an Arabic speaker who is not Egyptian and someone who is from Greater Syria, i.e., Syria itself, Lebanon, Palestine, Jordan; but "Shami" is also used to designate the Arabic dialect spoken by a Shami. Much more than my father, whose linguistic ability was primitive compared to hers, my mother had an excellent command of classical Arabic as well as the demotic. Not enough of the latter to disguise her as Egyptian, however, which of course she was not. Born in Nazareth, then sent to boarding school and junior college in Beirut, she was Palestinian, even though her mother, Munira, was Lebanese. I never knew her father, but he, I discovered, was the Baptist minister in Nazareth, although he originally came from Safad, via a sojourn in Texas.

Not only could I not absorb, much less master, all the meanderings and interruptions of these details as they broke up a simple dynastic sequence, but I could not grasp why she was not a straight English mummy. I have retained this unsettled sense of many identities—mostly in conflict with each other—all of my life, together with an acute memory of the despairing feeling that I wish we could have been all-Arab, or all-European and American, or all–Orthodox Christian, or all-Muslim, or all-Egyptian, and so on. I found I had two alternatives with which to counter what in effect was the process of challenge, recognition, and exposure, questions and remarks like "What are you?"; "But Said is an Arab name"; "You're American?"; "You're American without an American name, and you've never been to America"; "You don't look American!"; "How come you were born in Jerusalem and you live *here*?"; "You're an Arab after all, but what kind are you? A Protestant?"

I do not remember that any of the answers I gave out loud to such probings were satisfactory or even memorable. My alternatives were hatched entirely on my own: one might work, say, in school, but not in church or on the street with my friends. The first was to adopt my father's brashly assertive tone and say to myself, "I'm an American citizen," and that's it. He was American by dint of having lived in the United States followed by service in the army during World War I. Partly because this alternative meant his making of me something incredible, I found it the least convincing. To say "I am an American citizen" in an English school in wartime Cairo dominated by British troops and with what seemed to me a totally homogeneous Egyptian populace was a foolhardy venture, to be risked in public only when I was challenged officially to name my citizenship; in private I could not maintain it for long, so quickly did the affirmation wither away under existential scrutiny.

The second of my alternatives was even less successful than the first. It was to open myself to the deeply disorganized state of my real history and origins as I gleaned them in bits, and then to try to construct them into order. But I never had enough information; there were never the right number of well-functioning connectives between the parts I knew about or was able somehow to excavate; the total picture was never quite right. The trouble seemed to begin with my parents, their pasts, and names. My father, Wadie, was later called William (an early discrepancy that I assumed for a long time was only an Anglicization of his Arabic name but that soon appeared to me suspiciously like a case of assumed identity, with the name Wadie cast aside except by his wife and sister for not very creditable reasons). Born in Jerusalem in 1895—my mother said it was more likely 1893—he never told me more than ten or eleven things about his past, a series of unchanging pat phrases that hardly conveyed anything at all. He was at least forty at the time of my birth.

He hated Jerusalem, and although I was born and we spent long periods of time there, the only thing he ever said about it was that it reminded him of death. At some point in his life his father was a dragoman who because he knew German had, it was said, shown Palestine to Kaiser Wilhelm. And my grandfather—never referred to by name except when my mother, who never knew him, called him Abu-Asaad—bore the surname Ibrahim. In school, therefore, my father was known as Wadie Ibrahim. I still do not know where "Said" came from, and no one seems able to explain it. The only relevant detail about his father that my father thought fit to convey to me was that Abu-Asaad's whippings were much severer than his of me. "How did you endure it?" I asked, to which he replied with a chuckle, "Most of the time I ran away." I was never able to do this, and never even considered it.

As for my paternal grandmother, she was equally shadowy. A Shammas by birth, her name was Hanné; according to my father, she persuaded him—he had left Palestine in 1911—to return from the States in 1920 because she wanted him near her. My father always said he regretted his return home, although just as frequently he averred that the secret of his astonishing business successes was that he "took care" of his mother, and she in return constantly prayed that the streets beneath his feet would turn into gold. I was never shown her likeness in any photograph, but in my father's regimen for bringing me up she represented two contradictory adages that I could never reconcile: mothers are to be loved, he said, and taken care of unconditionally. Yet because by virtue of selfish love they can deflect children from their chosen career (my father wanted to remain in the United States and practice law), so mothers should not be allowed to get too close. And that was, is, all I ever knew about my paternal grandmother.

I assumed the existence of a longish family history in Jerusalem. I based this on the way my paternal aunt, Nabiha, and her children inhabited the place, as if they, and especially she, embodied the city's rather peculiar, not to say austere and constricted, spirit. Later I heard my father speak of us as Khleifawis, which I was informed was our real clan origin; but the Khleifawis originated in Nazareth. In the mid-1980s I was sent some extracts from a published history of Nazareth, and in them was a family tree of one Khleifi, probably my great-grandfather. Because it corresponded to no lived, even hinted-at, experience of mine, this startlingly unexpected bit of information—which suddenly gave me a whole new set of cousins—means very little to me.

My father, I know, did attend St. George's School in Jerusalem and excelled at football and cricket, making the First Eleven in both sports over successive years, as center forward and wicket keeper, respectively. He never spoke of learning anything at St. George's, nor of much else about the place, except that he was famous for dribbling a ball from one end of the field to the other, and then scoring. His father seems to have urged him to leave Palestine to escape conscription into the Ottoman army. Later I read somewhere that a war had broken out in Bulgaria around 1911 for which troops were needed; I imagined him running away from the morbid fate of becoming Palestinian cannon fodder for the Ottoman army in Bulgaria.

None of this was ever presented to me in sequence, as if his pre-American years were discarded by my father as irrelevant to his present identity as my father, Hilda's husband, U.S. citizen. One of the great set stories, told and retold many times while I was growing up, was his narrative of coming to the United States. It was a sort of official version, and was intended, in Horatio Alger fashion, to instruct and inform his listeners, who were mostly his children and wife. But it also collected and put solidly in place both what he wanted known about himself before he married my mother and what thereafter was allowed into public view. It still impresses me that he stuck to the story in its few episodes and details for the thirty-six years he was my father until his death in 1971, and that he was so successful in keeping at bay all the other either forgotten or denied aspects of his story. Not until twenty years after his death did it occur to me that he and I were almost exactly the same age when we, precisely forty years apart, came to the United States, he to make his life, I to be directed by his script for me, until I broke away and started trying to live and write my own.

My father and a friend called Balloura (no first name ever given) went first from Haifa to Port Said in 1911, where they boarded a British freighter to Liverpool. They were in Liverpool for six months before they got jobs as stewards on a passenger liner to New York. Their first chore on board was to clean portholes, but since neither of them knew what a porthole was, despite having pretended to "great sea-going experience" in order to get the jobs, they cleaned everything but the portholes. Their supervisor was "nervous" (a word my father used regularly to signify anger and general bother) about them, overturned a pail of water, and set them to floor swabbing. Wadie was then switched to waiting on tables, the only memorable aspect of which was his description of serving one course, then rushing out to vomit as the ship heaved and pitched, then staggering back to serve the next. Arriving in New York without valid papers, Wadie and the shadowy Balloura bided their time, until, on the pretext of leaving the ship temporarily to visit a nearby bar, they boarded a passing streetcar "going they had no idea where," and rode it to the end of the line.

Another of my father's much repeated stories concerned a YMCA swimming race at an upstate New York lake. This provided him with an engaging moral: he was the last to finish, but persisted to the end ("Never give up" was the motto)—in fact until the next race had already begun. I never questioned, and was duly submissive to, the packaged homily "Never give up." Then, when I was in my early thirties, it dawned on me that Wadie was so slow and stubborn he had in fact *delayed* all the other events, not a commendable thing. "Never giving up," I told my father—with the uppitiness of a recently franchised but still powerless citizen—could also mean a social nuisance, obstructing others, delaying the program, maybe even giving impatient spectators an opportunity to hoot and boo the offendingly slow and heedlessly stubborn swimmer. My father shot me a surprised, even slightly uncomfortable, smile, as if I had finally cornered him in a small way, and then he turned away without a word. The story was not repeated again.

He became a salesman for ARCO, a Cleveland paint company, and he studied at Western Reserve University. Hearing the Canadians were sending a battalion "to fight the Turks in Palestine," he crossed the border and enlisted. When he discovered that there was to be no such battalion he simply deserted. He then signed up for the American Expeditionary Force and was consigned to the rigors of Camp Gordon, Georgia, where his reaction to a battery of inoculations meant that he spent most of basic training ill and in bed. The scene then shifts to France, where he did time in the trenches; my mother had two photographs of him in the military dress of that time, a Cross of Lorraine hung round his neck in one of them, attesting to his French service. He used to speak of being gassed and wounded, then quarantined and interned in Mentone (he always used the Italian pronunciation). Once when I asked him what it was like to be in a war I recall him telling me about a German soldier whom he had killed at close range, "raising up his hands in a great cry before I shot him;" he said that he had recurring nightmares about the episode over several years of tormented sleep. After his death, when we had some reason to recover his army discharge papers (lost for half a century) I was stunned to discover that as a member of the quartermaster's corps he was recorded as having participated in no known military campaigns. This was probably a mistake, since I still believe my father's version.

He returned to Cleveland after the war and set up his own paint company. His older brother, Asaad ("Al"), was then working as a sailor on the Great Lakes. Even back then it was the younger brother, "Bill"—the name change occurred in the army—who supplied the older one with money and also sent his parents half his salary. Asaad once threatened to attack Bill with a knife: he needed more money from his prosperous younger brother in order to marry a Jewish woman, whom my father guessed that he abandoned but did not divorce when he suddenly also came back to Palestine in the twenties.

Curiously, nothing of my father's American decade survived except his extremely lean retellings of it, and such odd fragments as a love of apple pie à la mode and a few often repeated expressions, like "hunky-dory," and "big boy." Over time I have found that what his stint in the United States really expressed in relation to his subsequent life was the practice of self-making with a purpose, which he exploited in what he did and what he made others around him, chiefly me, do. He always averred that America was his country, and when we strenuously disagreed about Vietnam, he would fall back comfortably on "My country, right or wrong." But I never met or heard about friends or acquaintances from that time; there was one tiny photograph of Wadie at a YMCA camp plus a few laconic and uninformative entries in a soldier's log from the war year, 1917–18. And that was it. After he died I wondered whether, like Asaad, he hadn't had a wife and perhaps even a family that he too had left behind. Yet so powerfully instructive was his story for the shape my youth took under his direction that I cannot recall ever asking anything like a critical question.

After America the story gathers immediacy and somehow loses even a suggestion of Horatio Alger romance: it was as if, having returned to Palestine in 1920 armed with U.S. citizenship, William A. Said (formerly Wadie Ibrahim) had quite abruptly turned sober pioneer, hard-working and successful businessman, and Protestant, a resident first of

Jerusalem then of Cairo. This was the man I knew. The nature of the early relationship with his older cousin Boulos Said—who was also his sister Nabiha's husband—was never completely given, though clearly it was Boulos who founded the Palestine Educational Company, which Wadie entered (and invested in) on his return home. The two men became equal partners, although it was Wadie who in 1929 branched off from Palestine into Egypt, where, in a matter of no more than three years, he established the successful Standard Stationery Company, with two retail stores in Cairo, one in Alexandria, and various agencies and subdealerships in the Suez Canal Zone. There was a flourishing Syrian (Shami) community in Cairo, but he seems to have stayed clear of it, choosing instead to work long hours and play an occasional game of tennis with his friend Halim Abu Fadil; he told me that they played at two p.m., the hottest time of day, from which I was to conclude that an iron discipline, punishing in its rigors, ruled his efforts in everything he did, even sports.

My father alluded infrequently to those years before his marriage in 1932, but it seemed that fleshly temptations—Cairo's rococo nightlife, its brothels, sex shows, and opportunities for general profligacy offered to prosperous foreigners—were of little interest to him; his celibacy was virtuous and without a whiff of debauchery. My mother—who of course didn't know him then—used to tell how he would come home to his modest Bab el Louk flat, eat a solitary dinner, then spend the evening listening to classical records, reading his Home Library and Everyman's Library classics, which included many of the Waverley novels as well as the *Ethics* of G. E. Moore and Aristotle (during my adolescence and after, however, he confined his reading to works on war, politics, and diplomacy). He was well-off enough in 1932 to get married, and to take his much younger wife—she was eighteen and he was thirty-seven—for a three-month honeymoon in Europe. The marriage was brokered by my aunt Nabiha through her contacts in Nazareth and, to some degree, by my mother's aunt in Cairo, Melia Badr (Auntie Melia), a formidable spinster who with her amiable chauffeur, Saleh, became an important part of my childhood landscape. All these details came from my mother, who must have heard them as a sort of preparation for entering the state of matrimony with an older man she had not met, who lived in a place she knew virtually nothing about.

And then he turned into the model husband and father whose ideas, values, and of course methods were to shape me.

Whatever the actual historical facts were, my father came to represent a devastating combination of power and authority, rationalistic discipline, and repressed emotions; and all this, I later realized, has impinged on me my whole life, with some good, but also some inhibiting and even debilitating effects. As I have grown older I have found a balance between these effects, but from my childhood through my twenties I was very much controlled by him. With the help of my mother, he tried to create a world very much like a gigantic cocoon, into which I was introduced and maintained at, as I look back over it half a century later, exorbitant cost. What impresses me now is not that I survived it, but that by biding my time within his regime I somehow managed to connect the strengths of his basic lessons to my own abilities, which he seemed unable to affect, perhaps even to reach. What also remained of him in me, unfortunately, was his relentless insistence on doing something useful, getting things done, "never giving up," more or less all the time. I have no concept of leisure or relaxation and, more particularly, no sense of cumulative achievement. Every day for me is like beginning a new term at school, with a vast and empty summer behind it, and an uncertain tomorrow before it. Over time "Edward" became a demanding taskmaster, registering lists of flaws and failures with as much energy as accumulated obligations and commitments, the two lists balancing and in a sense canceling each other. "Edward" still has to begin every day anew and by the end of it normally feels that very little has gone right.

My mother was certainly my closest and most intimate companion for the first twenty-five years of my life. Even now, I feel imprinted and guided by several of her long-standing perspectives and habits: a paralyzing anxiety about alternative courses of action; chronic, mostly self-inflicted sleeplessness; a deep-seated restlessness accompanied by an unending supply of mental and physical energy; a profound interest in music and language as well as in the aesthetics of appearance, style, and form; a perhaps overelaborate sense of the social world, its currents, delights, and potential for happiness and grief; and finally, a virtually unquenchable, incredibly various cultivation of loneliness as a form both of freedom and of affliction. Were my mother to have been only a simple refuge, or a kind of intermittent safe haven, from the day's passage I cannot tell what the results might have been. But she had the most deep-seated and unresolved ambivalence toward the world, and me, I have ever known. Despite our affinities, my mother required my love and devotion, and gave them back doubled and redoubled; but she also could turn them away quite suddenly, producing in me a metaphysical panic I can still experience with considerable unpleasantness and even terror. Between my mother's empowering, sunlike smile and her cold scowl or her sustained frowning dismissiveness, I existed as a child both fortunate and hopelessly miserable, neither completely one nor the other.

She represented herself to me as an uncomplicated, gifted, loving, and beautiful young woman, and until I was twenty—when she was only forty—I saw her that way; if she abruptly turned into something else, I blamed myself. Later our relationship darkened a good deal. But for my early life I was in an enraptured state of precarious, highly provisional rapport with my mother, so much so that I really had no friends of my age, and my relationships with my younger sisters, Rosemarie, Jean, Joyce, and Grace, were attenuated and, to me at least, not very satisfactory. It was exclusively to my mother that I turned for intellectual and emotional companionship. She used to say that since her first child died in the hospital shortly after she gave birth to him, I was given extra doses of care and attention. But this excess could not disguise her strong underlying pessimism, which often neutralized her radiant affirmation of me.

Though for very different reasons, my mother, like my father, revealed very little about her origins and her past as I was growing up. Born in 1914, she was the middle child of five, the others being four boys, with all of whom I had highly problematic ties as my maternal uncles. Everyone who knew my mother in Nazareth concurs in her claim that she was her father's favorite; though she described him as a "good" man, he sounded to me unappealing, a fundamentalist Baptist minister who was both a harsh patriarch and a repressive husband. Hilda, my mother, was sent to boarding school in Beirut, to the American School for Girls, or ASG, a missionary institution that tied her to Beirut first and last, with Cairo as a long interlude between. Undoubtedly a star there and at the Junior College (now Lebanese American

University), she was popular and brilliant—first in her class—in most things. There were no men in her life, though, so thoroughly virginal was her existence in those two basically religious schools. Unlike my father, who seemed independent of all early attachments except for those of family, she maintained close friendships with classmates and contemporaries until her death: being a student in Beirut for five years was the happiest part of her life and stamped everyone and everything she knew or did then with a sense of lasting pleasure. Of someone whose company she enjoyed in the years after she was widowed she would say disappointedly and, to me, maddeningly, "Wadad is not really my friend, since she wasn't in school with me."

In 1932 she was plucked from what was—or was retrospectively embellished as—a wonderful life and the successes of Beirut and returned to dour, old Nazareth, where she was deposited into an arranged marriage with my father. No one of us today can have a full grasp of what that marriage was or how it came about, but I was trained by her—my father generally being silent on that point—to see it as something difficult at first, to which she gradually adjusted over the course of nearly forty years, and which she transformed into the main event in her life. She never worked or really studied again, except for taking French lessons in Cairo and, years later, a humanities course at her old Beirut college. There were stories of her anemia and seasickness on the honeymoon voyage, all of them interspersed with comments on my father's patience and kindness to her, the young, very vulnerable and naïve maiden-bride. She never spoke about sex without shuddering dislike and discomfort, although my father's frequent remarks about the man being a skilled horseman, the woman a subdued mare, suggested to me a basically reluctant, if also exceptionally fruitful, sexual partnership that produced six (five surviving) children.

But I also never doubted that at the time of her marriage to this silent and peculiarly strong middle-aged man she suffered a terrible blow. She was wrenched from a happy life in Beirut. She was given to a much older spouse—perhaps in return for some sort of payment to her mother—who promptly took her off to strange parts and then set her down in Cairo, a gigantic and confusing city in an unfamiliar Arab country with her maiden aunt, Emelia ("Melia") Badr. Melia had come to Egypt early in the century and, as my mother was to do in her own way, had hewn out a life in essentially foreign territory. Melia's father (my great-grandfather), Yousif Badr, was the first native Evangelical minister in Lebanon, and through him perhaps, Melia had been hired by the American College for Girls in Cairo, an essentially missionary establishment, as local staff to teach Arabic.

She was a tiny woman but had the strongest will of anyone I knew. She made the Americans call her *Miss* Badr (as opposed to a patroniz-ing title reserved for the natives, Teacher Melia), and early on demon-strated her radical independence by boycotting the church services, an integral part of school and mission life. "Is there a god?" I asked her in 1956 a short while before her death. "I very much doubt it," she said wearily and even dismissively, with that strange finality she switched on when she no longer wished to be exercised by the topic at hand.

Melia's presence in the Said family life, before and after my birth, was of central importance. We did not live next to or with our rela-tives. We were alone as a family in Cairo, except for Melia, and later in the forties her sister, my grandmother, Munira, who lived with us. Melia helped my mother understand the complicated Cairo social sys-tem, which was so tumultuously different from anything Hilda had ever experienced as a sheltered girl in Nazareth and Beirut. And Melia intro-duced the couple to various friends of hers, mostly Copts and Syrians ("Shawam," plural of "Shami") whose daughters were her students. Melia didn't seem overly attentive to my sisters, but she doted on me, although she never really let herself go as was normally the case with female family members: no effusions, extended embraces, or exagger-ated declarations of ritual concern. I was uniquely conceded the right to ask her questions like "Are you married to Saleh?" the driver who seemed to practically live with her, and occasionally I was even allowed to look through her complicated little handbag.

Between the years of 1945 and 1950, I saw her in action several times at the college. Slight and barely five feet tall, she always dressed in black, her head covered with a black turban, and she never wore anything on her feet except for delicate black patent leather pumps. Her gestures were economical in the extreme, and she never raised her voice nor expressed the slightest hesitation or uncertainty. She had a distinct method for every social class and subclass, but underlying each was a sense of formality that could not be violated, as well as a carefully and coldly sustained distance that allowed no one to pass beyond a point of familiarity that only she determined. She terrified maids and students; she forced even distinguished parents—including at least two prime ministers—to accept her strictures and judgments as unappealable and final; by her perseverance, longevity, and air of infallibility she compelled the American teachers (also spinsters) to conform to her way, rather than she to theirs. Through half a century at the college—she lived there as well, ruling her floor like a queen—no one ever got the better of her. She stopped teaching before I was born and became "director" of the college, a position created in deference to her ability to rule Egyptian students and staff as no American could.

Auntie Melia took Hilda in hand, showed her where to shop, where to send her children to school, whom to talk to when she needed something. She supplied her with maids, piano teachers, tutors, names of ballet schools, dressmakers, and, of course, endless, very quietly stated advice. She always appeared for lunch on Tuesday, a habit begun before I was born and continued until she left Egypt in 1953 for her brief period of retirement in Lebanon, where she died in 1956. I was particularly fascinated by two things about her. One was her way of eating. Perhaps because of defects in her molars, tiny morsels of food were carefully deposited between her gums and her front teeth; they did not make their way back to where they could be chewed and then swallowed. Instead she worked on the food in the front part of her mouth by pressing it down with her tongue and then sucking from it a minuscule portion of juice and, say, a grain of rice, or a tiny chunk of meat, which she abruptly and almost imperceptibly gulped down. Then with her fork she extracted what was left—which always looked pretty intact to me—and laid it down precisely on the plate's far corner. By the end of the meal, which she was always the last to finish, her plate contained seven or eight little mounds of food, neatly ringing the surface, as if they had been put there by a guileful chef.

The second thing that transfixed me were her hands, always encased in black or white lace gloves, depending on the season. She wore bracelets but not rings. Her left hand always held a small rolled-up handkerchief in the palm next to the thumb, where she could open and reroll it all day. Whenever she offered me candy—*bastilia,* she called it—it always emerged from the hankie, always smelling of lavender cologne, always covered in cellophane, always of some gentle, unassertive flavor like quince or tamarind. Her right hand either carried her bag or rested on it.

Auntie Melia's relationship with my father was very correct, respectful, even at times cordial; it was quite unlike his attitude toward her sister, the kind and patient and hopelessly good Munira, whom he called *mart ʿammi,* mother-in-law (literally, "my paternal uncle's wife"), and whom he always treated with a sort of playful condescension. As for his four brothers-in-law, he seemed to have qualified affection, and a great deal of criticism, for them. Hilda's brothers—Munir, Alif, Rayik, and Emile—lived in Palestine, and we would visit them there with some regularity; after 1948 they flowed in and out of Cairo, refugees mostly, variously "hard up," as my father would say, in need of help. They were more numerous than my father's relatives, especially if to their Palestinian number were added a whole host of Hilda's Lebanese relatives. One of my father's ironclad rules was never to discuss the Said family at all; he often told me that a man's family is his honor. But he had no qualms about discussing his wife's family, for whom (this must have greatly complicated my mother's life) he seemed to be, according to him, an unending source of loans. He was always wealthy, whereas Hilda's brothers were not. One of them borrowed money from my father to get married. The others borrowed sums for various unsuccessful business enterprises, and I was led to believe that these sums were never returned. My father told me all these things with distaste, and because of that information I must have subliminally developed a sense of discomfort and mild disapproval that made my adolescent interaction with them awkward and just short of pleasant.

But his main objection to them over the years started with his marriage to Hilda. I never had all the details, but it had something to do with the fact that my mother's oldest brother, Munira's favorite, had sold off the small plot of family land in order to get married. This left the widowed Munira, plus Hilda and her other three brothers, without adequate means to live. I have long (perhaps inaccurately) supposed that part of the marriage arrangements made with my father by Hilda's family included stipulations for Munira's subsistence. She ended up spending many years with us, but it was quite routine for us to hear stories of her mistreatment at her oldest son's house, or of her other sons' inability—my father always called it unwillingness—to contribute to her upkeep. My father had a righteous sense of achievement after he had persuaded one of her sons to take my grandmother out to Groppi's for ice cream once a week.

For my father all this represented a classic, not to say definitive, example of how sons should *not* treat their mother—and, he began after 1948 regularly to say, "their sister." This kind of talk, expressed in my father's laconic style, pervaded the family ambience for me in both a general and acutely personal way. Not only did it seem to put my mother's family under a permanent cloud of disapproval and fundamental disqualification, but as a brother and son I felt acute discomfort. The implicit syllogism, according to which I grew up, ran as follows: "Edward" resembles his maternal uncles (*talih* *mikhwil* is the Arabic expression for the process; it also suggests that the older one got, the more strong the resemblance); his uncles are irrecusably bad sons and brothers; therefore "Edward" is far too likely to end up like them, and must thus be broken in his course, reeducated, re-formed to be less like them.

This was awful for my mother, of course. To have her son, her mother (whom she always treated in my presence with an almost sneeringly cold dislike), and her brothers singled out for such a Darwinian fate turned her into an intolerable mix of defender-cum-agent of her original family, executor of my father's injunctions in her new one, and prosecutor of, as well as defense lawyer for, me. Whatever she did fell into these three categories of judgment simultaneously, and ended up tangled inside her, with very disorienting consequences for me, her admired and yet unfortunately wayward son, the child who confirmed the worst of her lineage. Her love for me was both beautiful and withheld, and also endlessly patient.

I grew up sliding between being—in my estimation of my father's attitude to me—a delinquent son and my uncles' all-too-dutiful nephew. I called my father Daddy until his dying day, but I always sensed in the phrase how contingent it was, how potentially improper it was to think of myself as his son. I never asked him for anything without great apprehension or hours of desperate preparation. The most terrible thing he ever said to me—I was twelve then—was, "You will never inherit anything from me; you are *not* the son of a rich man," though literally of course I was. When he died he left his entire estate to my mother. From the moment I became conscious of myself as a child, I found it impossible to think of myself as not having both a discrediting past and an immoral future in store; my entire sense of self during my formative years was always experienced in the present tense, as I frantically worked to keep myself from falling back into an already established pattern, or from falling forward into certain perdition. Being myself meant not only never being quite right, but also never feeling at ease, always expecting to be interrupted or corrected, to have my privacy invaded and my unsure person set upon. Permanently out of place, the extreme and rigid regime of discipline and extracurricular education that my father would create and in which I became imprisoned from the age of nine left me no respite or sense of myself beyond its rules and patterns.

And thus I became "Edward," a creation of my parents whose daily travails a quite different but quite dormant inner self was able to observe, though most of the time was powerless to help. "Edward" was principally the son, then the brother, then finally the boy who went to school and unsuccessfully tried to follow (or ignore and circumvent) all the rules. His creation was made necessary by the fact that his parents were themselves self-creations: two Palestinians with dramatically different backgrounds and temperaments living in colonial Cairo as members of a Christian minority within a large pond of minorities, with only each other for support, without any precedent for what they were doing except an odd combination of prewar Palestinian habit; American lore picked up at random in books and magazines and from my father's decade in the United States (my mother did not even visit the United States until 1948); the missionaries' influence; incompleted and hence eccentric schooling; British colonial attitudes that represented both the lords and the general run of "humankind" they ruled; and, finally, the style of life my parents perceived around them in Egypt and which they tried to adapt to their special circumstances. Could "Edward's" position ever be anything but out of place?

II

EVEN THOUGH THEY LIVED IN CAIRO IN 1935, MY PARENTS
made sure that I was born in Jerusalem, for reasons that were stated
quite often during my childhood. Hilda had already given birth to a
male child, to be called Gerald, in a Cairo hospital, where he developed
an infection and died soon after birth. As a radical alternative to another
hospital disaster, my parents traveled to Jerusalem during the summer,
and on the first of November, I was delivered at home by a Jewish midwife, Madame Baer. She regularly visited us to see me as I was growing up: she was a big, bluff woman of German provenance who spoke
no English but rather a heavily accented, comically incorrect Arabic.
When she came there were lots of hugs and hearty pinches and slaps,
but I remember little else of her.

Until 1947 our off-and-on sojourns in Palestine were entirely familial in character—that is, we did nothing as a family alone but always
with other members of the extended clan. In Egypt, it was exactly the
opposite; there, because we were by ourselves in a setting to which we
had no real connection, we developed a far greater sense of internal
cohesion. My early memories of Palestine itself are casual and, considering my profound later immersion in Palestinian affairs, curiously
unremarkable. It was a place I took for granted, the country I was from,
where family and friends existed (it seems so retrospectively) with un-

reflecting ease. Our family home was in Talbiyah, a part of West Jerusalem that was sparsely inhabited but had been built and lived in exclusively by Palestinian Christians like us: the house was an imposing two-story stone villa with lots of rooms and a handsome garden in which my two youngest cousins, my sisters, and I would play. There was no neighborhood to speak of, although we knew everyone else in the as yet not clearly defined district. In front of the house lay an empty rectangular space where I rode my bike or played. There were no immediate neighbors, although about five hundred yards away sat a row of similar villas where my cousins' friends lived. Today, the empty space has become a park, and the area around the house a lush, densely inhabited upper-class Jewish neighborhood.

When we stayed with my widowed aunt Nabiha, my father's sister, and her five grown children, I was routinely a straggler behind the twins, Robert and Albert, who were about seven years older than I; I had neither any independence nor a particular role to play, except that of the younger cousin, occasionally used either as an unthinking, blindly obedient loudspeaker to yell insults and nasty messages to their friends and enemies from atop a wall, or as an assenting audience to extremely tall tales. Albert, with his rakish air and sporty sense of fun, was the closest I came to having an older brother or good friend.

We also went to Safad, where we stayed for weeklong visits with my maternal uncle Munir, a doctor, and his wife, Latifeh, who had two boys, and a girl roughly my age. Safad belonged to another, less-developed, world: the house had no electricity, the narrow, carless streets and steep climbs made for a wonderful playground, and my aunt's cooking was exceptionally delicious. After the Second World War, our visits to Jerusalem and to a greater extent Safad provided an escape from the regimen already forming around me with cumulative daily reinforcement in Cairo. The Safad visits were mostly idyllic times for me, broken occasionally by school or a tutorial, but never for very long.

As we increasingly spent time in Cairo, Palestine acquired a languid, almost dreamlike, aspect for me. There I did not as acutely feel the solitude I began to dread later, at eight or nine, and although I sensed the absence of closely organized space and time that made up my life in Egypt, I could not completely enjoy the relative freedom from it that I had in Jerusalem. I recall thinking that being in Jerusalem was pleasant but tantalizingly open, temporary, even transitory, as indeed it later was.

The more significant and charged geography and atmosphere of Cairo were concentrated for us in Zamalek, an island in the Nile between the old city in the east and Giza in the west, inhabited by foreigners and wealthy locals. My parents moved there in 1937, when I was two. Unlike Talbiyah, whose residents were mainly a homogeneous group of well-to-do merchants and professionals, Zamalek was not a real community but a sort of colonial outpost whose tone was set by Europeans with whom we had little or no contact: we built our own world within it. Our house was a spacious fifth-floor apartment at 1 Sharia Aziz Osman that overlooked the so-called Fish Garden, a small, fence-encircled park with an artificial rock hill (*gabalaya*), a tiny pond, and a grotto; its little green lawns were interspersed with winding paths, great trees, and, in the *gabalaya* area, artificially made rock formations and sloping hillsides where you could run up and down without interruption. Except for Sundays and public holidays, the Garden, as we all called it, was where I spent all of my playtime, always supervised, within range of my mother's voice, which was always lyrically audible to me and my sisters.

I played Robinson Crusoe and Tarzan there, and when she came with me, I played at eluding and then rejoining my mother. She usually went nearly everywhere with us, throughout our little world, one little island enclosed by another one. In the early years we went to school a few blocks away from the house—GPS, Gezira Preparatory School. For sports there was the Gezira Sporting Club and, on weekends, the Maadi Sporting Club, where I learned how to swim. For years, Sundays meant Sunday School; this senseless ordeal occurred between nine and ten in the morning at the GPS, followed by matins at All Saints' Cathedral. Sunday evenings took us to the American Mission Church in Ezbekieh, and two Sundays out of three to Evensong at the cathedral. School, church, club, garden, house—a limited, carefully circumscribed segment of the great city—was my world until I was well into my teens. And as the timetable for my life grew more demanding, the occasional deviations from it were carefully sanctioned respites that strengthened its hold over me.

One of the main recreational rituals of my Cairo years was what my father called "going for a drive," as distinguished from his daily drive to work. For more than three decades, he owned a series of black American cars, each bigger than its predecessors: a Ford, then a deluxe Plymouth sedan, then in 1948 an enormous Chrysler limousine. He always employed drivers, two of whom, Faris and Aziz, I was allowed to chat with only when he was not there: he insisted on complete silence as he was being driven to and from his office. On the occasions I rode with him, he started the journey from home very much in a domestic mood, so to speak, relatively open to conversation, and would even vouchsafe me a smile, until we reached the Bulaq bridge that connected Zamalek to the mainland. Then he would gradually stiffen and grow silent, pulling out some papers from his briefcase and beginning to go over them. By the time we reached the ʾAsa ʿaf and Mixed Courts intersection that bordered Cairo's European business center, he was closed to me completely, and would not answer my questions or acknowledge my presence: he was transformed into the formidable boss of his business, a figure I came to dislike and fear because he seemed like a larger and more impersonal version of the man who supervised my life.

At night and on holidays, without a driver he would take us on "the drives," all chatter and jokes, all entertaining patriarchy, which I recognized half consciously as a liberation for him above all. Minus coat and tie, in summer shirtsleeves or winter sports jacket, he headed for one of a handful of designated fun destinations. On Sunday afternoons it was to Mena House for tea and a modest concert. Saturday afternoons it was the Barrages, a pocket-size British-constructed dam in the Delta. Surrounded by verdant parks crisscrossed by a simple trolley system whose mysterious purpose always stimulated my fantasies of escape (and the impossibility thereof), we might wander about where we wished, eating a sandwich here, an apple there, over a period of two and perhaps even three hours. On holidays we invariably trailed out past the Pyramids into the Western Desert, there to stop at an anonymous milepost, unfold our blankets, unpack an elaborate picnic lunch, throw stones at a target, skip rope, toss a ball. Just the five, six, or seven of us, as the family grew. Never, except for Mena House, at a public place like a café or restaurant. Never with anyone else. Never at any recognizable place—just a spot off the Desert Road. Holiday evenings we toured the streets south of Bab el Louk where most of the government buildings were located. Lit up with thousands of sandy yellow bulbs and bright-green neon lights, the buildings constituted "the illuminations," as my father called them, that we visited on the king's birthday or the opening of Parliament.

Beyond these boundaries of habit and minutely plotted excursions I felt that a whole world was held at bay, ready to tumble in, engulf us, perhaps even sweep us away, so protected and enclosed was I inside the little world my parents created. Cairo was a fairly crowded city in the early forties: during the World War II years thousands of Allied troops were stationed there, in addition to numerous expatriate communities of Italians, French, English, and the resident minorities of Jews, Armenians, Syro-Lebanese (the Shawam), and Greeks. Various unannounced parades and displays by the troops could be encountered by chance all over Cairo, and though my father talked occasionally of taking me to a jamboree—a scheduled parade—this never happened. In both Jerusalem and Cairo I saw British and ANZAC troops marching, their trumpets blaring and drums thumping inexorably, but I never understood why or for whom: I supposed that their purpose in life was much grander than mine, and therefore too significant for me to understand. I always noticed the facades of forbidden restaurants and cabarets decorated with signs like "All Ranks Welcome," but did not understand their meaning, either. One such place, Sauld's, in the Immobilia building downtown, happened to be near my uncle Asaad's Arrow Stationery Company (a gift to him from my father), and he took me there often. "Feed the boy," he would announce to a sleepy-eyed counter clerk, and I would gorge myself on cheese sandwiches and turnip pickles. I first thought that "all ranks" meant that civvies like me were licensed to enter, but soon realized that I had no rank at all. Sauld's and Uncle Al, as we called him, symbolized a momentary, all-too-brief, and, given the rigid dietary laws imposed by my mother, entirely fugitive moment of freedom.

By 1943, my parents had begun to impose their disciplinary regime so fully that when I left Egypt for the United States in 1951, Uncle Al's hearty "Feed the boy" had already taken on a nostalgically irrecoverable sweetness, stupid and happy at the same time. When Uncle Al died in Jaffa four years later, Sauld's had also ceased to exist.

During the first part of the war we spent more time than usual in Palestine. In 1942 we rented a summer house in Ramallah, north of Jerusalem, and did not return to Cairo until November. That summer

altered our family life dramatically, as a change occurred in our otherwise rather unpredictable and cumbersome movements between Cairo
and Jerusalem. We usually traveled by train from Cairo to Lydda with
at least two servants, a large amount of luggage, and a generally frenetic
air; the return trip was always slightly easier and more subdued. In 1942,
however, my mother, my two sisters, Rosemarie and Jean, my father,
and I did not travel by train but by car. Instead of boarding the luxury
Wagons-Lits train in Cairo's Bab-el-Hadid Station for the twelve-hour
overnight journey to Jerusalem, in May of that year we were on the run
from the rapidly approaching German army, in my father's black Plymouth, its headlights blued out, our quickly packed leather suitcases piled
on the luggage rack and in the trunk. Driving to the Suez Canal Zone
took many hours as we encountered numerous British convoys con-
verging on Cairo: we would be pulled over and forced to wait as tanks,
trucks, and personnel carriers trailed past us headed for what was to be
an Allied defeat followed by the British counteroffensive that culminated in the battle of el-Alamein in November.

We made the long drive in complete silence right through the night.
My father negotiated the unmarked Sinai roads after having crossed the
Suez Canal without ceremony or fuss at the Qantara bridge; the customs post there was deserted when we arrived at about midnight. It was
at that point that we met up with the only civilian car going the same
way, a convertible driven by a Jewish businessman from Cairo, with no
passengers, and with only several bottles of iced water and a revolver
for luggage. He recognized my father, and even suggested that he might
relieve the Plymouth of some of its cargo—several large suitcases were
duly transferred to him—but asked in return that he be allowed to follow in our tracks. I vividly remember the haggard, weary expression on
my father's face as he assented to this lopsided arrangement, and so we
proceeded silently through the night, the second car following hard
upon the first, with my father left on his own, both to excavate the
sand-blown, meandering, narrow road in the blackest of black nights
and also to endure the pressure of his little family inside the car, and
outside the Egyptian Jewish businessman, convinced that he was running for his life, constantly bearing down upon us.

Earlier that winter I had heard the sirens blaring "alarm" and "all
clear." Bundled in blankets and transported in my father's arms to the

garage-shelter during a German night bombing raid, I felt a vague premonition that "we" were threatened. The political, to say nothing of
the military, meaning of our situation, were beyond me at age six and
a half. As an American in Egypt, where the Germans under Rommel
were predicted to descend first on Alexandria then on Cairo, my father
must have thought he was targeted for an unpleasant fate. A whole wall
in our house's entrance room was covered with large maps of Asia,
North Africa, and Europe. Every day my father moved red (for the
Allies) and black (for the Axis) pins to reflect advances and retreats on
the warring sides. For me, the maps were disquieting rather than informing, and though I occasionally asked my father to explain, it
seemed hard for him to do so: he was distracted, bothered, distant. And
then suddenly we left for Jerusalem on that difficult night ride. The day
he decided to leave, he came home for lunch and told my mother simply to pack and get ready, and by five that afternoon we were off,
driving slowly through Cairo's half-deserted streets. A desolate, baffling
time, my familiar world inexplicably being abandoned as we headed off
into the cheerless dusk.

The images of my father's withdrawal and silence that followed
during the long, perplexing and strange summer in Ramallah continued
to haunt me for years. He sat on the balcony gazing off into the distance, smoking incessantly. "Don't make noise, Edward," my mother
would say. "Can't you see your father is trying to rest?" Then she and
I would go out for a walk through the leafy and comfortable, largely
Christian, town north of Jerusalem, with me clinging nervously to her.
The Ramallah house was unattractive to me, but nevertheless a perfect
setting for the stillness and bleakness of my father's mysterious ordeal.
A steep outdoor staircase went up diagonally from the garden, which
was divided in the center by a stone path, on either side of which lay
furrows of brown earth in which nothing but a few brambles grew. A
pair of skinny quince trees stood close to the house by the first-floor
balcony, where my father spent most of his time. The bottom floor was
closed and empty. Having been forbidden to walk on the furrows, I was
left with the ungenerous stony line going from gate to stairs as my playground.

I had no idea what was wrong, but Ramallah was where I first heard
the phrase "nervous breakdown." Associated with that was the protec-

tion of my father's "peace of mind," a phrase he got from a book of that name, which provided the topic of many conversations with his friends. The tiresome languor of our Ramallah summer was closed to scrutiny and explanation, both of which as a bright six-and-a-half-year-old I needed quite naturally. Was Daddy afraid of something, I wanted first of all to ask: Why does he sit there for so long, and say nothing? Either I was led off to some useful or punitive activity, or I was thrown a few enigmatic and generally incomplete hints for an answer. There was talk of extreme anxiety about his suddenly higher blood pressure. There was also reference to having sent off my cousins Abie (Ibrahim) and Charlie—Uncle Asaad's boys—to Asmara, where, my father worried himself sick, they might be killed. A shady Cairo businessman was said to have tried unsuccessfully to tempt my father into some business scheme for war profiteering. (I understood that my father refused.) Were those events enough to cause a nervous breakdown?

Whatever the reason, once we returned to Cairo a process of change in my life began as a result, and indeed I was encouraged by my mother in particular to believe that a happier, less problematic period had ended. I sank more and more into generalized truancy—"You're very clever," I'd be told over and over, "but you have no character, you're lazy, you're naughty," etc.—and was also made aware of an earlier Edward, sometimes referred to as "Eduardo Bianco," whose exploits, gifts, and accomplishments were recounted to me as signs of pre-1942 early promise betrayed. From her I learned that at the age of one and a half the former Edward had memorized thirty-eight songs and nursery rhymes, which he could sing and recite perfectly. Or that when cousin Abie, a fluent harmonica player, purposely introduced a wrong note in his rendition of "John Peel," Edward would clench his fists, close his eyes, and bawl out first his annoyance at the mistake and then the correct version. Or that except for the odd use of "you" for "me," Edward spoke perfect sentences in English and Arabic by the age of fifteen months. Or that his ability to read simple prose was quite developed by the age of two and a half or three. Or that math and music were as natural to him aged three or four as they were to eight- and nine-year-olds. Cute, playful, preternaturally fast and smart, this early Edward enjoyed roistering play with his happy father. I recalled none of this myself, but my mother's frequent rehearsal of it plus a couple of photo albums from those years—including an idyllic summer in Alexandria—supported the claim.

None of this, except as regretted memory, was meant to survive the dark days of 1942. We returned to Cairo after the battle of el-Alamein in November, and I went back to GPS, to become a thoroughgoing problem boy for whom one unpleasant antidote after another was devised, until by the age of nine and right through my fifteenth birthday I was constantly engaged in private remedial therapies after school and on weekends: piano lessons, gymnastics, Sunday School, riding classes, boxing, plus the mind-deadening rigors of relentlessly regulated summers in Dhour el Shweir. After 1943 we started to spend every summer in this dreary Lebanese mountain village that my father seemed more attached to than any other place on earth. My parents were at the heart of the entire administered system that determined my time minute by minute and my father's attitude toward me for the rest of his life, a system that allowed me only the smallest of spots of relief to enjoy and feel that I was out of its clutches.

He managed to combine harshness, unreadable silence, and odd affection laced with surprising generosity which somehow never gave me enough to count on, and which until very recently I could neither dismiss as no longer threatening nor fully understand. But as the core of the disciplinary structure devised for my life emerged out of the depredations of 1942, the danger of not keeping to its various prescriptions produced in me a fear of falling back into some horrible state of total disorder and being lost, and I still have it.

This dangerous state soon came to be embodied for me in the physical and moral temptations of Cairo, which lay just beyond the carefully plotted, rigidly administered routine of my life. I never went out with girls; I wasn't ever allowed to visit, much less frequent, places of public entertainment or restaurants; and I was always warned by both my parents not to get close to people on the bus or tram, not to drink or eat anything from a shop or stand, and above all to regard our home and family as the only refuge in that vast sty of vices all around us.

Saving me from what was already happening: this was the paradox I lived. The only thing worse, I imagined, was total breakdown, perhaps of the kind my father experienced in the summer of 1942. After that my father began the serious task of reorganizing his business and his leisure, with a new emphasis on the latter, as his fortunes increased considerably. By 1951, he had stopped going to his office at all after lunch. Instead he started to play bridge, which, seven days a week, every week in the year except when he traveled, became his obsession. He would come home for lunch at one-thirty, eat, then sleep until four, when he would be driven to the club to play until seven-thirty or eight. He might play again after dinner.

After our summer in Ramallah a large number of Ely Culbertson books appeared all over the Cairo apartment, in addition to several solo bridge sets and a new green felt cover for use on the two folding card tables we had. On Tuesday evening my father would go to Philip Souky's house near the Pyramids to play bridge. When we started to spend our summers in Dhour el Shweir, he would play bridge in the morning at a café, then again in the afternoon, and finally at night he would preside over a game at our house or at a friend's. The distance between us grew even greater as I, and alas he, discovered that I had no talent for or even interest in bridge. He seemed to have a phenomenal capacity for all indoor games, none of which I ever mastered. He tried to teach me backgammon, or *tawlah,* with, to me, appalling results. After watching me as I counted spaces laboriously, he would impatiently snatch the counter from under my finger and move it rapidly to the correct space: "Why are you counting like that"—here he would mimic my counting by affixing a crude moronic contortion to his face, as if I were a cretin trying hopelessly to go from three to four—"when *this* is the way it should be done?" Later he would ask me to play again but would end up playing the entire game for me. "It's faster this way!" I was there just to sit opposite him and do nothing: he played both parts.

There wasn't a card game he didn't know, or a casino ritual he didn't unsuccessfully try to teach me. Having had them explained thirty times has not after all enabled me to play either poker or baccarat. During the summer of 1953, after a year of learning how to play pool at my American boarding school, I thought I managed slyly to cajole him into a game of 8-ball at a little café in Dhour across from the Cirque Café. I attributed his initial reluctance to apprehension that he might be beaten, but it was a trick. I realized later that he feigned reluctance, and even a little admiration, just to get me going. "This is the way we play it in the States," I crowed to him, as professional to novice. "If you hit the ball on the side, it's called English." I put in two balls, then missed the third. Taking up the cue, my father seemed suddenly transformed from humbly nodding apprentice into fearsome pro. It was no contest at all, not even after we moved to the adjoining 3-ball billiard table, where I thought I might have a chance. I was reduced to a state of complete confusion, and a kind of babbling helplessness as I blamed the cue, the mocking waiter, the absence of practice. "So it's called English," he said caustically on the way home, and this from a player who seemed to have every spin and twist at his command.

Games did not require him to say very much nor make more than a minimal emotional investment, and perhaps for this reason cardplaying became an obsessional and apparently life-sustaining habit. It was a way of sublimating his anxieties in an area of life in which the rules were set, and a routine order prevailed; an escape from any kind of confrontation with people, business, or problems.

Bridge, and card games generally, were part of his regeneration from the ravages of 1942. "It's a relaxation," he said once or twice over the years, describing a pastime that occupied at least twelve hours a day during the summer holidays and up to four hours during his periods of work. I remember nothing with quite the same dispiriting blankness as those times when as a young boy I was compelled to watch him play. While I sat by his side, every card flipped onto the table, every bid, every laconic postmortem after the hand was played out signified my mental and moral subordination and increased my sense of his authority over me. He would not speak to me at all, nor point out what in a given hand might have been interesting; there was just the unending monotony of the card game, and his express desire to be in it for reasons I could never fully understand.

Standing or sitting next to him during the first few years after 1942 was my punishment for misbehaving, and it constituted my parents' primitive idea for keeping me out of trouble at times when I wasn't at school and, worse, when we summered in Lebanon. Being forced to watch him playing bridge or *tawlah* for hours on end was a mind-numbing experience. These periods of enforced boredom were early avatars of a larger scheme to curtail my potential mischief-making: "Wadie, please take the boy with you," my mother would say exasperatedly. "He's causing a lot of trouble." When Wadie's services were not available, my mother would either send me on a long and pointless errand or pronounce the words "Take off your clothes and go *right* to bed." Books, music, diversion of any kind were forbidden in bed, as were food and drink. I was forbidden to lock the bedroom door, allowing my mother unimpeded, extremely sudden, and unannounced entrances into the room to ascertain whether I was complying. The only benefit of this particularly deadening punishment was that having discovered three chessmen lying in the back of a drawer I practiced throwing them up and catching them until I had taught myself to juggle.

My parents' early disciplinary practices I associate first with the long vacations, when extended intervals of leisure might have allowed my inquiring and radically naughty self to go where it might be risky to trespass. But they soon extended to my Cairo life as well. I had an amazingly resourceful curiosity about people and things. I was frequently upbraided for reading books I shouldn't have, and more damningly I was often found looking in the autograph books, notepads, pamphlets and comics, scribbled messages, and notes of my sisters, schoolmates, and parents. "Curiosity killed the cat" was the frequent verdict on me, but I wanted to get beyond the various cages in which I found myself placed, and which made me feel so dissatisfied, and even distasteful to myself. Having to do my schoolwork, to play games like soccer at which I was manifestly unsuccessful, to be a dutiful, church-going son and brother, I soon began to take secret delight in doing and saying things that broke the rules or took me beyond the boundaries set by my parents. I always looked around doors that were ajar; I read books to find out what propriety kept hidden from me; I peered into drawers, cupboards, bookshelves, envelopes, scraps of paper, to glean from them what I could about characters whose sinful wantonness corresponded to my desires.

I soon began to cherish the act of discovery that reading provided. About half our family business in Palestine—the Palestine Educational Company—was bookselling, and a small amount was publishing; in Egypt, however, my father ran a company (in partnership with his cousin Boulos and his children) entirely devoted to office equipment and stationery, some of which we also sold in Jerusalem and Haifa.

Whenever some member of our Jerusalem family visited I would get presents of suitable books taken off the shelf with their price tags and inventory labels still in them. These suitable books seemed to fall into two general categories: children's books in the A. A. Milne and Enid Blyton mold, and useful books of information like the *Collins Junior Book of Knowledge,* which was given to me when I was between nine and ten. It entertained me for long hours as I tried to grasp the mysteries of one Kalita, the girl fakir who performed miracles of strength and self-punishment at the Bertram Mills Circus. I had not yet even been to a circus—the Circo Togni was not to appear in Cairo until four years later—nor, apart from the anodyne suggestions provided in Blyton's Mr. Galliano's Circus books, did I have any conception of what life in a European circus was all about. It was enough for me that Kalita was of mysterious origin; in the tiny, grainy, and blurred photographs provided in the text, she wore what appeared to be a two-piece costume such as I had never seen, and she was able to do amazing, unimaginable things with her body.

All of this defied the positive laws of respectability and decency under which I chafed. Her contortions were also at odds with nature, but that increased their excitement. She was described as lying on her back supporting a gigantic stone slab on her bare stomach; a large half-naked man in a turban stood over her with an enormous sledgehammer, which he brought down on the stone. A picture of the whole scene, with utensil caught in mid-descent, confirmed this feat. Kalita was also capable of walking in her bare feet on broken glass, lying on nails, and, for her major adventure, being buried underground for many minutes. Another photograph represented her in her bathing suit with a discernible smile of almost sensual satisfaction on her face and carrying a large and extremely fearsome-looking crocodile.

I read and reread the three grittily printed pages on Kalita and I examined and reexamined the two photographs that drew me in every time I opened the book. But it was their very insufficiencies—their minuscule size, the impossibility of actually being able to see the woman's body, the alienating distance between them and me—that paradoxically compelled, indeed enthralled, me for weeks and weeks. I dreamed of knowing her, being taken into her "caravan," being shown some more horrible feats (for example, her imperviousness to, perhaps even enjoyment of, other forms of extreme pain and unknown types of pleasure, her disdain for domestic life, her capacity for diving to unusual depths, eating live animals and disgusting fruits) and hearing from her about her freedom from the ordinary talk and responsibilities of everyday life. It was from my experiences of Kalita that I developed the habit of mentally extending the story presented in a book, pushing the limits to include myself; gradually I realized that I could become the author of my own pleasures, particularly those that took me as far away as possible from the choking impingements of family and school. My ability to appear to be studying, reading, or practicing the piano and at the same time to be thinking about something completely different and completely mine, like Kalita, was one of the features of my life that irritated teachers and parents but impressed me.

There were two main sources of stories whose boundaries I could expand: books and films. Fairy tales and biblical stories were read to me by my mother and grandmother but I had also been given an illustrated book of the Greek myths as a birthday present when I was seven. It opened an entire world to me, not only the stories themselves but the wonderful connections that might be made between them. Jason and the Argonauts, Perseus and the Gorgon, Medusa, Hercules and his twelve adventures: they were my friends and partners, parents, cousins, uncles, and mentors (like Chiron). I lived with them and meticulously imagined their castles, chariots, and triremes. I thought about them when they were *not* killing lions or monsters. I released them for a life of easy grace free of obnoxious teachers and hectoring parents, Perseus talking with Jason on some airy patio about what it was like to see Medusa in his shield, Jason telling Perseus about the pleasures of Colchis, the two of them marveling at Hercules' killing of the serpents in his cradle.

The second source was films, particularly those like the Arabian Nights adventures that regularly featured Jon Hall, Maria Montez, Turhan Bey, and Sabu, and the Johnny Weissmuller *Tarzan* series. When I was in good favor with my parents, the pleasures of Saturday included an afternoon cinema performance, fastidiously chosen for me by my mother. French and Italian films were taboo. Hollywood films were suitable only if declared "for children" by my mother. These were Laurel and Hardy, lots of Abbott and Costello, Betty Grable, Gene

Kelly, Loretta Young, many, many musicals and family comedies with Clifton Webb, Claudette Colbert, and Jennifer Jones (acceptable in *The Song of Bernadette,* forbidden in *Duel in the Sun*), Walt Disney fantasies and Arabian Nights films preferably with only Jon Hall and Sabu (Maria Montez was frowned on), war films, some Westerns. Sitting in the plush cinema seats, much more than in viewing the Hollywood films themselves—which struck me as a weird form of science fiction corresponding to nothing at all in my life—I luxuriated in the sanctioned freedom to see and not be seen. Later I developed an irrecusable attachment to Johnny Weissmuller's whole Tarzan world, especially to the uxorial and, in *Tarzan and His Mate* at least, virginally sensual Jane cavorting in their cosy tree house, whose clever Wemmicklike comforts seemed like a pure, uncomplicated distillation of our life as a family alone in Egypt. Once "The End" appeared on the screen in *Tarzan Finds a Son* or *Tarzan's Secret Treasure,* I began my ruminations on what happened afterward, on what the little family did in the tree house, on the "natives" they cultivated and befriended, on members of Jane's family who might have visited, on the tricks that Tarzan taught Boy, and on and on. It was very odd, but it did not occur to me that the cinematic Aladdin, Ali Baba, and Sinbad, whose genies, Baghdad cronies, and sultans I completely possessed in the fantasies I counterpointed with my lessons, all had American accents, spoke no Arabic, and ate mysterious foods—perhaps "sweetmeats," or was it more like stew, rice, lamb cutlets?—that I could never quite make out.

One of the rare moments of complete satisfaction I enjoyed before I was eighteen occurred during my first year at Cairo's School for American Children (I was ten and a half). I was standing on the first landing of a grand staircase, looking down at a roomful of faces, and masterfully reciting narratives, drawing out the stories of Jason and Perseus. I gloried in finicky, unending detail—the identity of the Argonauts, what the Golden Fleece was, the reasons for Medusa's horrible affliction, the later story of Perseus and Andromeda—and experienced for the first time the joys of virtuosity and emancipation denied me by the French and English language and history classes I seemed so poor at. I had a fluency and concentration in the telling and thinking through of these stories that supplied me with a unique pleasure I could find nowhere else in Cairo. I was also beginning to enjoy classical music quite seriously, but in my piano lessons, which began when I was six, my gifts of memory and melody ran aground on the need to practice scales and Czerny exercises, with my mother standing over or sitting next to me; the result was a feeling of being interrupted in developing a musical identity. Not until I was fifteen could I buy records and enjoy the operas I chose on my own. The Cairo musical season of operas and ballets was still out of bounds to me: I therefore relied on what the BBC and Egyptian State Broadcasting had to offer, my greatest pleasure being the BBC's forty-five-minute Sunday afternoon program "Nights at the Opera." Using Gustave Kobbé's *Complete Opera Book* I discovered quite early on that I really disliked Verdi and Puccini but loved the little I knew of Strauss and Wagner, whose works I did not see in an opera house until I was in my late teens.

III

SCHOOLTEACHERS WERE SUPPOSED TO BE ENGLISH, I THOUGHT. Students, if they were fortunate, might also be English or, as in my case, if they were not, not. I attended the Gezira Preparatory School (GPS) from the autumn of 1941 till we left Cairo in May 1942, then again from early 1943 till 1946, with one or two longer Palestinian interruptions in between. During that period I had no Egyptian teachers at all, nor was I conscious of any Arab Muslim presence in the school: the students were Armenians, Greeks, Egyptian Jews, and Copts, as well as a substantial number of English children, including many of the staff's offspring. Our teachers were, to mention the two most prominent, Mrs. Bullen, headmistress, and Mrs. Wilson, the ubiquitous all-purpose general head teacher. The school itself was located in a large Zamalek villa, once intended for living on a grand scale, its main floor now converted into several classrooms, all of which were entered from an enormous central hall with a platform at one end and an imposing entrance portal at the other. The hall was two floors high with a glass ceiling; a balustrade surrounded another set of rooms located directly above our classrooms. I only ventured there once, and not very happily at that. These struck me as secret places where mysterious English meetings took place and where the redoubtable Mr. Bullen, a large red-faced man only rarely glimpsed on the lower floor, might be found.

I had no way of knowing then that Mrs. Bullen, the headmistress, whose daughter Anne was in the class immediately senior to mine, was in Egypt as a school concessionaire who held a franchise to run for the GPS British Council, not as an educator. After the 1952 Free Officers' Revolution the school slowly lost its European cachet and by the 1956 Suez crisis had become something else altogether. Today it is a career language training school for young adults, without a trace of its English past. Mrs. Bullen and her daughter later appeared in Beirut as principals of another English-type school, but they seem to have been even less successful than they were in Cairo, where they were dismissed for inefficiency and Mr. Bullen's drinking habits.

GPS conveniently sat at the end of Sharia Aziz Osman, our relatively short Zamalek street, a walk of exactly three blocks. The time I took to get there or to come home was always an issue with my teachers and parents, associated forever in my mind with two words, "loitering" and "fibbing," whose meaning I learned in connection with my meandering, fantasy-filled traversal of that short distance. Part of the delay was to put off my arrival at either end. The other part was sheer fascination with the people I might encounter, or with glimpses of life revealed as a door opened here, a car went by there, or a scene was played out briefly on a balcony. As my day began at seven-thirty, what I witnessed was invariably stamped with night's end and day's beginning—the black-suited *ghaffeers,* or evening watchmen, slowly divesting themselves of blankets and heavy coats, sleepy-eyed *suffragis* shuffling off to market for bread and milk, drivers getting the family car ready. There were rarely any other grown-ups about at that hour, although once in a while I'd see a parent marching along with a GPS child, dressed in our uniform of cap, trousers, and blazer, all in gray with light-blue piping. What I cherished in those dawdling walks was the opportunity to elaborate on the scanty material offered me. A redheaded woman I saw one afternoon seemed—just by walking by—to have persuaded me that she was a poisoner and (I had without specific comprehension heard the word recently) a divorcee. A pair of men sauntering about one morning were detectives. I imagined that a couple standing on a balcony overhead spoke French and had just had a leisurely breakfast with champagne.

Fantasizing about other lives and especially other people's houses was stimulated by my quite rigid confinement in our own. I can count on the fingers of one hand the number of times I actually set foot in a classmate's apartment or house as I was growing up. And I cannot remember any occasion at all when one of my friends—"friend" is probably too strong a word to describe the children of my own age with whom I had contact—from either school or the club came to my house. One of my earliest and most long-lasting passions therefore has been an almost overpowering desire to imagine what other people's houses were like. Did their rooms resemble ours? Did their kitchens work the way ours did? What did their cupboards contain, and how were those contents organized? And so on, down to the smallest details—night tables, radios, lamps, bookshelves, rugs, etc. Until I left Egypt in 1951 I assumed that my sequestration was (in an extremely imprecise way) "good" for me. Only later did it occur to me that the kind of discipline my parents devised for me meant I was to regard our life and house as somehow the norm and not, as it most certainly was, fantastically isolated and almost experimental.

As a rare escape I was sometimes allowed to go skating on Saturday mornings at a rink, the Rialto, near "B" Branch—a small shop maintained by my father mainly to sell pens and expensive leather gifts—on Fuad al-Awwal Street. The area was packed with bustling shops and department stores: Chemla and Cicurel across the street, Paul Favre, the large shoe shop next to "B" Branch, where, from a tired mustachioed middle-aged Armenian clerk in waistcoat and green eyeshade, we bought shoes for summer (sandals and light shoes) and winter (button- or lace-ups, black and dark brown). Tennis shoes and loafers were "bad," and hence permanently disallowed.

School always began in the big hall with the singing of hymns—"All Things Bright and Beautiful" and "From Greenland's Icy Mountains" were the two that recurred most frequently—accompanied at the piano by omnicompetent Mrs. Wilson and directed by Mrs. Bullen, whose daily homilies were simultaneously condescending and cloying, her bad British teeth and ungenerous lips shaping the words with unmistakable distaste for the mongrel-like collection of children who stood before her. Then we filed into our classes for a long morning's lessons. My first teacher at GPS was Mrs. Whitfield, whom I suspected of being not really English, though she mimicked the part. Besides, I envied her her name. Her son, Ronnie (Mrs. Wilson had a son, Dickie, and a daughter, Elizabeth; Mrs. Bullen had Anne, of course), like the Wilson children, was enrolled at GPS; all of them were older than I, and this added to their privileged remoteness and *hauteur*. Our lessons and books were mystifyingly English: we read about meadows, castles, and Kings John, Alfred, and Canute with the reverence that our teachers kept reminding us they deserved. Their world made little sense to me, except that I admired their creation of the language they used, which I, a little Arab boy, was learning something about. A disproportionate amount of attention was lavished on the Battle of Hastings along with lengthy explanations of Angles, Saxons, and Normans. Edward the Confessor has ever since remained in my mind as an elderly bearded gentleman in a white gown lying flat on his back, perhaps as a consequence of having confessed to something he shouldn't have done. There was never to be any perceived connection between him and me, despite our identical first name.

These lessons in English glory were interspersed with repetitive exercises in writing, arithmetic, and recitation. My fingers were always dirty; then, as now, I was fatally attracted to writing with an ink pen that produced an ugly scrawl, plus numerous smudges and blots. I was made acutely conscious of my endless infractions by Mrs. Whitfield in particular. "Sit up straight and do your work properly"—"Don't fidget," she then added almost immediately. "Get on with your work." "Don't be lazy" was the habitual clincher. To my left Arlette was a model student; to my right it was the ever-obliging and successful Naki Rigopoulos. All around me were Greenvilles, and Coopers, and Pilleys: starchy little English boys and girls with enviably authentic names, blue eyes, and bright, definitive accents. I have no distinct recollection of how I sounded in those days, but I know that it was not English. The odd thing though was that we were all treated as if we should (or *really* wanted to) be English, an unexceptionable program for Dick, Ralph, and Derek, less so for locals like Micheline Lindell, David Ades, Nadia Gindy, and myself.

All our time outside class was spent in a little enclosed yard completely shut off from Fuad al-Awwal, the bustling main street into which Aziz Osman—our house sat at the bottom left-hand side—ran. Fuad al-Awwal was lined with shops and vegetable stands; it carried a healthy flow of traffic as well as an extremely noisy tram line and occasional public buses. Not only was it distinctly urban and busy, but it welled up from the older parts of Cairo, crossed into Zamalek from Bulaq, traversed the quietly wealthy and smug Gezira island, where we lived, and then disappeared across the Nile into Imbaba, another teeming antithesis to Zamalek, with its quiet tree-lined streets, its foreigners, and its carefully plotted, shopless streets like Sharia Aziz Osman. The GPS's "playground," as it was called, constituted a frontier between the native urban world and the constructed colonial suburb we lived, studied, and played in. Before school began we would line up by class in the yard, and then again during recess, lunch, and dismissal. It is a sign of how lasting was the impression on me made by those exercises that I still remember *left* as the side nearest the school building, *right* as the Fuad al-Awwal side.

We stood there supposedly to be counted and greeted or dismissed: "Good morning, children" or "Good-bye, children." This seemed a polite ritual camouflaging the travails of being in line, where all sorts of unpleasant things took place. Forbidden to utter a word in class except in answer to the teacher's questions, the line was simultaneously a bazaar, auction house, and court, where the most extravagant of offers and promises were exchanged, and where the younger children were verbally bullied by older boys who threatened the direst punishment. My particular bane was David Ades, a boy two or three years older than me. Dark and muscular, he was ruthlessly focused on my pens, my pencil box, my sandwiches and sweets, which he wanted for himself, and was fearsomely challenging to everything I was or did. He didn't like my sweaters; he thought my socks were too short; he hated the look on my face; he disapproved of my way of talking. Coming to or leaving the school represented a daily challenge to me, of how to avoid getting caught or waylaid by David Ades, and for the years I was at GPS I was quite successful. But I could never escape him in the class lines, when despite the supervising teacher's presence, pushy, ruffianlike behavior was tolerated and Ades would whisper and mutter his threats and general disapprobation across the row of fidgeting children that kept us mercifully apart.

I have retained two phrases from Ades in my memory. One I parroted for years thereafter, "I promise you"; the other I haven't forgotten, because it frightened me so much when he uttered it: "I'll bash your face after school." Sometimes separately, often together, both were pronounced with fervent, not to say menacing, earnestness, even though it must have been at most a month after he first hurled them at me that I noticed how empty and unfulfilled they both were. Despite its soporific and sometimes repressive class atmosphere, the "school" that Ades promised to bash my face "after" protected me from him. His older brother Victor was a famous swimmer and diver who attended English Mission College (EMC) in Heliopolis; I admired his performances at meets around Cairo to which GPS took us, but I never liked the look of him any more than I ever warmed up to David, who would occasionally ask me to play a game of marbles with him.

I tried out both phrases at home—"I promise you" on my sisters, "I'll bash your face after school" in front of a mirror. (I was too timid to use it on a real person.) In the bickering squabbles I had with the two oldest of my younger sisters, "promising" meant trying to get something on loan ("I promise you I'll give it back") or working hard to convince them of some preposterous "fib" I was telling ("I promise you I saw the crazy poisoner with red hair today!") But I was prevented from pronouncing it as much as I wanted by Auntie Melia, who said I should vary its idiotic insincerity and monotony by saying "I assure you" instead.

For some infraction in class when I was eight I was sent out of the room by one of the women teachers (there weren't any males) who never used physical punishment except for a few polite taps of a ruler on our knuckles. The teacher left me outside the door, then summoned Mrs. Bullen, who with a dour expression on her face jostled me along to a staircase leading up from the main hall. "Come along now Edward. You've got to see Mr. Bullen upstairs!" She went up ahead of me. At the top of the stairs she stopped, placed her hand on my left shoulder, and steered me toward a closed door. "Wait here," she said, and then entered. A moment later she was back, signaling for me to go in; she then closed the door behind me, and I was, for the first and last time in my life, in the presence of Mr. Bullen.

I was instantly frightened of this large, red-faced, sandy-haired and silent Englishman who beckoned me toward him. Not a word passed between us as I approached him slowly where he stood near the window. I remember a blue vest and a white shirt, suede shoes, and a long flexible bamboo stick, something between a riding crop and a cane. I was apprehensive, but I was also aware that having reached this nadir of awfulness I must not break down or cry. He pulled me forward by the back of my neck, which he then forced down away from him so that I was half bent over. With his other hand he raised the stick and whacked me three times on the behind; there was a whistle as the stick cut the air, followed by a muffled pop as it hit me. The pain I felt was less than the anger that flushed through me with every one of Bullen's silently administered strokes. Who was this ugly brute to beat me so humiliatingly? And why did I allow myself to be so powerless, so "weak"—the word was beginning to acquire considerable resonance in my life—as to let him assault me with such impunity?

That five-minute experience was my sole encounter with Bullen; I knew neither his first name nor anything else about him except that he embodied my first public experience of an impersonal "discipline." When the incident was brought to my parents' notice by one of the teachers, my father said to me, "You see, you see how naughty you're becoming. When will you learn?" and there was not in their tone the slightest objection to the indecency of the punishment. Father: "We pay a lot of money for you to go to the finest schools; why do you waste the opportunity so?" as if overlooking how he had in fact paid the Bullens to treat me in this way. Mother: "Edward, why do you always get yourself into trouble like that?"

So I became delinquent, the "Edward" of punishable offenses, laziness, loitering, who was regularly expected to be caught in some specific unlicensed act and punished by being given detentions or, as I grew older, a violent slap by a teacher. GPS gave me my first experience of an organized system set up as a colonial business by the British. The atmosphere was one of unquestioning assent framed with hateful servility by teachers and students alike. The school was not interesting as a place of learning but it gave me my first extended contact with colonial authority in the sheer Englishness of its teachers and many of its students. I had no sustained contact with the English children outside the school; an invisible cordon kept them hidden in another world that was closed to me. I was perfectly aware of how their names were just *right,* and their clothes and accents and associations were totally different from my own. I cannot recall ever hearing any of them refer to "home," but I associated the idea of it with them, and in the deepest sense "home" was something I was excluded from. Although I didn't like the English as teachers or moral examples, their presence at the end of the street where I lived was neither unusual or unsettling. It was simply an unremarkable feature of Cairo, a city I always liked yet in which I never felt I belonged. I discovered that our apartment was rented, and that although some of the GPS children thought we were Egyptian, there was something "off" and out of place about us (me in particular), but I didn't yet quite know why.

Bullen remained fixed in my memory, as unchanged and undeveloped as an ogre in a child's story. He was the one figure in my childhood whose sole function was to whip me, never becoming more complicated than that. Exactly fifty years later during a short visit to Cairo I was leafing through a book written by an Egyptian scholar about two hundred years of British cultural interest in Egypt, and Bullen's name leapt up at me off the page. This time he was referred to as Keith Bullen, one of a group of minor British writers known as the *Salamander* poets who were resident in wartime Cairo. *Salamander* was a literary review whose name derived from Anatole France's inane observation that "one must be a philosopher to see a SALAMANDER"; an obliging Cairo friend later sent me a photocopy of the March 1943 issue, which must have appeared just as Mr. Bullen was whipping me, or perhaps another boy. Having already ascertained that my Bullen was indeed the *Salamander* Keith Bullen, I read his free English translation of "Summer Hours" by one Albert Samain. The opening:

> Bring me the cup of gold,
> The crystal, colour of a dream;
> In perfumes violent, extreme
> Our love may still unfold

This is followed by:

> Crushed is the golden summer's vine
> Let the cut peach incarnadine
> Stain the white splendour of your breast
>
> Sombre the woods are, void and vain. . . .
> This empty heart that finds no rest
> Aches with an ecstasy of pain . . .

How mannered, even precious, such verse is, with its fancy words and word order ("peach incarnadine,") and its exaggerated, unrealistic, and bathetic sentiment ("aches with an ecstasy of pain"). For me the poem's first line—"Bring me the cup of gold"—suggested a weird cartoon revision of my caning experience with Mr. Bullen: Could Keith have uttered those words to his wife as she opened the door to bring me in for the caning, "in perfumes violent . . . Our love may still unfold"? But no matter how much I try I still cannot reconcile the silent, terrorized submission I was physically forced into as he whipped me with the simpering poetaster who had disciplined me in the morning and who produced the appalling "Summer Hours" in the afternoon, and who doubtless was an admirable fellow who listened to Chaminade at night.

A short time after I was caned, I had an even more acute, and much more explicit, colonial encounter. Coming home at dusk across one of the vast outlying fields of the Gezira Club, I was accosted by a brown-suited Englishman with a pith helmet on his head and a small black briefcase hanging from his bicycle handlebars. This was Mr. Pilley, known to me in writing as "Hon. Sec'y" of the club, and also as the father of Ralph, a GPS contemporary of mine. "What are you doing here, boy?" he challenged me in a cold, reedy voice. "Going home," I said, trying to be calm as he dismounted from the bicycle and walked toward me. "Don't you know you're not supposed to be here?" he asked reprovingly. I started to say something about being a member, but he cut me off pitilessly. "Don't answer back, boy. Just get out, and do it quickly. Arabs aren't allowed here, and you're an Arab!" If I hadn't thought of myself as an Arab before, I now directly grasped the significance of the designation as truly disabling. When I told my father what Mr. Pilley had said to me he was only mildly disquieted. "And he wouldn't believe that we were members," I pleaded. "I'll speak to Pilley about this," was the noncommittal answer. The subject was never discussed again: Pilley had gotten away with it.

What troubles me now, fifty years later, is that although the episode remained with me for such a long time and although it smarted both then and now, there seemed to be a fatalistic compact between my father and myself about our necessarily inferior status. He knew about it; I discovered it publicly for the first time face to face with Pilley. Yet neither of us saw it then as worth a struggle of any kind, and that realization shames me still.

Such disparities in perception and reality could only become apparent to me decades and decades after I had left GPS. Very little of what surrounded me at the school—lessons, teachers, students, atmosphere—was sustaining or helpful to me. The best memories I have from my years at GPS belong to the end of the school day when my mother was always there for me to talk and listen to, as she enveloped my waking hours with an interpretation of everything taking place. She explained my teachers, my reading, and me. Except for activities like penmanship and art, I was a clever albeit erratic student, quick as well as perceptive, but my mother seemed unconsciously to take away from my achievements after initially celebrating them, by saying, "Of course you're clever, you're so so intelligent, but"—and here I was brought up short—"but that isn't a real accomplishment of yours since God gave you those gifts." Unlike my father, she communicated a kind of melting softness and supportive sentiment that sustained me for as long as it lasted. In her eyes, I felt, I was blessed, whole, marvelous. One compliment from her about my brightness, or my musicality, or my face caused me such a lift as momentarily to give me a feeling of actually belonging somewhere good and solid, although, alas, I soon became aware of how brief that feeling would be. Immediately then, I would start to worry about whether I could give myself permission to *be* secure, and pretty soon I had lost confidence again, and the old insecurities and anxieties set in. I have never doubted that my mother really loved me as she said she did, but by the time I was twelve or thirteen, I also knew that in some unspoken and mysterious way she was deeply critical of me. She had developed an extraordinary capacity to draw one in, convincing you of her total commitment and then, with scarcely a moment's notice, making you realize that she had judged and found you wanting. No matter how close I was to her she could always reveal a mysterious reserve or objectivity that never fully explained itself but nevertheless exercised harsh judgment and was simultaneously dispiriting and maddening to me.

And when I returned home in the afternoon there was always the risk of a telephoned report about what mischief I had been up to or what class I hadn't prepared for, to poison the respite from school supervision that I longed for. In this way I gradually lost my confidence, retaining only a fragile sense of security in self or surroundings, making me more dependent than ever on my mother's approval and love. My father was quite a remote figure during the week. He seemed to have no domestic responsibilities except shopping for fruits and vegetables in enormous quantities, all of which arrived home by delivery boy, and all of which my mother quite routinely bewailed. "We're drowning in oranges, bananas, cucumbers, tomatoes, Wadie. Why did you buy five kilos more today?" "You're crazy!" he'd sometimes respond coldly and bury himself back in his evening paper, unless of course I had been "reported" by the school, or if my monthly "report" expressed the usual reservations about my misbehavior, carelessness, loitering, or fidgeting. Then he would confront me ferociously for an awful moment or two, and withdraw. The confrontations worsened later, especially when I went to Victoria College.

I did have some lasting moments of unexpected well-being at GPS, however, the most notable of them having to do with my introduction to the theater, which took place in early 1944. It was an odd business coming back to school in the early evening, the classrooms dark and empty, the central hall dimly lit, beginning to be crowded with people filling the fastidiously arranged chairs. The slightly raised platform from which Mrs. Bullen made her morning pronouncements had been converted into a stage, complete with a wrinkled white curtain strung along the front. It was to be a performance of *Alice's Adventures in Wonderland;* the novel had been passed on to me by my mother at about the same time, but I found it tiresomely arch and largely incomprehensible, except for the illustrations, one in particular, of a mouse swimming up a stream, his little nose barely above water, which mysteriously intrigued me. My mother's rather vague and disappointed recommendation when I didn't press on with the book—"But it's for children, Edward!"—hadn't changed my mind, although I was excited that I might find something different in the book if it was presented and realized on the stage. "Is it like the cinema?" I remember asking an older boy who pushed me along into one of the front rows.

I can still see and hear bits of that school production of *Alice,* especially the tea party, the Red Queen playing croquet and bellowing "Off with their heads," and above all, Alice wandering in and out of situations we found funny but that alarmed and disoriented her. I could not grasp what the whole thing was about except that it totally transformed and gave an aura of irreducible glamour and strangeness to the actors, who during the day had been children at the GPS like myself. For no one was this more powerfully true than for Micheline Lindell, the girl who played Alice. The others—the Mad Hatter and March Hare, the Queen of Hearts—were older students I didn't have much to do with; Colette Amiel, a preternaturally large girl who seemed born to play the Queen, was the sister of Jean-Pierre Amiel, an exact contemporary and neighbor of David Ades, so I knew her by affiliation, and with only a little familiarity. The others were just "big" boys and girls whom I had glimpsed around the school. Micheline, on the other hand, was no more than a year older than me; she had once or twice sat one row away from me in French when, for unknown reasons, different classes were combined. She had a mole on the left side of her mouth, was about my height, and had the most beautifully clear voice, fluent in perfect English and Cairo French.

In *Alice* she was dressed in a white dress, with long white stockings and white ballet slippers. She was supposed to look virginal but did not at all, so artfully did her underlyingly seductive message get through the tight primness of her clothes, appealing very directly to a completely transfixed and, it must be added, mystified boy of nine. I felt no defined sexual attraction since I simply had no conception of what sex was, but looking at Micheline I did feel stirred and excited at how completely transformed she was and, even more exciting, how easily during the three days of performances she glided between being one of us, average, humdrum, uninteresting, to being a creature with so unmistakable an aura of glamour and elevation. During the day I would watch Micheline being ordinary, marveling at how like us she spoke, bore the teachers' criticism, had trouble with her lessons. No allowances seemed to be made for her success as an actress. Then at night she became the isolated and gifted girl, aglow with her power and skill. I saw every performance, although my parents demurred each time, but then reluctantly gave in on the grounds identified by my father as "it's a part of his education." I liked to stand quietly and unnoticed just outside the school gate to watch her leave, her eyes gleaming with the excitement of having won the evening for herself, her white dress only partly hidden beneath the black coat held around her shoulders by her father. I felt some guilt at my "sneakiness," but it was overridden by the thrill of concealment and of having seen Micheline exiting from one life into another.

There were no such passages for me. Something was clearly wrong in my life for which systematic remedies were devised, all of them out of school, many of them extensions of it. For a few months when I was in my last year at GPS (1946) I found myself deposited for two afternoons a week across the tramway tracks at the Greenwoods' house for extra exercises and sport. Like all the English children at school whose parents were not teachers, Jeremy Greenwood was the son of a company executive whose Zamalek villa, which I never entered, was surrounded by both a large garden and a high wall. On the lawn, and led by a wiry Egyptian instructor dressed impeccably in cricket whites, a few boys were guided through an hour of calisthenics, followed by some running and ball-throwing. I learned no skills at the Greenwood sessions, but as the only non-English boy I did learn something about "fair play" and "sportsmanship," a word I distinctly recall our instructor's pronouncing with an accent on the *man* and a heavily rolled *r*. I understood that both were about appearances; "fair play" meant complaining loudly to an adult that something your opponent did was "not fair," and sports*man*ship meant never revealing your real feelings of anger and hatred. I was the only non-English boy at the Greenwood afternoons, and felt awkward and forlorn as a result.

After a few unhappy and aimless weeks of exercise I was switched to the Cubs, whose bedraggled rump—the whole troop never seemed to turn up—met its two scoutmasters behind a shed somewhere on the Gezira Club grounds. There was a lot of squatting and bellowing into the wind: *"Ak-e-la, we will do our best."* I was particularly proud of this ritual of loyalty since it put me explicitly for the first time into a front-line position with the English boys *and* with the distasteful Ades, to whose whispered threats I was impervious in the Cub ranks. We met on Wednesday and Saturday afternoons, when I proudly wore my khaki shirt and shorts, my red kerchief and brown leather knot, my smart green stockings and red garters. My mother didn't like what she took to be the militarization of my spirit; having read about Mowgli, Kaa, Akela, and even Rikki-tikki-tavi with me, she couldn't accept the hierarchies and authorities imposed on her boy by the English, and she scarcely cared for my costume. My sisters Rosemarie and Jean, who were seven and four, respectively, were cowed into momentary awe by my rousing whoops and cries.

My father said nothing very much until the day he heard me practicing the oath, in particular the part about God and King. "Why are you saying that?" he asked me, as if I had devised the words myself. "You're an American, and we have no king, only a president. You are loyal to the President. God and President." Momentarily taken aback by this (I had no idea who the president was or what role he played in my life: the king after all was the latest I had studied in a long line from Edward the Confessor to the Plantagenets, the Stuarts, and beyond) I stammered a few words of mild objection: "'God and President' doesn't work," I volunteered at first. Then I wailed, "I can't say that, Daddy, I can't." He seemed puzzled by my pathetic refusal, since he clearly could not imagine what it would mean for a nine-year-old boy to challenge the Cub Scout authorities on a fine point of exact allegiance. He turned to my mother, who, as always, was nearby, and said to her in Arabic: "Hilda, come, try to figure out what's wrong with your son."

For the first time I took in what it meant to have failed his expectations; there was soon to be a second, also associated with the Cubs. On a fine Saturday afternoon in March a group of Cubs were taken to the nearby football field on the other, more open side of our Gezira Club shed. Our match against the Heliopolis Cubs had been announced a week earlier, so I had naïvely alerted my father—a great football forward himself as a young man thirty years ago in Jerusalem—to attend in order to watch me carry on the family tradition. Albert, my cousin, who played on, as had his uncle Wadie, the St. George's First Eleven, was lithe, powerful, a very fast runner—much like my father in appearance and his interest in sports. I would have liked to have been like him. In any event, I associated Albert with my father as he had been, and assumed, with considerable encouragement from my debonair cousin, that my father was in fact a great player who would appreciate my playing. Please come and see me play, I said, and he, not surprisingly, came.

The Cubmaster and I had overlooked the matter of football shoes, so I ended up as the only player on the field running about in immaculate brown Paul Favre shoes. Assigned to one of the halfback positions,

I suddenly found myself at a complete loss as to what I was meant to be doing. I was brought up short even more intensely when I grasped, as if for the first time, that I had never actually played on a team before, and that my father, standing impassively about fifty feet away from me, was watching not only a very incompetent but a doubtless shamingly awkward son playing a position he had no business occupying. My feet seemed gigantic, and extremely heavy at the same time. I kicked at, but completely missed, the first ball to come my way, all in all the perfect beginning for what was to be a thoroughly undistinguished performance. "Said [pronounced *Side*]," one of the masters announced to me, "move about a bit more. Can't have you just standing there!" I later saw him giving me a disapproving look for having three or four, instead of one or two, orange slices during half-time. During the second half, I was just as immobilized by timidity and uncertainty. We lost.

After church the next day my father intercepted me in the corridor leading to the dining room. Lunch was about to be served—on rare occasions we had "people," i.e., family, in for the main Sunday meal, which enlivened an otherwise monotonous day of enforced piety—but I could tell the encounter with my father was going to be a little less than pleasant. He held my shoulder after he had turned me around in front of him: together we faced down the corridor. As he swung his right leg to emulate a football kick, he began: "I watched you yesterday." Pause. "You kick the ball and then you stop. You should go after it, move, move, move. Why do you stand still? Why don't you rush after it?" This last question was accompanied by a great shove as he propelled me down the corridor in supposed pursuit of a nonexistent ball. All I could do was to stumble badly as I ungracefully recovered my balance. There was nothing I could say at all.

I do not know whether my feelings of physical incompetence, which came from a sense that neither my body nor my character naturally inhabited my assigned spaces in life, derived from this quite unpleasant ordeal at my father's hands, but certainly I have always found myself tracing these feelings back to that event. Body and character were, I began to discover, interchangeable so far as his scrutiny was concerned. One particularly durable theme in his comments from early youth right through to the end of my undergraduate education was my penchant for never going far enough, for skimming the surface, for not "doing your best." Whenever he drew my attention to each of these failings he made a particular gesture with his hands, a clenched fist pulled back toward his shoulder in the first instance, a fluttering pass from left to right in the second, a wagging finger in the third. Most of the time he would cite my experience at the scout football game as an illustration of what he meant, from which I concluded that I did not have the moral force actually to do what was necessary for "my best." I was weak in all senses of the word, but especially (I made the unspoken connection myself) with reference to him.

A little later in the same year (1944) that I was so captivated by Micheline Lindell in *Alice,* I was to have another extraordinary theatrical experience. My mother announced that John Gielgud was coming to Cairo to perform *Hamlet* at the Opera House. "We must go," she said with infectious resolve, and indeed it was duly set up, although of course I had no idea who John Gielgud was. I was nine at the time, and had just learned a bit about the play in the volume of Shakespeare stories by Charles and Mary Lamb I had been given for Christmas a few months earlier. Mother's idea was that she and I should gradually read through the play together. For that purpose a beautiful one-volume complete Shakespeare was brought down from the shelf, its handsome red morocco leather binding and delicate onion-skin paper embodying for me all that was luxurious and exciting in a book. Its opulence was heightened by the pencil or charcoal drawings illustrating the dramas, *Hamlet*'s being an exceptionally taut tableau by Henry Fuseli of the Prince of Denmark, Horatio, and the Ghost seeming to struggle against each other as the announcement of murder and the agitated response to it theatrically gripped them.

The two of us sat in the front reception room, she in a big armchair, I on a stool next to her, with a smoky smoldering fire in the fireplace on her left, and we read *Hamlet* together. She was Gertrude and Ophelia, I, Hamlet, Horatio, and Claudius. She also played Polonius as if in implicit solidarity with my father, who often admonishingly quoted "neither a borrower nor a lender be" to me as a reminder of how risky it was for me to be given money to spend on my own. We skipped the whole play-within-a-play sequence as too bewilderingly ornate and complicated for the two of us. There must have been at least four, and perhaps even five or six, sessions when, sharing the book, we read and tried to make sense of the play, the two of us completely alone and together, for four afternoons after school, with Cairo, my sisters, and father totally shut out.

I only half-consciously understood the lines, though Hamlet's basic situation, his outrage at his father's murder and his mother's remarriage, his endless wordy vacillation, did come through. I had no idea what incest and adultery were, but could not ask my mother, whose concentration on the play seemed to me to have drawn her in and away from me. What I remember above all was the change from her normal voice to a new stage voice as Gertrude: it went up in pitch, smoothed out, became exceptionally fluent and, most of all, acquired a bewitchingly flirtatious and calming tone. "Good Hamlet," I remember her clearly saying to me, not to Hamlet, "cast thy nighted colour and let thine eye look like a friend on Denmark." I felt that she was speaking to my better, less disabled, and still fresh self, hoping perhaps to lift me out of the sodden delinquency of my life, already burdened with worries and anxieties that I was now sure were to threaten my future.

Reading *Hamlet* as an affirmation of my status in her eyes, not as someone devalued, which I had become in mine, was one of the great moments in my childhood. We were two voices to each other, two happily allied spirits in language. I knew nothing conscious of the inner dynamics that linked desperate prince and adulterous queen at the play's interior, nor did I really take in the fury of the scene between them when Polonius is killed and Gertrude is verbally flayed by Hamlet. We read together through all that, since what mattered to me was that in a curiously un-Hamlet-like way, I could count on her to be someone whose emotions and affections engaged mine without her really being more than an exquisitely maternal, protective, and reassuring person. Far from feeling that she had tampered with her obligations to her son, I felt that these readings confirmed the deepness of our connection to each other; for years I kept in my mind the higher than usual pitch of her voice, the unagitated poise of her manner, the soothing, altogether conclusively patient outline of her presence as goods to be held on to at all costs, but rarer and rarer as my delinquencies increased in number and her destructive and certainly dislocating capacities threatened me more.

When I did see the play at the Opera House I was jolted out of my seat by Gielgud's declaiming, "Angels and ministers of grace defend us," and the sense it conveyed of being a miraculous confirmation of what I had read privately with Mother. The trembling resonance of his voice, the darkened, windy stage, the distantly shining figure of the ghost, all seemed to have brought to life the Fuseli drawing that I had long studied, and it raised my sensuous apprehension to a pitch I do not think I have ever again experienced at quite that intensity. But I was also disheartened by the physical incongruencies between myself and the men, whose green and crimson tights set off fully rounded, perfectly shaped legs, which seemed to mock my spindly, shapeless legs, my awkward carriage, my unskilled movements. Everything about Gielgud and the blond man who played Laertes communicated an ease and confidence of being—they were English heroes, after all—that reduced me to inferior status, curtailing my capacities for enjoying the play. A few days later, when an Anglo-American classmate called Tony Howard invited me to meet Gielgud at his house, it was all I could do to manage a feeble, silent handshake. Gielgud was in a gray suit, but said nothing; he pressed my small hand with an Olympian half-smile.

It must have been the memory of those long-ago *Hamlet* afternoons in Cairo that made my mother, during the last two or three years of her life, enthusiastic once again about our going to the theater together. The most memorable time was when—her cancer afflictions already pronounced—she arrived in London from Beirut on her way to the United States to consult a specialist; I met her at the airport and brought her to Brown's Hotel for the one night she had to spend there. With barely two hours to get ready and have an early supper she nevertheless said an unhesitating yes to my suggestion that we see Vanessa Redgrave and Timothy Dalton as Anthony and Cleopatra at the Haymarket Theatre. An understated, unopulent production, the long play positively transfixed her in a way that surprised me; after years of Lebanese war and Israeli invasion she had become distracted, often querulous, worried about her health and what she should do with herself. All of this, however, went into abeyance as we watched and heard Shakespeare's lines—"Eternity was in our lips and eyes, Bliss in our brows bent"—as if spoken in the accents of wartime Cairo, back in our little cocoon, the two of us very quiet and concentrated, sharing the language and communion despite the disparity in our ages and the fact that we were nevertheless mother and son, for the very last time. Eight months later she began her final descent into the disease that killed her,

her mind ravaged by metastases that before striking her completely silent for the two months before she died caused her to speak fearsomely of plots around her, then to utter what was the last lucidly intimate thing she ever said to me, "My poor little child," pronounced with such sad resignation, a mother taking final leave of her son.

When I was growing up I always wished that she might have been the one to watch me play football or tennis, or that she alone could have talked to my teachers, relieved of her duties as my father's partner in the joint program for my reform and betterment. After she died, and I no longer wrote her my weekly letter nor (when she was in Washington nursing her illness) spoke directly to her in our daily phone call, I kept her as a silent companion anyway. To be held in her arms when she wished to cuddle and stroke me as a small boy was bliss indeed, but such attention could never be sought or asked for. Her moods regulated mine, and I recall one of the most anguished moods of my childhood and early adolescence was trying, with nothing to guide me and no great success at all, to distract her from her role as taskmaster, and to tease her into giving me approval and support. A good deed, a decent grade, a well-executed passage on the piano might nevertheless cause in her a sudden transfiguration of her face, a dramatic elevation in her tone, a breathtakingly wide opening of arms, as she took me in with "Bravo Edward, my darling boy, bravo, bravo. Let me kiss you." Yet most of the time she was so driven by her sense of duty as mother and supervisor of household life that the habitual voice of those years that has also stayed with me is the one she used to call out injunctions: "Practice your piano, Edward!"; "Get back to your homework"; "Don't waste time: begin your composition"; "Have you had your milk, your tomato juice, your cod liver oil?"; "Finish your plate"; "Who ate the chocolates? A full box has disappeared. Edward!"

IV

MY FATHER'S STRENGTH, MORAL AND PHYSICAL, DOMINATED the early part of my life. He had a massive back and a barrel chest, and although he was quite short he communicated indomitability and, at least to me, a sense of overpowering confidence. His most striking physical feature was his ramrod-stiff, nearly caricaturelike upright carriage. And with that, in contrast to my shrinking, nervous timidity and shyness, went a kind of swagger that furnished another browbeating contrast with me: he never seemed to be afraid to go anywhere or do anything. I was, always. Not only did I not rush forward, as I should have done in the unfortunate football game, but I felt myself to be seriously unwilling to let myself be looked at, so conscious was I of innumerable physical defects, all of which I was convinced reflected my inner deformations. To be looked at directly, and to return the gaze, was most difficult for me. When I was about ten I mentioned this to my father. "Don't look at their eyes; look at their nose," he said, thereby communicating to me a secret technique I have used for decades. When I began to teach as a graduate student in the late fifties I found it imperative to take off my glasses in order to turn the class into a blur that I couldn't see. And to this day I find it unbearably difficult to look at myself on television, or even read about myself.

When I was eleven, this fear of being seen prevented me from doing something I really wanted to do. It was perhaps my second opera performance in the Cairo house that was a miniature replica of the Paris Garnier behemoth and had canonized *Aida*. I was excited by the solemn rituals of the stage and costumed people, but also by the music itself, its enactments and formality. I was particularly intrigued by the orchestra pit and, at its center, the conductor's podium, with its enormous score and long baton. I wanted a closer look at both during intermission, which our center *baignoire* seats did not afford. "Can I look at them?" I asked my father. "Go ahead. Go down there," he responded. The idea of walking alone through the parquet suddenly struck me as impossible: I was too ashamed, my physical vulnerability to inquiring (perhaps even condemning) looks too great. "All right," he said with exasperation. "I'll go." I saw him commandeer the aisle, almost strutting toward the podium, which he very slowly, deliberately, reached; then, adding to my discomfort, he pretended to turn the pages of the score with curiosity and daring all over his face. I sank further into my seat, allowing myself only a peep over the banister, unable to bear the combined embarrassment, perhaps even fear, at my father's exposure, and my shrinking timidity.

It was my mother's often melting warmth which offered me a rare opportunity to be the person I felt I truly was in contrast to the "Edward" who failed at school and sports, and could never match the manliness my father represented. And yet my relationship with her grew more ambivalent, and her disapproval of me became far more emotionally devastating to me than my father's virile bullying and reproaches. One summer afternoon in Lebanon when I was sixteen and in more than usual need of her sympathy, she delivered a judgment on all her children that I have never forgotten. I had just spent the first of two unhappy years at Mount Hermon, a repressive New England boarding school, and this particular summer of 1952 was critically important, mainly because I could spend time with her. We had developed the habit of sitting together in the afternoons, talking quite intimately, exchanging news and opinions. Suddenly she said, "My children have all been a disappointment to me. All of them." Somehow I couldn't bring myself to say, "But surely not me," even though it had been well established that I was her favorite, so much so (my sisters told me) that during my first year away from home she would lay a place for me at table on important occasions like Christmas Eve, and would not allow Beethoven's Ninth (my preferred piece of music) to be played in the house.

"Why," I asked, "why do you feel that way about us?" She pursed her lips and withdrew further into herself, physically and spiritually. "Please tell me why," I continued. "What have I done?"

"Someday perhaps you will know, maybe after I die, but it's very clear to me that you are all a great disappointment." For some years I would re-ask my questions, to no avail: the reasons for her disappointment in us, and obviously in me, remained her best-kept secret, as well as a weapon in her arsenal for manipulating us, keeping us off balance, and putting me at odds with my sisters and the world. Had it always been like this? What did it mean that I had once believed our intimacy was so secure as to admit few doubts and no undermining at all of my position? Now as I looked back on my frank and, despite the disparity in age, deep liaison with my mother, I realized how her critical ambivalence had always been there.

During the GPS years my two oldest younger sisters, Rosy and Jean, and I began slowly, almost imperceptibly, to develop a contestatory relationship that played or was made to play in to my mother's skills at managing and manipulating us. I had felt protective of Rosy: I helped her along, since she was somewhat younger and less physically adept than I; I cherished her and would frequently embrace her as we played on the balcony; I kept up a constant stream of chatter, to which she responded with smiles and chuckles. We went off to GPS together in the morning, but we separated once we got there since she was in a younger class. She had lots of giggling little girlfriends—Shahira, Nazli, Nadia, Vivette—and I, my "fighting" classmates like Dickie Cooper or Guy Mosseri. Quickly she established herself as a "good" girl, while I lurked about the school with a growing sense of discomfort, rebelliousness, drift, and loneliness.

After school the troubles began between us. They were accompanied by our enforced physical separation: no baths together, no wrestling or hugging, separate rooms, separate regimens, mine more physical and disciplined than hers. When Mother came home she would discuss my performance in contrast to my younger sister's. "Look at Rosy. All the teachers say she's doing very well." Soon enough, Jean—exceptionally pretty in her thick, auburn pigtails—changed from a tagalong younger version of Rosy into another "good" girl, with her own circle of apparently like-minded girlfriends. And she also was complimented by the GPS authorities, while I continued to sink into protracted "disgrace," an English word that hovered around me from the time I was seven. Rosy and Jean occupied the same room; I was down the corridor; my parents in between; Joyce and Grace (eight and eleven years younger than I) had their bedrooms moved from the glassed-in balcony to one or another of the other rooms as the apartment was modified to accommodate the growing children.

The closed door of Rosy and Jean's room signified the definitive physical as well as emotional gulf that slowly opened between us. There was once even an absolute commandment against my entering the room, forcefully pronounced and occasionally administered by my father, who now openly sided with them, as their defender and patron; I gradually assumed the part of their dubiously intentioned brother, a role of course pioneered (in my father's eyes) by my maternal uncles. "Protect them," I was always being told, to no effect whatever. For Rosy especially I was a sort of prowling predator-target, to be taunted or cajoled into straying into their room, only to be pelted with erasers, hit over the head with pillows, and shrieked at with terror and dangerous enjoyment. They seemed eager to study and learn at school and home, whereas I kept putting off such activities in order to torment them or otherwise fritter the time away until my mother returned home to a cacophony of charges and countercharges buttressed by real bruises to show and real bites to be cried over.

There was never complete estrangement though, since the three of us did at some level enjoy the interaction of competing, but rarely totally hostile, siblings. My sisters could display their quickness or specialized skill in hopscotch, and I could try to emulate them; in memorable games of blind man's buff, ring-around-the-rosy, or clumsy football in a very confined space, I might exploit my height or relative strength. After we attended the Circo Togni, whose lion tamer especially impressed me with his authoritative presence and braggadoccio, I replicated his act in the girls' room, shouting commands like *"A posto, Camelia"* at them while waving an imaginary whip and grandly thrusting a chair in their direction. They seemed quite pleased at the charade, and even managed a dainty roar as they clambered onto bed or dresser with not quite feline grace.

But we never embraced each other, as brothers and sisters might ordinarily have: for it was exactly at this subliminal level that I felt a withdrawal on all sides, of me from them, and them from me. The physical distance is still there between us, I feel, perhaps deepened over the years by my mother. When she returned from her afternoons at the Cairo Women's Club she invariably interjected herself between us. With greater and greater frequency my delinquency exposed me to her angry reprobation: "Can't I ever leave you with your sisters without your making trouble?" was the refrain, often succeeded by the dreaded appendix, "Wait till your father gets home." Precisely because there was an unstated prohibition on physical contact between us, my infractions took the form of attacks that included punching, hair-pulling, pushing, and the occasional vicious pinch. Invariably I was "reported" and then "disgraced"—in English—and some stringent punishment (a further prohibition on going to the movies, being sent to bed without dinner, a steep reduction in my allowance and, at the limit, a beating from my father) was administered.

All this heightened our sense of the body's peculiar, and problematic, status. There was an abyss—never discussed, nor examined, nor even mentioned during the crucial period of puberty—separating a boy's body from a girl's. Until I was twelve I had no idea at all what sex between men and women entailed, nor did I know very much at all about the relevant anatomy. Suddenly, however, words like "pants" and "panties" became italicized: "I can see your pants," said my sisters tauntingly to me, and I responded, heady with danger, "I can see *your* panties." I quite clearly recall that bathroom doors had to be bolted shut against marauders of the opposite sex, although my mother was present for both my dressing and undressing, as well as for theirs. I think she must have understood sibling rivalry very well and the temptations of polymorphous perversity all around us. But I also suspect that she played and worked on these impulses and drives: she kept us apart by highlighting our differences, she dramatized our shortcomings to each other, she made us feel that she alone was our reference point, our most trusted friend, our most precious love—as, paradoxically, I still believe she was. Everything between me and my sisters had to pass through her, and everything I said to them was steeped in her ideas, her feelings, her sense of what was right or wrong.

None of us of course ever knew what she really thought of us, except fleetingly, enigmatically, alienatingly (as when she told me about our all being a disappointment). It was only much later in my life that I understood how unfulfilled and angry she must have felt about our life in Cairo and, retrospectively, its busy conventionality, its forced rigors and the absence (in her and in her children) of openness, its limitless manipulations, and its peculiar lack of authenticity. A lot of this had to do with her fabulous capacity for letting you trust and believe in her, even though you knew that a moment later she could either turn on you with incomparable anger and scorn or draw you in with her radiant charm. "Come and sit next to me, Edward," she would say, thereby letting you into her confidence, and allowing you an amazing sense of assurance; of course you also felt that by doing this she was also keeping out Rosy and Jean, even my father. There was a kind of demonic possessiveness and, at the same time, an infinitely modulated responsiveness that accepted you not just as a son but as a prince. I once confessed to her my belief in myself as someone both gifted and unusual, despite the almost comic lineup of failures and endless troubles I found myself in at school, and everywhere else. It was a very timidly volunteered affirmation of a force, perhaps even another identity underneath "Edward." "I know," she said softly to me, in the most confidential and reassuring of fugitive *sotto voces*.

But who was she really? Unlike my father, whose general solidity and lapidary pronouncements were a known and stable quantity, my mother was energy itself, in everything, all over the house and our lives, ceaselessly probing, judging, sweeping all of us, plus our clothes, rooms, hidden vices, achievements, and problems into her always expanding orbit. But there was no common emotional space. Instead there were bilateral relationships with my mother, as colony to metropole, a constellation only she could see as a whole. What she said to me about herself, for instance, she also said to my sisters, and this characterization formed the basis of her operating persona: she was simple, she was a good person who always did the right things, she loved us all unconditionally, she wanted us to tell her everything, which only she could keep hidden from everyone else. I believed this unquestioningly. There was nothing so satisfying in the outside world, a merry-go-round of changing schools (and hence friends and acquaintances), numerous lives, being a non-Egyptian of uncertain, not to say suspicious, composite identity habitually out of place, and representing a person with no recognizable profile and no particular direction. My mother seemed to take in and sympathize with my general predicament. And that was enough for me. It worked as a provisional support, which I cherished tremendously.

It was through my mother that my awareness of my body as incredibly fraught and problematic developed, first because in her intimate knowledge of it she seemed better able to understand its capacity for wrongdoing, and second because she would never speak openly about it, but approached the subject either with indirect hints or, more troublingly, by means of my father and maternal uncles, through whom she spoke like a ventriloquist. When I was about fourteen I said something she thought was tremendously funny; I did not realize at the time how unknowingly astute I was. I had left the bathroom door unlocked (a telling inadvertence, since I had gained some privacy as an adolescent, but for some reason wanted it occasionally infringed upon), and she suddenly entered. For a second she didn't close the door, but stood there surveying her naked son as he hastily dried himself with a small towel. "Please leave," I said testily, "and stop trying to catch up where you left off." This injunction carried the day, since she burst out laughing, quickly closed the door, and walked briskly away. Had she ever really left off?

I knew much earlier that my body and my sisters' were inexplicably taboo. My mother's radical ambivalence expressed itself in her extraordinary physical embrace of her children—covering us with kisses, caresses, and hugs, cooing, making expostulations of delight about our beauty and physical endowments—and at the same time offering a great deal of devastating negative commentary on our appearance. Fatness became a dangerous and constant subject when I was nine and Rosy was seven. As my sister gained weight it became a point of discussion for us throughout childhood, adolescence, and early adulthood. Along with that went an amazingly detailed consciousness of "fattening" foods, plus endless prohibitions. I was quite skinny, tall, coordinated; Rosy didn't seem to be, and this contrast between us, to which was added the contrast between her cleverness at school and my shabby performance there, my father's special regard for her versus my mother's for me (they always denied any favoritism), her greater savoir faire when it came to organizing her time, and her capacity for pacing herself, talents I did not at all possess—all this deepened the estrangement between us, and intensified my discomfort with our bodies.

It was my father who gradually took the lead in trying to reform, perhaps even to remake, my body, but my mother rarely demurred, and regularly brought my body to a doctor's attention. As I look back on my sense of my body from age eight on, I can see it locked in a demanding set of repeated corrections, all of them ordered by my parents, most of them having the effect of turning me against myself. "Edward" was enclosed in an ugly, recalcitrant shape with nearly everything wrong with it. Until the end of 1947, when we left Palestine for the last time, our pediatrician was a Dr. Grünfelder, like Madame Baer, the midwife, a German Jew, and known to be the finest in Palestine. His office was in a quiet, clean, orderly, and leafy area of the parched city that seemed distinctly foreign to my young eyes. He spoke to us in English, although there was a good deal of confidential whispering between him and my mother that I was rarely able to overhear. Three persistent problems were referred to him, for which he provided his own, idiosyncratic solutions; the problems themselves indicate the extent to which certain parts of my body came in for an almost microscopic, and needlessly intense, supervision.

One concerned my feet, which were pronounced flat early in my life. Grünfelder prescribed the metal arches that I wore with my first pair of shoes; they were finally discarded in 1948, when an aggressive clerk in a Dr. Scholl's store in Manhattan dissuaded my mother from their use. A second was my odd habit of shuddering convulsively for a brief moment every time I urinated. Of course I was asked to perform the shudder for the doctor, but just as certainly was unable either to urinate or to shudder. My mother observed me for a couple of weeks, then brought the case to the world-renowned "child specialist." Grünfelder shrugged his shoulders. "It is nothing," he pronounced, "probably psychological"—a phrase I didn't understand but could see worried my mother just a little more, or was at least to worry *me* until I was well into my teens, after which the issue was dropped.

The third problem was my stomach, the source of numerous ills and pains all my life. It began with Grünfelder's skepticism about my mother's habit of wrapping and tightly pinning a small blanket around my midsection in both summer and winter. She thought this protected me against illness, the night air, perhaps even the evil eye; later, hearing about it from different friends, I realized it was common practice in Palestine and Syria. She once told Grünfelder about this strange prophylactic in my presence, his response to which I distinctly remember was a knitted, skeptical brow. "I don't see the need," he said, whereupon she pressed on with a rehearsal of all sorts of advantages (most of them preventive) that accrued to me. I was nine or ten at the time. The issue was also debated with Wadie Baz Haddad, our family GP in Cairo, and he too tried to dissuade her. It took another year for the silly thing to be removed once and for all; Hilda later told me that still another doctor had warned her against sensitizing my midsection so much, since it then became vulnerable to all sorts of other problems.

My eyes had grown weaker because I had spring catarrh and a bout with trachoma; for two years I wore dark glasses at a time when no one else did. At age six or seven, I had to lie in a darkened room every day with compresses on my eyes for an hour. As my shortsightedness developed I saw less and less well, but my parents took the position that glasses were not "good" for you, and were positively bad if you "got used" to them. In December of 1949 at the age of fourteen, I went to see *Arms and the Man* at the American University of Cairo's Ewart Hall, and was unable to see anything taking place on stage, until my friend Mostapha Hamdollah loaned me his glasses. Six months later, after a teacher's complaint, I did get glasses with express parental instructions not to wear them all the time: my eyes were already bad enough, I was told, and would get worse.

At the age of twelve I was informed that the pubic hair sprouting between my legs was not "normal," increasing my already overdeveloped embarrassment about myself. The greatest critique, however, was reserved for my face and tongue, back, chest, hands, and abdomen. I did not know I was being attacked, nor did I experience the reforms and strictures as the campaigns they were. I assumed they were all elements of the discipline that one went through as part of growing up. The net effect of these reforms, however, was to make me deeply self-conscious and ashamed.

The longest running and most unsuccessful reform—my father's near obsession—was my posture, which became a major issue for him just as I reached puberty. In June of 1957, when I graduated from Princeton, it culminated in my father's insisting on taking me to a brace and corset maker in New York in order to buy me a harness to wear underneath my shirt. What distresses me about the experience is that at age twenty-one I uncomplainingly let my father feel entitled to truss me up like a naughty child whose bad posture symbolized some objectionable character trait that required scientific punishment. The clerk who sold us the truss remained expressionless as my father amiably declared, "See, it works perfectly. You'll have no problems."

The white cotton and latex truss with straps across my chest and over the shoulders was the consequence of years of my father trying to get me to "stand up straight." "Shoulders back," he would say, "shoulders back," and my mother—whose own posture, like her mother's, was poor—would add in Arabic, "Don't slump." As the offense persisted she resigned herself to the notion that my posture came from the Badrs, her mother's family, and would routinely emit a desultory sigh, fatalistic and disapproving at the same time, followed by the phrase *"Herdabit beit Badr,"* or "the Badr family humpback," addressed to no one in particular, but clearly intended to fix the blame on my ancestry, if not also on her.

The Badrs' or not, my father persisted in his efforts. These later included "exercises," one of which was to slip one of his canes through both my armpits and make me keep it there for two hours at a stretch. Another was to make me stand in front of him and for half an hour respond to his order, "One," by thrusting my elbows back as hard and as quickly as possible, supposedly straightening my back in the process. Whenever I wandered across his line of vision he would call out, "Shoulders back"; this of course embarrassed me when others were around, but it took me weeks to ask him to please not call out to me so loudly on the street, in the club, or even walking into church. He was reasonable about my objection. "Here's what I'll do," he said reassuringly. "I'll just say 'Back,' and only you and I will know what it means." And so "Back" I endured for years and years until the truss.

A corollary to the struggle over my posture was how it affected my chest, whose disproportionately large size and prominence I inherited from my father. Very early in my teens I was given a metal chest expander with instructions to use it to develop the size and disposition of the front of my body, sorely affected by my posture's continuing misdemeanor. I was never able to master the gadget's crazy springs, which leapt out at you threateningly if you did not have the strength to keep them taut. The real trouble, as I once explained to my mother who listened sympathetically, was that my chest was already too large; thrusting it forward aggressively, making it even bigger, turned me into a grotesque, barrel-chested caricature of a well-developed man. I seemed to be caught between the hump and the barrel. My mother understood and tried to persuade my father of this without any observable result. When he was in the United States before World War I, my father had been influenced by Gregory Sandow, the legendary strongman who even turns up in *Ulysses,* and Sandow featured an overdeveloped chest and erect back. What was good for Sandow, my father once told me, ought to do "for you too."

Yet on several occasions my resistance exasperated my father enough for him to pummel me painfully around my shoulders, and once even to deliver a solid fist into my back. He could be physically violent, and threw heavy slaps across my face and neck, while I cringed and dodged in what I felt was a most shameful way. I regretted his strength and my weakness beyond words, but I never responded or called out in protest, not even when, as a Harvard graduate student in my early twenties, I was bashed by him humiliatingly for being rude, he said, to my mother. I learned how to sense that a cuff was on its way by the odd fashion he drew his top lip into his mouth and the heavy breath he suddenly took in. I much preferred the studied care he took with my canings—using a riding crop—to the frightening, angry, and impulsive violence of his slaps and swinging blows to my face. When she suddenly lost her temper, my mother also flailed at my face and head, but less frequently and with considerably less force.

As I write this now it gives me a chance, very late in life, to record the experiences as a coherent whole that very strangely have left no anger, some sorrow, and a surprisingly strong residual love for my parents. All the reforming things my father did to me coexisted with an amazing willingness to let me go my own way later on; he was strikingly generous to me at Princeton and Harvard, always encouraging me to travel, continue piano studies, live well, always willing to foot the

bill (in his own special way, of course), even though that took me further from him as an only son and the only likely successor in the family business, which he quietly sold the year I got my Ph.D. in literature.
What I cannot completely forgive, though, is that the contest over my
body, and his administering of reforms and physical punishment,
instilled a deep sense of generalized fear in me, which I have spent most
of my life trying to overcome. I still sometimes think of myself as a
coward, with some gigantic lurking disaster waiting to overtake me for
sins I have committed and will soon be punished for.

My parents' fear of my body as imperfect and morally flawed
extended to my appearance. When I was about five, my long curly hair
was chopped down into a no-nonsense very short haircut. Because I
had a decent soprano voice and was considered "pretty" by my doting
mother, I felt my father's disapproval, even anxiety, that I might be a
"sissy," a word that hovered around me until I was ten. A strange motif
of my early teens was an assault on the "weakness" of my face, particularly my mouth. My mother used to tell two favorite stories; the first
was about how Leonardo da Vinci used the same man as a model for
Jesus and, after years of the man's dissipation, for Judas. The other had
her quoting Lincoln, who, after condemning a man for his awful looks
and being challenged by a friend that no one is responsible for being
ugly, was reported to have responded, "Everyone is responsible for his
face." When I was being upbraided for delinquency against my sisters,
or lying about having eaten all the candy, or having spent all the
money, my father would swiftly thrust his hand out, put his thumb and
second finger on either side of my mouth, press in, and hold the area
with a number of energetic short jerks to the left and right, all the while
producing a nasty, buzzing sound like "mmmmmm," quickly followed
by "that weak mouth of yours." I can recall staring at myself disgust-
edly in the mirror well past my twentieth birthday, doing exercises
(pursing my mouth, clenching my teeth, raising my chin twenty or
thirty times) in an effort to bring "strength" to my weak droop. Glenn
Ford's way of flexing his jaw muscles to signify moral fortitude and the
travails of being "strong" was an early model, which I tried to imitate
when responding to my parents' accusation. And it was as a subsidiary
aspect of my weak face and mouth that my parents disapproved of my
wearing glasses; my mother, ever ready to condemn and praise at the

same time, stipulated that glasses obscured "that beautiful face of yours."

As for my torso, there wasn't much said about it until I was thirteen, a year before I went to Victoria College in 1949. My father met a gentleman at the Gezira Club called Mr. Mourad who had just opened a gymnasium in an apartment on Fuad al-Awwal Street in Zamalek, about half a mile from where we lived. Soon thereafter I found myself enrolled in three exercise classes a week, along with half a dozen Kuwaitis who had come to Egypt to attend the university. These classes included knee bends, medicine-ball raises and lifts, sit-ups, jogging, and jumping (all inside a tiny square room). I was soon the butt of our wiry instructor, Mr. Ragab. "More effort," he would call out hectoringly at me in English—"Up, down, up, down," etc. Then, a few weeks into the course, came the bombshell. "Come on Edward," he said contemptuously of my sit-ups, "we must get that stomach of yours into shape." When I said that I thought the purpose of my being at the gym was my back, he said that it was, but my midsection was not firm enough. "Anyway, it's what your parents want us to do." I was too embarrassed knowing what they thought about my midsection ever to raise the matter with my parents. Another tear opened in the relationship to my body. And as I accepted the verdict I internalized the criticism, and became even more awkward about and uncertain of my physical identity.

My problematic hands became my mother's special province of critical attention. Although I was only dimly aware that physically I noticeably resembled neither the Saids (short, stocky, very dark) nor her family, the Musas (white-skinned, of medium height and build, with longer than average fingers and limbs), it was clear to me that I had endowments of strength and athletic ability denied anyone else. By the age of twelve I was a good deal taller than everyone else in my family, and, thanks to my father's curious persistence, I had amassed knowledge and practice of numerous sports, including tennis, swimming, football (despite my noted failure at it), riding, track and field, cricket, Ping-Pong, sailing, boxing. I was never outstanding in any of them, being too timid to be able to dominate an opponent, but I had developed an already considerable natural competence. This allowed me over time to develop my strength, certain muscles, and—something I still possess—

a very unusual stamina and wind. My hands in particular were large, exceptionally sinewy, and agile. And to my mother, they represented objects both of adoring admiration (the long, tapered fingers, the perfect proportions, the superb agility) and of often quite hysterical denunciation ("Those hands of yours are deadly instruments"; "They're going to get you into trouble later"; "Be very careful").

To my mother they were almost everything except a pair of hands: they were hammers, pliers, clubs, steel wires, nails, scissors, and when she wasn't angry or agitated, instruments of the most refined and gentle kind. For my father my hands were noteworthy for the fingernails, which I chewed on and which for decades he tried to get me not to chew, even to the point of having them painted with a vile-tasting medicine and to promising me a fancy manicure at Chez Georges, the plush barbershop he frequented on Kasr el Nil Street. All to no avail, though I often found myself hiding my hands in my pockets, as I tried not to expose myself to my father's gaze so that my "back" would not obtrusively draw his, and everyone else's, attention.

The moral and the physical shaded into each other most imperceptibly of all when it came to my tongue, which was the object of a dense series of metaphorical associations in Arabic, most of which were negative and, in my particular case, recurred with great frequency. In English one hears mainly of a "biting" or "sharp" tongue, in contrast with a "smooth" one. Whenever I blurted out something that seemed untoward, it was my "long" tongue that was to blame: aggressive, unpleasant, uncontrolled. The description was a common one in Arabic and signified someone who did not have the required politeness and verbal savoir faire, important qualities in most Arab societies. It was my state of being repressed that caused my occasional outbursts as I compensated too much in the wrong direction. In addition, I violated all sorts of codes for the proper way to address parents, relatives, elders, teachers, brothers and sisters. This was noted by my mother, who would escalate my offense into a portent of truly dire things to come. Added to that, I was also singularly unable to keep secrets or to do what everyone else did by way of choosing what *not* to say. In the context of Arabic, therefore, I was regarded as outside the range of normal behavior, a rogue creature of whom other people should be wary.

Perhaps the real issue was sex, or, rather, my parents' defense against its onset in my life and, when it could no longer be staved off, its taming. Even when I left for the United States in 1951 at fifteen, my existence had been completely virginal, my acquaintance with girls nonexistent. Movies like *The Outlaw, Duel in the Sun,* even the Michèle Morgan costume drama *Fabiola,* which I desperately wanted to see, were forbidden as being "not for children"; such bans existed until I was fourteen. There were no visibly available sex magazines or pornographic videos in those days; the schools I went to in Egypt or the States until I was seventeen and a half infantilized and desexualized everything. This was also true of Princeton, which I attended until I was twenty-one. Sex was banned everywhere, including books, although there my inquisitiveness and the large number of volumes in our library made a complete prohibition impossible to enforce. The experience of lovemaking was described in convincing detail in the World War I memoirs of Wilfred de Saint-Mandé, a British officer of whom I never learned anything at all except that he went from battle to sexual encounter for well over six hundred pages. Saint-Mandé in effect became one of the silent, secret companions of my adolescence. As a rake, bloody-minded British soldier, and upper-class barbarian he was an appalling role model, but I did not care—I liked him all the more. So in my above-ground life I was steered carefully away from anything that might excite sexual interest, without really talking about it at all. It was my own powerful need to know and experience that broke through my parents' restrictions, until an open confrontation took place whose memory, forty-six years later, still makes me shudder.

One chilly Sunday afternoon in late November 1949, at three o'clock, a few weeks after I had turned fourteen, there was a loud knock on my bedroom door, followed immediately by a sternly authoritative wrenching of the handle. This was very far from a friendly parental visit. Performed with unimpeachable rectitude "for your own good," it was *the* rigorous assault on my character that had been building to this climax for almost three years. My father stood near the door for a moment; in his right hand he clutched my pajama bottoms distastefully, which I despairingly remembered I had left in the bathroom that morning. I held out my hands to catch the offending article, expecting him as he had done once or twice before to scold me for leaving my things around ("Please put them away; don't leave them for someone else to pick up"). The servants, he would add, were not for my personal comfort.

Since he kept the garment in his hand I knew that this must be a more serious matter, and I sank back into the bed, anxiously awaiting the attack. When he was halfway into the room, just as he began to speak, I saw my mother's drawn face framed in the doorway several feet behind him. She said nothing but was present to give emotional weight to his prosecution of the case. "Your mother and I have noticed"— here he waved the pajama—"that you haven't had any wet dreams. That means you're abusing yourself." He had never said it accusingly before, although the dangers of "self-abuse" and the virtues of wet dreams had been the subject of several lectures and were first described to me on a walk around the deck of the *Saturnia* en route to New York in July of 1948.

These lectures were the result of my asking my mother about a stout little pair of Italian opera singers, fellow passengers on the *Saturnia*. She wore very high heels, a tight white dress, heavily painted lips; he was in a shiny brown suit and elevated heels, with carefully slicked-back hair; both exuded a bountiful sexuality to which I could attach no specific practices. In an unguarded moment I had asked my mother confusedly and inarticulately how such people as those actually did "it." I had no words for "it," none for penis or vagina, and none for foreplay; all I could do was to enlist urination and defecation in my question, which, I had somehow gleaned, bore some pleasurable meaning as well. My mother's look of alarm and disgust set me up for the "man-to-man" talk with my father. A great part of his massive authority, and his compelling power over me, was that strange combination of silence and the ritual repetition of clichés picked up from assorted places—*Tom Brown's Schooldays,* the YMCA, courses in salesmanship, the Bible, evangelical sermons, Shakespeare, and so on.

"Just think of a cup slowly filling up with liquid," he began. "Then once it is full"—here he cupped one hand and with the other skimmed off the hypothetical excess—"it naturally flows over, and you have a wet dream." He paused for a bit. Then he continued, again metaphorically. "Have you ever seen a horse win a race without being able to maintain a steady pace? Of course not. If the horse starts out too quickly, he gets tired and fades away. The same thing with you. If you abuse yourself your cup will not run over; you can't win or even finish the race." On a similar occasion later he added warnings about going bald and/or mad as a result of "self-abuse," which only very rarely did he refer to as masturbation, a word pronounced with quite dreadful admonishment: *"maaasturbation"* (the *a*'s almost *o*'s).

My father never spoke of making love, and certainly not of fucking. When I tried to bring up the question of how children were produced the answer was schematic. My mother's frequent pregnancies, and especially her alarmingly protuberant stomach during them, never settled the question. Her line to me was always "We wrote a letter to Jesus and he sent us a baby!" What my father told me after his solemn shipboard warning about "self-abuse" was a few, almost dismissive words about how the man puts his "private parts" in the woman's "private parts." Nothing about orgasm or ejaculation or about what "private parts" were. Pleasure was never mentioned. As for kissing, he referred to it only once in all my years of being with and knowing him. "You must marry a woman," he told me when I was in college, "who has never been kissed before you kiss her. Like your mother." There was not even a mention of virginity, an abstruse concept that I had heard about in Sunday school and then through catechism and that acquired some concrete meaning for me only when I was about twenty.

After we returned from the United States in the autumn of 1948, there were two and perhaps three occasions when we had man-to-man talks, each time with a growing sense on my part of encroachment and guilt. I once asked him how one would know that the wet dream had occurred. "You would know in the morning," was his first answer. As with most things then, I was hesitant to ask more, but I did when he next brought it up, along with a still more embellished account of the evils of "self-abuse" (the man becoming "useless" and a "failure" as the degeneracy took final hold). "A wet dream is a nocturnal emission," he said. The phrase sounded as if he were reading it off a page. "Is it like going to the bathroom?" I asked, using the euphemism we all used for urinating ("pee-pee" was the definitely riskier alternative, which my mother always admonished me against: I used it when trying to be "naughty," along with "I can see your pants!" to one of my sisters, as a further act of insubordination and intransigence).

"Yes, more or less, but it's thicker and sticks to your pajamas," he said then. So this was why the pajama was being clinically transported in his left hand as he stood a few feet away from my bed. "There's nothing on these pajamas at all," he said to me with a look of scowling disgust, "nothing. Haven't I told you many times about the dangers of self-abuse? What's the matter with you?" There was a pause, as I looked furtively past my father toward my mother. Although I knew in my heart that she sympathized with me most of the time, she rarely broke ranks with him. Now I couldn't detect any support at all; just a shyly questioning look, as if to say: "Yes, Edward, what *are* you doing?" plus a little bit of "Why do you do nasty things to hurt us?"

I was immediately seized with such terror, guilt, shame, and vulnerability that I have never forgotten this scene. The most important thing about these feelings is how they coalesced around my father, whose cold denunciation of me in my bed had me utterly silenced, defeated. There was nothing to confess to that he didn't already know. I had no excuse: the wet dreams hadn't in fact occurred, even though for a time during the past year I did wake up anxiously, searching bed and nightclothes for evidence that they might have. I was already down the road to perdition, perhaps even baldness. (I was alarmed after a bath once to notice that my wet hair, normally quite thick, appeared to show a couple of patches of what appeared to be baldness. I also suspected that my father's insistence on frequent haircuts was connected to deterring the premature effects of self-abuse. "Have your hair cut often and short, like your father," he'd say, "and it'll remain strong and full.") My secret, such as it was, had been found out. All I could think of was that I had no place to go as the dreadful retribution was about to occur. Somehow, the vague, if also overpowering, anxiety I was experiencing held an extremely concrete sense of threat, and for a moment I felt as if I was clinging to "Edward" to save him from final extinction.

"You have nothing to say, do you?" A quick breath, then the climax. He threw the pajama bottom at me with vehemence and what I thought was exasperated disgust. "All right then. Have a wet dream!" I was so taken aback by this peremptory order—could one, in fact, if one wanted, just have a wet dream?—that I shrank back even further into the bed. Then, just as I thought he was going to leave, he turned toward me again.

"Where did you learn how to abuse yourself?" As if by a miracle I was given an opening to save myself. I recalled in a flash that only a few weeks earlier, near the end of summer and just before school started, I had been loitering in the boys' dressing room at the Maadi Club. Although it was at the time my father's favorite club for golf and bridge, I knew relatively few people, and, with my usual shyness, would go into the dressing room to get into my bathing suit but would also take my time, hoping to strike up a friendship perhaps, or meet a stray acquaintance. My feeling of loneliness was unallayed. This time, however, a gaggle of older boys, wet from swimming, burst in. They were led by Ehab, a very tall and thin boy with a deep voice that exuded confidence. Rich, secure, at home, and in place. "Come on Ehab, do it," he was urged by the others. I had seen him before but had not really met him: our fathers did not know each other and I was still dependent on this kind of parental introduction. Ehab lowered his trunks, stood on the bench, and while peering over the wall at the pool's designated sunbathing area, began to masturbate. I heard myself blurt out, "Do it on Colette," Colette being a voluptuous young woman in her twenties who always wore a black bathing suit and had graced my own private fantasies. No one heard me; I felt like an ass and blushed uncontrollably though no one seemed to notice. We were all watching Ehab as he rubbed his penis slowly until, at last, he ejaculated, also slowly, at which point he started to laugh smugly, displaying his sticky fingers as if he had just won a sports trophy.

"It was at the club. Ehab did it," I blurted out to my father, who had no idea who Ehab was or what it was I was trying to say. I realized that he was not asking me for anything concrete: it was only a rhetorical question. Of course I was guilty. Of course he now knew it. My sins had also been exposed to my mother, who never said a word, but showed signs of scarcely comprehending horror and even bereavement.

My father did not seem particularly interested either in my explanation or in listening for a few seconds to my clumsy expressions of determined self-reform, my future action. He had found me out and found me wanting; he knew what harm I was doing myself, and he had judged me both weak and radically unreliable. That was all. He had told me about the cup and the race horse, about baldness and madness. He had repeated the homilies perhaps eight times, so all he could do now would be to repeat them yet again or, "wisely" (a word he liked to use), he could register the crime and move on, his authority and moral judgment remaining formidably intact. I was neither punished nor even reminded of my secret vice. But I didn't think I had escaped lightly. This particular failure of mine, embodied in that exquisitely theatrical scene, added itself, like a new and extremely undermining fault line, to the already superficially incoherent and disorganized structure of "Edward."

During the many years we lived in Cairo my father practiced surveillance of a more public kind as the proud owner, and one of the very first in Egypt, of a Kodak 8-millimeter camera. Father was remarkably busy recording scene after repetitive scene of "Edward," his mother, cousins, aunts, and uncles (never anyone outside of the family) at play or at rest, appearing to be happy, idyllic, and without any problems. I was fascinated with the flat rectangular machine that smelled of plastic, its complicated insides and its meandering passages for the film to pass through requiring patience in loading, threading, and unloading. Neither of my parents was particularly dexterous, a disability I seem to have inherited where practical things are concerned, but my father was positively clumsy. He bought films in tiny spools and put them in the camera so sloppily that they jammed, whereupon another would be fished out, the old one pulled angrily through the machine and then thrown away, the fresh one put in, and finally he could begin filming. Every couple of weeks he walked over to the Kodak shop on Adly Pasha Street to deliver a handful of films for developing; when I was eight I'd accompany him, as he collected them four or five to a large spool, a more convenient size that allowed thirty minutes of continuous running time on his projector.

Once or twice a month we performed the ritual of drawing the living-room shutters closed and setting up the elaborate, ever-shiny projector on the small modern coffee table and the tripod-borne screen; while the smell of polished, mechanical newness wafted through the air, we turned off the lights and settled snugly into the large overstuffed living-room chairs and sofas to watch ourselves at the zoo, on a Desert Road picnic, or at the pyramids. Six months after my mother died in 1990 a sizable batch of films, each one carefully encased in the white and blue boxes that my father had had made for them by his stationery and binding staff, were found at the bottom of one of her cupboards in Beirut. There must have been thirty-five of them, containing 120 of the individual films taken between 1939 and 1952, some of them marked in my father's scrawl "Cairo 1944," "Jerusalem 1946," "Yousif's wed-

ding," all of them still exuding the smells and even the feel of those projection evenings so long ago. I took them home to New York, where
for a couple of years they sat in a nondescript brown cardboard box,
provoking my curiosity every now and then as to what portion of our
old life was preserved in them as they slowly sank into oblivion and
final disuse.

A coincidence made them available once again: a pair of young
BBC directors, making a documentary on the writing of my book
Culture and Imperialism, asked me for some old family pictures, and
quite by some mysterious impulse I thought of the box of patiently
waiting films. The films were taken back to London and transferred to
videotape.

It was not so much that I was disappointed at how badly they had
been shot or how jerky and unsatisfying the sequences they contained
were, or at how the print was either too light or too dark, but rather
that the films exclude so much, seem contrived and rigid as they positively ban any trace of the effort and uncertainty of our lives. The smiles
on everyone's faces, the impossibly cheery and at times even sturdy pre-
sentation of my mother (whom I remember as more slender and
moody), highlight the artificial quality of what we were, a family determined to make itself into a mock little European group despite the
Egyptian and Arab surroundings that are only hinted at as an occasional
camel, gardener, servant, palm tree, pyramid, or tarbushed chauffeur is
briefly caught by the camera's otherwise single-minded focus on the
children and assorted relatives. The earliest films consist of scenes showing Rosy and me at play: I place her on one end of a seesaw, rush to
the opposite side, pump up and down, abruptly stop, then dash back to
her and kiss her curls. Then there was a whole sequence of films taken
below our house on Gabalaya Street, at right angles to Aziz Osman,
alongside the Fish Garden, whose fence has remained unchanged for
over fifty years now. On an essentially deserted street, with scarcely a
soul in sight—today, the same sidewalks are crowded with parked cars,
and the street has become a permanent traffic jam—we see Edward and
Rosy, aged six and four, standing thirty yards from the camera, two
tiny, excited little figures, jumping up and down as they await an
unseen cue off camera, which catches their grotesquely enlarged faces
covered in all kinds of theatrically engendered smiles.

This same scene is reenacted dozens of times: in Zamalek, Jerusalem, at the zoo, in the desert, at the club, on other streets in Cairo. Always the eager run, the happy faces, the inconclusive conclusion. At first I thought, and indeed remembered, that this was an elementary way of demonstrating the difference between a still and a motion picture camera. There are a number of sequences showing Edward at age ten coaxing older cousins out of what appears to be a transfixed immobilized pose in front of the camera. In their seemingly limitless repetitiveness the films of course are, and for my father seem to have been, a kind of regulated prerehearsed scene, which we performed in front of him as he recorded indefatigably. My father wanted us always to appear face-front. There are no side views in the films, and consequently there was no risk of giving any of us the unwanted exposure of an unguarded look or unpredictable trajectory. The camera was always there when we left the house for a walk or drive. It must also have been my father's way of capturing as well as confirming the ordered family domain he had created and now ruled.

I remember that as I grew older—certainly by age eleven or twelve—I felt that the ritual of doing the same thing over and over in front of my father's camera was becoming more and more disconcerting. This awareness coincided with my wish somehow to be disembodied. One of my recurrent fantasies, the subject of a school essay I wrote when I was twelve, was to be a book, whose fate I took to be happily free of unwelcome changes, distortions of its shape, criticism of its looks; print for me was made up of a rare combination of expression in its style and contents, absolute rigidity, and integrity in its looks. Passed from hand to hand, place to place, time to time, I could remain my own true self (as a book), despite being thrown out of a car and lost in a back drawer.

Occasionally, however, a very few eccentric glimpses of our life escaped through my father's unforgiving optical grid. There is one scene of loitering boys (including me) watching a rehearsal of bride and groom coming down the front stairs of our Jerusalem house in 1947. It is as if my father's movie camera subverted the even more demanding rigor of Khalil Raad's hooded tripod camera, always summoned by my aunt and her sons to an important family occasion. A slightly built white-haired man, Raad took a great deal of time as he arranged the large group of family and guests into acceptable order. At such mo-

Wadie Said, my father,
in the American
Expeditionary Force
under General Pershing,
France, 1917

The wedding of my
parents, Wadie and
Hilda, at the Baptist
Church in Nazareth,
December 24, 1932

Right: My parents on their
honeymoon in London,
January 1933

Below: An exterior view of
the main branch of the
Cairo Standard Stationery
Company, established by
Wadie on Malika Farida
Street. Wadie is in a bow
tie in the doorway, and on
his right is Anna Mandel,
his secretary, 1932

Above: Interior shot of Standard Stationery, with Wadie in a white suit, sitting at right; standing directly behind him is Lampas, the store manager

Right: My mother and me, age one, in the Mena House gardens

With my father
on the beach at
Alexandria, 1936

Above: Aunt Melia
in her customary
hat, Cairo, late
1930s

Left: Displaying
early conducting
skills on the terrace
of the Cairo
apartment on Aziz
Osman Street

Right: Standing on one of the pyramids during a family outing to Giza, 1939. Front row, left to right: cousins George, Robert, me, and Albert; back row: Evelyn and Yousif

Below: A weekend drive to the Barrages Gardens north of Cairo in the delta near the Barrages Dam, 1939, included my mother's family, the Musas. Clockwise from bottom left: Rosy, Shukri Musa, Marwan held by Latifeh, her husband Munir, Hilda, Albert, Robert, me, and Wadie

Aunt Nabiha, with
her sons Robert and
Albert, Palestine,
1939

Age five, at the
Maadi Sporting
Club pool, 1940

With my sister Rosy in
traditional Palestinian
dress, Jerusalem, 1941

At seven with
Rosy in Gezira
Preparatory School
uniforms on the
Cairo apartment
terrace

A family shot of Saids and Mansours, my father's second cousins, photographed for the last time before everyone dispersed, Mansour House, circa 1946–47

Family portrait in Jerusalem, circa 1946–47. Left to right: Jean, Rosy, me at eleven, Joyce, and baby Grace

ments, endlessly prolonged by the man's finickiness and disregard for his subjects, standing still seemed by common agreement to be a required ordeal of these formal family occasions. No one then knew that Raad's photos would become perhaps the richest archival resource for Palestinians' lives until 1948—"before their diaspora," in Walid Khalidi's phrase. My father's interest in movement, perhaps as a result of exasperation with Raad, is another, at the time inadvertent, part of that unofficial record.

Then there are scenes he caught of my uncle Boulos, Aunt Nabiha's husband (and first cousin), Ellen Badr Sabra, Uncle Munir and his wife, Latifeh, Albert my cousin: they pass through my father's films smilingly, the premonition of death added retrospectively by the viewer, and in the blurred outlines of their forms they seem in effect to be moving sideways, away from the camera, as if walking to another rhythm, for another reason than the expected one.

No one in the films seems informally or lightly dressed, perhaps because my father did his shooting in winter, never in the terrifying brightness of the Middle Eastern sun. The women wear heavy dark satins and wools, the men are always in dark suits, the children in sweaters, caps, long stockings. Only my mother appears for some reason in sleeveless, sometimes polka-dotted dresses, her round arms and dazzling smile occasionally expressing a smiling protest, which I remember clearly from my childhood as being gently voiced against my father's attentions to her with his ever-continuing, whirring camera. My grandmother ("Teta") never appears at all, rigidly in keeping with her strenuous wish that she should never be photographed. I do not know why she felt this way, or why she always made a point of not eating chocolate, or wouldn't drink tea if the milk had not been poured into the cup first, or why each set of her personal belongings (hankies, notepaper, pajamas, pencils, playing cards, etc.) had to be housed (the word was hers) in a little cloth case, which she made and decorated with complicated petit point or embroidered patterns. But Teta felt very strongly about those things and resisted my father to the end of her life.

Unlike my grandmother, I never resisted at all; how could I when I felt I was a failure, both physically and morally? Are parents supposed to provide role models, or at least some concrete idea of where all the pushing and kneading into shape would ultimately lead, and where or when it might stop? There was only one intriguing scene in the many, many hours of videotaped films that showed me another version of "Edward," my childhood self. It was taken at the Maadi pool, probably on a late Sunday morning in June, and reveals a teeming, disorderly scene crisscrossed with bathers, divers, watching parents, all shooting past my father's camera as he, clearly perplexed by the bustle before him, jerks the camera rapidly from figure to figure, up to the sky and down again, and churns the already considerable disorder of the pool into a confusing, dizzying patchwork of light, bodies, and meaningless space (pavement, wall, cloud), flouting the prerehearsed images of order we had become so used to in our runs toward the camera.

Watching this maelstrom I suddenly detected myself, a little boy in a pair of dark swimming trunks with a white belt, slipping between a phalanx of much larger bodies, and diving into the pool with scarcely a splash. It was as if I had caught my father unaware; the camera followed quickly, having abruptly located me, but I seem to have swum out of shot. The camera returns to the general confusion, and then, from an unexpected angle, running toward him with my head down, arms outstretched, I appear, and almost immediately disappear into the pool. He had missed me entirely the second time, although of course I appeared in the camera for a split second.

This tiny, quite trivial episode elates me half a century later as I try to render the outlines and important details of a story I was immersed in with my father's plans and expectations, his drills and proverbs, shaping and directing me, my sisters, and my mother very much in the way his films record his unresting will to make us all move toward him, forward march, with all the unnecessary stuff clipped out. The great paradox is that he was such an immensely sustaining force in our lives—none of us ever had a day's worry about anything material, the cupboards were always full of food, we had the best education, were well dressed, our houses were perfectly run and staffed, we always traveled first class—that I never thought of him as repressive at the time. He pressured me constantly in that lapidary way of his, and I saw it again in the oddly episodic, repetitive, and reductive quality of his films. But that I managed occasionally to escape his fearsome strength, as in the little sequence at the pool, tells me something I only realized years later, when I had gone my own way: that there was more to "Edward" than the delinquent yet compliant son, submitting to his father's Victorian design.

It was my mother who often supplied the justifying gloss on his unyielding and cold exterior. It was as if he were a marble statue and it was her job to put words into his mouth to make him articulate and fluent; she spoke my father to me, miming all the sentiments he never expressed, drawing him out so much that he became a loving, caring man so very different from the harshly unyielding person whose authority over me was practiced almost to his death. "You should hear him talk about 'my son' to his friends," she said. "He's so proud of you." And yet, I could never directly engage, much less attract, his help. I was no more than four when he took me for a walk near the Fish Garden in Cairo (I do not think he ever entered the place, which seemed exclusively my mother's domain). I scampered along behind him, while he pressed on with his hands behind his back at a resolute pace. When I stumbled and fell forward, scratching my hands and knees badly, I instinctively called out to him, "Daddy . . . please," at which he stopped and turned around slowly toward me. He paused like that for a couple of seconds, then turned back, resuming his walk without a word. That was all. It was also how he died, turning his face to the wall, without a sound. Had he, I wonder, ever really wanted to say more than he actually did?

V

IT WAS AS AN AMERICAN BUSINESSMAN'S SON WHO HADN'T
the slightest feeling of being American that I entered the Cairo School
for American Children (CSAC) in the fall of 1946, the first day made
easier by the fact that the Greek bus driver who picked me up very
early on a sunny October morning in Zamalek and drove me with a lot
of totally unfamiliar, loud, unself-conscious American children in gaily
colored shirts, skirts, and shorts was a driver at my Auntie Melia's college. He recognized me at once and always treated me—as no one else
did—with deferential, if familiar, courtesy. I had never seen such an
assortment, or concentration, of Americans before. Gone were the gray
uniforms and subdued, conspiratorial whispers of the GPS's English and
mostly Levantine children; gone too were English names like Dickie,
Derek, and Jeremy, as well as Franco-Arab names like Micheline,
Nadia, or Vivette. Now there were Marlese, Marlene, Annekje, several
Marjies, Nancy, Ernst, Chuck, and lots of Bobs. No one paid any attention to me.

"Edward Sigheed" did pass muster, and I was soon able in some way
to belong, but every morning when I stepped on the bus I felt a
seething panic when I saw the colored T-shirts, striped socks, and
loafers they all wore, while I was in my primly correct gray shorts, dress
white shirt, and conventionally European lace-ups. For the class I'd

settle my inner consternation into an efficient, albeit provisional, identity, that of bright, yet often wayward, pupil. Then at lunch, as they unwrapped the same neatly cut white-bread sandwiches of peanut butter and jelly—neither of which I had ever tasted—and I my more interesting cheese and prosciutto in Shami bread, I fell back into doubt and shame that I, an American child, ate a different food, which no one ever asked to taste, nor asked me to explain.

One evening we were sitting on the veranda when my father reached into his jacket pocket and pulled out a pair of striped socks. "An American flier gave them to me," he said. "Why don't you wear them?" It was like a sudden lifeline to better days. I wore them the next day and the day after with a noticeable lift in my spirits. Yet no one on the bus really noticed, and the socks had to be washed. With only one pair of socks to give my claim to being an American any credence, I felt let down brusquely. I tried explaining to my mother that it might be nice to have sandwiches cut into rectangles with jam and butter, but that got me a dismissive "We only use toast bread and jam for breakfast. I want you to be nourished. What's wrong with our food anyway?"

Founded after the war to accommodate the children of American oil company, business, and diplomatic personnel in Cairo's newly expanded expatriate community, the Cairo School for American Children was housed at the outer western perimeter of Maadi, parallel to the train station and about a mile from the great river. Like GPS, which was only a primary school, the new school occupied a large villa, but with a two-acre garden, gardener's shed, and, on the south side of the house, a dirt expanse half the size of a football field, half of which during my first year, 1946–47 (interrupted by a long spring sojourn in Jerusalem), was asphalted over and became a basketball court. Being a school for smaller children, GPS confined itself to netball, a gentle perfumed equivalent of basketball, intended mainly for girls—and, on festive occasions like the king's birthday, to Maypole dancing, a pastime I found both curious (why so many ribbons, and what did they represent?) and idiotic (going round in a circle to Mrs. Wilson's hand claps and an extremely shrill recording of English country music was for me a low point in the idea of disciplined physical movement). CSAC introduced me not only to basketball, but to softball, sports my father really knew nothing about. As honorary chairman of the Cairo YMCA, which mounted games between Cairo teams like the Armenian Houmentmen and the Jewish Maccabees, matched against an excellent visiting U.S. Army team, he would take us to games he had never played himself. Certainly softball interested me enough to turn me into a decent pitcher and batter; "rounders" was what my father persisted in calling it, but mercifully he took no serious interest in it, nor in ever seeing me hit the plump ball with a Louisville Slugger bat.

Postwar Cairo gave me, for the first time, a sense of highly differentiated social strata. The major change was the replacement of British institutions and individuals by the victorious Americans, the old empire giving way to the new, while my father enjoyed even greater business success. At GPS ceremonies a fuss would be made over Lady Baden-Powell or Roy Chapman-Andrews, who were symbols of British authority requiring no Egyptian or Arab counterpart to offset their foreignness as they stood at the podium; Britannia ruled supreme, and all of us took it for granted. The appearance of Shafiq Ghorbal, a noted Egyptian historian and Ministry of Education executive, at the first CSAC ceremony that I remember marked the difference in imperial approach. We Americans were partners of the Egyptians, and what was more appropriate than to let them appear as speakers at functions like the opening of the Egyptian parliament, or King Farouk's birthday, of which no notice was taken at GPS. "All things bright and beautiful" had meant bright and beautiful England, the distant lodestar of good for all of us: that was over, and the hymn disappeared from my repertory forever. I was struck by the fact that part of the American approach was to institute the teaching of Arabic for all children, and having pretended that "Sigheed" was an American name, I had some of my worst moments in Arabic class. Somehow I had to conceal my perfect command of what was my mother tongue in order to fit in better with the inane formulas given out to American youngsters for what passed for spoken (but was really kitchen) Arabic. I never volunteered, rarely spoke, often crouched near the back of the room. There were provocations, however, like the pretty young Arabic teacher who, while describing her adventures at the just-opened amusement park in Gezira, placed particular emphasis on an airplane ride called "Saida," after the newly formed Egyptian airline company. In a tiny class of four people, she planted herself in front of me and proceeded to detail her excitement at "Saida," which she repeated again and again, as if emphasizing the lurking Arab quality in my name, which I had laboriously tried to scale down to the prevailing norms of American pronunciation. "No, Edward," she said emphatically, "you couldn't have been on the best rides if you haven't tried Saida. Do you know how many times I rode Saida? At least four. Saida is the ride. Saida's just great." In other words, stop pretending that you're Sigheed: You're Said, as in Saida. The connection was undeniable.

I was assigned to the sixth grade in a second-floor classroom whose plants and window flower boxes gave it the atmosphere of a family room. The class was ruled by the first great martinet and sadist of my life, a Miss Clark, whose single-minded persecution of me crippled my already uncertain sense of self. Miss Clark's demeanor was extremely restrained, quiet, and composed to the point of unpleasantness. She was in her mid-thirties and seemed, as I thought about her over the years, to be a WASP from the Northeast, very much a creature of that world's fully paid up citizens—morally righteous, confident, generally patronizing. I never knew what it was about me that so gripped her, but it only took a week or ten days for her to declare herself my enemy in a class that contained no more than a dozen boys and girls.

After the hierarchical and rigid English system, the American school was informal in every sense. In the classrooms chairs and tables were scattered about, whereas at GPS we had sat in military rows of cramped little desks and benches. Except for the French, Arabic, and art teachers, the instruction was by American women (heavily made up in loud, colored dresses, totally different from the scrubbed plain faces and sensible skirts affected by Mrs. Wilson and her cohorts) and one man, a Mark Wannick, who also doubled as softball and basketball coach. On one occasion he donned a bright yellow Ohio State basketball uniform to play with us: in the torrid Cairo afternoon, surrounded by brown fields with brown peasants in *galabiyahs* leading donkeys and water buffaloes round as they have done for millennia, Mr. Wannick cut a surrealistic sight in his overpoweringly colored uniform, hairy arms and legs, military crew cut, black sneakers, and delicate rimless glasses.

I encountered American education as a regimen designed to be attractive, homey, and tailored down to the level of growing children.

Books at GPS were uniformly in small print, without illustrations, unrelentingly dry in tone; history and literature, for instance, were presented as matter-of-factly as possible, making each page a challenging task just to read through. No concessions were made in arithmetic to the world of lived experience: we were given rows of figures to add, subtract, divide, and multiply, plus a large number of rules and tables (multiplication, weights and measures, distances, meters, yards, and inches) to memorize. The goal of all this was to do "sums," a task whose difficulty for us was commensurate with its programmatic dullness. At CSAC we were all given "workbooks," in marked contrast to the GPS's "copybooks," which were lined exercise books as anonymous as bus tickets; workbooks had charming, chatty questions, illustrations, pictures to be appreciated, enjoyed, and, when relevant, filled in. To write in one of our GPS textbooks was a serious misdemeanor; in American workbooks, the *idea* was to write in them.

More attractive still were the textbooks handed out by Miss Clark at the beginning of each day. At the core of each subject there seemed to be a family to whom one was introduced at the outset: there was always a Sis, a Mom and a Dad, plus assorted family and household members, including a large black woman housekeeper with an extremely exaggerated expression of either sadness or delight on her face. Through the family one learned about adding and subtracting, or civics, or American history (literature was treated separately). The idea seemed to be to make learning a painless process, on a par with getting through the day on a farm or in a suburb of St. Louis or Los Angeles. References to the drugstore, the hardware or dime stores, mystified me completely but did not need explaining to my classmates, all of whom had actually lived in places like St. Louis or LA. For me, however, such locations corresponded to nothing in my experience, which was barren of soda fountains and soda jerks, the two items that intrigued me the most.

I was meant to find this "fun," and for a month I did. But I was never left alone by Miss Clark nor by the other children, with whom I quickly became quite antagonistic; after that first pleasurable month I found myself longing for the GPS, with its clear lines of authority, its cut and dried lessons, its very strict rules of deportment. Teachers at CSAC never used or threatened violence, but male students were extremely rough with each other, since the boys were quite big and were willing to use their strength against each other in contests of will and turf. By Christmastime, every day at the school was an ordeal in which I had to make my way through a gauntlet of flailing arms and fists on the bus, followed by the chilly put-downs and severe scoldings I received from Miss Clark in the classroom.

The most humiliating moment in my first year came the day after the class had been on a field trip—for me the concept was an entirely novel one—to a large sugar refinery across the Nile from Maadi. I admit that after the first twenty minutes the excursion was simply too boring to warrant much of my attention, but I had no choice but to stick with the group, steered from boiling vat to storehouse to cutting room, to the accompaniment of our guide's voluble enjoyment— thirty-minute explanations where only one minute would have been sufficient, an overabundance of technical language, an extraordinary air of self-satisfaction—to make matters even less compelling. He was a middle-aged gentleman wearing a tarbush who was seconded to us from one of the ministries expressly for this trip. Miss Clark was there of course. I paid very little attention to her, a great mistake. When she entered my field of vision I saw her nodding (was it agreement, or understanding, or satisfaction at the torrent of information about sugar cane, its history and structure, the chemistry of sugar, etc.?) but I gave her no other heed. The whole trip was so bizarrely unlike anything my English colonial schools were likely to mount that I had not even begun to dwell on the differences between the authoritarian Brits and the benevolent Americans, who were so much more eager to give the Egyptians a democratic chance to be themselves.

The next day we convened as usual in the classroom. Miss Clark was already behind her desk and seemed as composed and as inscrutable as ever. "Let's spend some time talking about yesterday's field trip," she began, then turned immediately to B.J., a short-haired girl whose clipped tone and businesslike manner quickly established her as the class touchstone. B.J. provided a detailed appreciation of the day's events. "How about you, Ernst?" she asked Ernst Brandt, the class's somewhat inarticulate but biggest and strongest boy. There was little more anyone could add to B.J.'s strenuous recital, and Ernst scarcely made the effort. "It was okay," was all he said. I sat there slowly drifting off into some idle daydream, once again paying Miss Clark's predatory instincts insufficient attention. "You were all very well behaved yesterday: I'm proud of you," she said, and I thought she would then press on with our

English assignment. "All except one person, that is. One person only paid no heed to Ibrahim Effendi's very helpful and fascinating commentary. One person only always lagged behind the rest of the group. One person only fidgeted the entire time. One person only never looked at all the machines and vats. One person only bit his nails. One person alone disgraced the entire class." She paused, even as I wondered who that person might be.

"You, Edward. You behaved abominably. I have never seen anyone so unable to concentrate, so inconsiderate, so careless and sloppy. What you did yesterday made me very angry. I watched you every minute of the time, and there was nothing you did that could possibly redeem you. I am going to speak to Miss Willis [the headmistress] about you, and I shall ask her to call your parents in for a conference." She stopped, looking at me with unconcealed distaste. "Had you been one of the good students in this class," she began again, "I would have perhaps forgiven your conduct. Had you been someone like B.J., for instance. But since you are undoubtedly the worst student in this class, what you did yesterday is simply unforgivable." The emphases were delivered with definitive italicized dispassion.

Miss Clark had purposely, deliberately, even fastidiously, defined me, caught me, as it were, from within, had seen me as I could or would not see myself, and she had made her findings extremely public. I was riveted to my chair, blushing, trying to look both sorry and strong at the same time, hating the by now thoroughly concentrating class, each one of them, I felt, looking at me with justified dislike and curiosity. "Who is this person?" I imagined them saying, "a little Arab boy, and what is he doing in a school for American children? Where did he come from?" Meanwhile, Miss Clark was moving her books and pencils around on her desk. Then we returned to our recitation, as if nothing had happened. Although I glanced at her ten minutes later to see if there might have been a relenting look for me, she remained as unshaken and as imperviously unforgiving as ever.

The power of what Miss Clark said about me was that it collected all the negative and critical comments that had loosely surrounded me at home and at GPS, and concentrated the whole lot into one unpleasant steel container, into which I was placed, like Jell-O poured into a mold. I felt as if I had no history to shield me from Miss Clark's judgment or to resist my public disgrace. Even more than that passive exposure, I have always hated and feared the sudden delivery of bad news that allows me no chance to respond, to separate "Edward" in all his well-known infirmities and sins from the inner being I generally consider my real or best self (undefined, free, curious, quick, young, sensitive, even likable). Now I could no longer do this, being confronted with a single inescapable devalued and doomed self, not, no never quite right, and indeed very wrong and out of place.

I came to detest this identity, but as yet I had no alternative for it. So objectionable had I become that of course I was compelled to go and see Miss Willis, a white-haired, unforceful, late-middle-aged Middle Western woman who seemed more puzzled than angry at my malfeasance. Miss Clark was not present at the interview, but there was no comparison at all between Miss Clark's ontological condemnation of me and Miss Willis's ramblingly vague lecture on the virtues of good citizenship, an unthinkable phrase in the British colonial context I had just left, where we were subjects at most, and obedient as well as unquestioning ones. My parents also came by in due course; they saw Miss Clark and Miss Willis. The former made an extremely pronounced impression on my mother, who heard in the woman's penetrating accents a more well-sculpted and delivered account of her son's weakness than had ever been given before. What exactly was said about me I never knew, but it resonated in my mother's speeches to me for years and years. "Remember what Miss Clark said" was the refrain used to explain both my lack of proper focus and concentration and my chronic inability to do the right thing. So in effect Miss Clark's awful opinion of me was prolonged and given additional reach by my mother. It never occurred to me to ask my mother why she allied herself so unskeptically with someone who seemed to be moved not by pedagogical but by sadistic, instinctual imperatives.

I was supposed to be among my own kind at CSAC, but found it my lot to be even more the stranger than I had been at GPS. There was much bonhomie—"Good morning"'s and "Hi"'s were de rigueur among us, as they never were at GPS—and a good deal of emphasis was placed on who sat next to whom on the bus, in class, and at lunch. Yet there was a hidden but unanimously agreed-upon hierarchy of boys based not on seniority or position but on strength, will, and athletic prowess. The school leader was Stan Henry, a ninth-grader whose sister Paddy was a year behind me; they were the children of a senior Standard Oil executive. Stan was over six feet, radiated confidence and intelligence, and was a superb swimmer and all-round athlete. He had a horselike laugh that belied the keen competitive wit he used to dominate our frequent breaks in the garden. His only rival in size was Ernst Brandt, whom I once saw Stan humiliate by grabbing his hands and then squeezing him by the knuckles so as to force him to the ground. Ernst then stood up, and remained immobile with tears streaming down his face. Since Stan was also a "leader" (a word I learned at CSAC) it did not take very long for the rest of us to shake down around him, although that space remained a hotly contested one, with Stan unchallenged in his preeminence, the rest of us in constant flux.

I was in perpetual combat with two boys in particular. Alex Miller (the son of embassy parents, I think) and Claude Brancart, a Belgian-American whose father represented Caltex in Egypt. Both had attractive older sisters—brunette Amaryllis and blonde Monique—who seemed to me more like women than sixteen- or seventeen-year-olds. Amaryllis occasionally sat next to me on the bus, was always amiable if not actually friendly, and stunned me when I saw her wearing a two-piece bathing suit at a school outing to the Maadi pool; this was the first time in my closeted life I had ever seen that much of the female body so exposed, but I felt paradoxically that it increased the distance between us. Monique had a vague, dreamy manner about her, and floated around the school very fetchingly. Both girls had little to do with their younger brothers, who were not involved with me as friends at all, but as opponents in a ceaseless round of wrestling and boasting sessions whose object seemed both obscure and undiscussed. I remember being impressed at how one time Alex traded blows with me on the bus, standing on the other side of a seat, patiently, methodically, even slowly, delivering punches at my head and stomach while I, ever the impetuous and relatively uncontrolled fighter, pummeled him with the crosses and roundhouse upper cuts—most of them off target—I had learned from my YMCA boxing instructor, Sayed. It is bizarre indeed how such a scene, both pointless and extremely energetic, stays in my memory for such a long time, like a series of Muybridge photographs: what was I all about then, I keep asking myself, and why was I so driven and so prone to such intense antagonisms?

Unlike GPS, where there was no chance that a fight would last more than ten seconds before being broken up by several teachers, CSAC adopted a radically different philosophy, which was to provide a sanctioned space for fighting, and other boyish expenditures of excess energy. I can remember neither a single moment of peace during the lunch break, nor a pleasurable moment of camaraderie.

Claude Brancart and I were rivals—but for what, I have no idea—always ready for a spat, or a spitting or throwing contest, or a boasting spree in which our fathers, eminently unqualified in real life for such matters, were pitted against each other in imaginary tennis, wrestling, or rowing contests. At one point when Claude and I had reached a peak of enmity, this warranted an all-out fight, and we went at it on the dusty field, pulling, punching, and then, finally locked in a hugging embrace, we crashed to the ground together. He managed to get on top of me, fought vigorously to pin me back, and finally to make me say "I give up."

One of the onlookers, Jean-Pierre Sabet, a non-American Maadi resident who was enrolled at CSAC by some unintelligible dispensation, at that point matter-of-factly said of me, "He's straining. Can't you see he's straining? It isn't over." He was right: I felt I had been defeated in a sense because "Edward" had given up, he had let go and was now dominated by someone who should have dominated him. Strangely, though, there was another self beginning to surge inside me, just as "Edward" had passed and was now a prisoner of Claude Brancart, so this new self came from some region inside myself that I knew existed but could only rarely have access to. My body, instead of remaining supine and abject underneath Braucart, began to push up against him, first disengaging my arms, then pounding his chest and head until he was forced to defend himself, loose his grip on me, and finally roll over sideways as I got up and continued pummeling him. In a minute Mr. Wannick had appeared, pulled us apart, and with a disdainful "What is the matter with you two?" sent us back into the school building.

A year earlier I had had a similar experience of defeat and regeneration, and it is only now that they strike me as examples of the same unpredictable will to go on past rules and deadlines that had already been accepted by "Edward." I had met Guy Mosseri, a small, slim boy who lived in Maadi but who also went to GPS, at the Maadi swimming pool one weekend. We started a game of catch—I was to dive in and swim, then pull myself out of the pool, then dive in and swim some more, until, if he could, he caught me. I began exuberantly, threading my way through all the other swimmers, Guy in close pursuit. But soon I began to flag, whereas to my consternation Mosseri simply kept coming after me, inexorably, expressionlessly. The chase became even grimmer, blown out of proportion by my feeling of crushing failure. As he closed in I started to slow down, a sign that "Edward" had given up, only to discover that some new energy was propelling my legs and arms farther and farther away from Mosseri, who was perplexed by the sudden change in the relationship between hunter and hunted. A few minutes later he simply stopped and could not go on.

Such episodes were rare. CSAC forced me to take "Edward" more seriously as a flawed, frightened, uncertain construction than I ever had before. The overall sensation I had was of my troublesome identity as an American inside whom lurked another Arab identity from which I derived no strength, only embarrassment and discomfort. I saw in Stan Henry and Alex Miller the much more enviable, rocklike hardness of an identity at one with the reality. Jean-Pierre Sabet, Malak Abu-el-Ezz, even Albert Coronel—who, though obviously Egyptian and Jewish, carried a Spanish passport—all could be themselves, they had nothing to hide, had no American part to play. Once during my second year there, when a new older boy, Bob Simha, appeared, I thought I might have found a companion when my parents explained to me that the name Simha was Arab and Jewish. I tried to discover a hidden affinity between us, but he seemed mystified by my questions about relatives he might have had in Aleppo or Baghdad. "Nah," he told me with dismissive impatience, "I'm from New Rochelle." It was from him that I learned the expression "Your father's mustache."

Daily at school I felt the disparity between my life as "Edward," a false, even ideological, identity, and my home life, where my father's prosperity as an American businessman flourished after the war. After 1946, he and my mother began their at least twice-yearly European, later also Asian and American, travels, and because I was the only son, and my father never stopped being the owner and promoter of his far-flung business interests, I was expected to take an interest in his enterprises. A long series of companies, whose representative ("agent" was the word used then) he was, entered our lives, the house, and our daily speech; nearly all of their products found their way into number 1 Sharia Aziz Osman, apartment 20, fifth floor: Sheaffer pens and Scripp ink, Art Metal steel furniture, Sebel chairs and tables, Chubb safes, Royal typewriters, Monroe calculators, Solingen stainless-steel scissors and knives, Ellam's and A. B. Dick duplicators and spirit machines, Maruzen office supplies, Letts diaries, 3M tapes, copiers, and paints, Dictaphone recording and transcribing machines, plus English franking machines, a Swedish adding machine, a Chicago Automatic Typewriter, and the Weber-Costello globe company's more recent additions.

It was not only their products but their travelers that we came to know, especially one Alex Kaldor, a heavily accented Hungarian (or Rumanian: his origins were obscure and the subject of much speculation), a bachelor of roughly my father's generation, a Royal typewriter voyageur who lived first class all across the globe. He turned up at least twice a year in Cairo, routinely coming by for drinks and taking my parents and, when I got to be about fourteen, me out to dinner. Kaldor was the first hardbitten cynic and expense account free-loader I met, but I liked his way of appearing to have done everything (except perhaps marriage) and to have been impressed with nothing, not even my father, whom he treated with patronizing amusement. He was fat and seemed addicted to Melba toast. I think I found him fascinating because he sounded like Bela Lugosi, whose films I was not permitted to see ("not for children") but got to know a little about through the "coming attractions" snippets that accompanied films for children in the local cinemas.

My father started traveling regularly after the war to the various offices and factories of his principals, suppliers, and associates. He always sought and obtained exclusive representations, so that he in turn could sell these products to other dealers and customers as the local principal. By the time I left Egypt his had become by far the largest office equipment and stationery business in the Middle East. And I also developed the same keenly competitive sense that he had for rival products, whom we treated as private enemies: Olivetti, Roneo, Parker, Gestetner, and Adler, among others, whose inferiority to "our lines," as my father called them, we argued with considerable passion. By the same token, the principal salesmen and directors of divisions in the "shop" were also familiar to us as not quite family, but certainly more than just employees. Most of them endured, looking back on it now, with remarkable longevity; only one, a Mr. Panikian, the accountant, whose wife had protruding teeth and on their annual visit to our house showed off her musical skills by playing the piano with oranges, left for Australia in 1946 with their two sons; and, according to his successor in my father's office, a substantial amount of the firm's money turned out to be missing.

The rest stayed for years and years, an odd assortment of Levantine minorities, Egyptian Muslims and Copts, and, after 1948, an increasing number of Palestinian refugees whom Auntie Nabiha pressed on my father to employ, which he unhesitatingly did. I later appreciated that what my father produced in the way of rational organization and incentives for each member of his ever-larger staff was unique not only to him, but to the Middle East: Lampas, a voluble Greek who was my father's oldest employee, was shop manager; Peter, an Armenian, ran copiers and duplicating; Hagop and Nicola Slim, calculators; Leon Krisshevsky, typewriters; Sobhi, a Copt, furniture; Farid Tobgy, diaries and pens; Shimy was the storekeeper; Ahmad was the cashier. Each of them had a small battalion of assistants to command.

In his office across the street my father had one female personal secretary, and one male Arabic secretary, Mohammed Abu ʿOof, a short bespectacled man with incredible patience and the kind of fastidious anality that one associates with a ploddingly diligent, but not gifted, student who never graduated. During my childhood the female secretary was an alert, elegantly dressed Miss Anna Mandel, who would occasionally come to tea, then shortly after the battle at el-Alamein abruptly disappeared. She had started work for my father a year before his marriage in 1932, and I recall his conversation in my earliest years as dotted with frequent references to "Miss Mandel." I later discovered that she had been made to leave my father's employ by my mother, who, she told me quite calmly many years later, believed that Anna Mandel "had wanted to marry your father." Did they have an affair? I asked. "She'd have liked that. No, of course not," was the retort. I was never so sure. Most of the women (there were also a couple of men) who subsequently held the post with my mother's approval or acquiescence tended to be extremely young and clumsy, or else overweight and middle-aged, ponderous and slow—not at all like Miss Mandel, whom I dimly remember as a sleek, carefully put together woman.

Two other office divisions rounded off the small army of people my father employed: one was Accounts, which was run by Asaad Kawkabani, taken in by my father from an English accounting firm and made in effect his second in command. This did not prevent my father from treating Asaad like the merest dunce when he couldn't remember something, or when he misplaced or miscalculated bills. Asaad also ran a staff of his own, all of them following meticulous accounting procedures laid down by "Mr. Said," as everyone called my father. Lastly, there was Repairs, headed by a contemporary of Lampas's, a man called Hratch, an extremely taciturn Armenian whom I never saw without a leather apron; my father thought Hratch was a genius who could fix anything, including our toys, my mother's kitchen appliances, and furniture. In repairs and later service my father was also a pioneer, inventing the scheme of a service contract for every machine he sold; this allowed him to underbid his competitors, and then make up the difference plus some by persuading customers to buy the contract for several years. Hratch presided over thirty mechanics, supplied with motorcycles or bicycles, who sped all over town servicing virtually everything that the Standard Stationery Company—SSCo, as we called it—had sold.

The business also employed a battalion of "servants," as my father called them, or *farasheen* in Arabic, who worked as delivery boys, coffee makers, porters, cleaners; some of them also trundled about Cairo on tricycles and later in small delivery vans. Over this quite enormous, always expanding, domain, my father ruled as absolute monarch, a sort of Dickensian father figure, despotic when angered, benevolent when not. He knew more than anyone about the most minute aspects of his empire, remembered everything, would brook no back talk (he never engaged in personal discussion with anyone on the premises, as he called the place, not even with members of his family), and earned his staff's respect, if not affection, by the virtuosity and sheer infallible competence of his managerial and overall business skills. One of his achievements was to have transformed the Egyptian government bureaucracy by introducing typewriters, duplicators, copiers, and filing cabinets, replacing the haphazard methods of carbon paper, copying pencils, and papers stacked on window sills and table tops. With my mother's help, he developed—"invented" would not be wrong—the Arabic typewriter with Royal, whose aristocratic American owners, the John Barry Ryans, he came to know quite well. He had two formidable, unfailing capacities possessed by no one else in my experience: the power to execute extremely complicated arithmetical procedures in his head at lightning speed, and a perfect memory for the date acquired and cost of every object (many thousands of them) involved in his business. It was intimidating to watch him behind his desk, surrounded by Asaad, numerous secretaries, department heads, all of them rummaging through files and papers, while he reproduced the whole purchasing and marketing history of, say, a particular flat file, a line of calculators, or every model of Sheaffer pen entirely from memory.

This did not make him a patient, or even considerate, boss, but I believe he was always correct and fair, as well as generous, in the process inventing the idea of Christmas or Eid al-Adha or Rosh Hashanah bonuses for everyone, to say nothing of health and retirement plans. None of this made any significant impression on me then: I was too busy being managed or feeling persecuted to appreciate his extraordinary business genius, developed on his own in a provincial Third World capital still mired in colonial economics, feudal landowning, and disorganized (albeit at times successful) large- as well as small-scale peddling. It is only now, as I survey his accomplishments, that I realize how astounding and, sadly, how unsung and unrecorded they were. He was basically a modern capitalist with an extraordinary capacity for thinking systematically and institutionally, never afraid to take risks or incur expenses for long-range profit, a brilliant exploiter of advertising and public relations, and most of all a sort of organizer and shaper of his clients' business interests, providing them first with an articulation of their needs and goals, then with the necessary products and services to realize them.

One of his innovations was to produce an annual product catalogue of all his offerings, something literally no one in his business had ever done in Egypt. He once told me that his cousin and Jerusalem partner Boulos had scolded him for the expense involved. But as the business expanded he discontinued the practice of his own volition and instead printed lists of "satisfied customers" for each of the major lines he carried; at relatively little cost these made his clients in a sense work with and for him. Thus his business grew and grew, despite often calamitous setbacks; in consequence he allowed his family in his own special way the full benefit of his expanded wealth and influence.

Before I left for the United States in 1951, my parents had still not made the transition into Cairo society on a major scale. Despite their wealth, the circle of their acquaintances and friends was confined pretty much to various retainers and a few family members such as Isaac Goldenberg, the family jeweler; Osta Ibrahim, the amiable handlebar-mustachioed carpenter whose workshops produced furniture for the house and, on an increasing scale, for my father's business; Mahmud, Osta Ibrahim's son-in-law (his other son-in-law was Mohammed Abu-ʿOof); my mother's youngest brother, Emile, who was now working for my father; Mourad Asfour, a rising young employee at the YMCA who later saddled my father with thousands of pounds in debt when his sports shop failed and the loans my father had guaranteed were called in; Naguib Kelada, a genial Copt who was the YMCA's general secretary and an important associate of my father's. Kelada's daughter Isis possessed a phenomenal alto voice and sang at the American Mission Church. Their circle was completed by a small number of relatives, such as Auntie Melia, and Uncle Al and his strange giggling wife, Emily, their two sons and one daughter, plus the occasional Palestine-based relative on a sporadic visit to Cairo, mostly for shopping or business. These friends and acquaintances turned up for meals at appointed times and days (for instance, the carpenter for Saturday breakfast), and I came to know them best by their eating habits—Osta Ibrahim refused to eat white bread, loved garlic, preferred *foul* (fava beans) to meat, for example. I was meticulously observant of tiny superficial details and became more so as I lived the contrast between American and local environments with increasing intensity that first year at CSAC. Why did the Americans wear colored socks, Egyptians and Arabs not? We had no T-shirts, whereas "they" did.

Miss Clark's impassive dislike and disapproval of me dogged me at home as well. There were monotonous injunctions against my lack of concentration, seriousness, sense of purpose, and strength of character:

I never learned anything from these injunctions, having taught myself to resist them by reducing them in my mind to pure sound. All pleasures except for parentally certified ones like playing with my Lionel electric train—brought back from the United States by my father in 1946, an extremely complicated thing to set up, requiring the dining table to be cleared, plus the services of someone skilled at electricity, since the connections between cars were never just right—were so ringed with approbation as to seem impossible to enjoy. I was allowed two, and then three, radio programs a week: two from the Children's Corner, on Sunday afternoon and Wednesday evening, a horribly smarmy "good" collection of aunties and uncles, English during the war, Egyptian after it (all of them affecting ghastly imitation-British accents and revolting names like Auntie Loulou and Uncle Fouad), and one—"Nights at the Opera"—on the BBC every Sunday afternoon at 1:15, which is where I listened to a full-length opera for the first time. When Smetana's *The Bartered Bride* was broadcast I was entranced, my mind desperately trying to imagine Czech wedding festivities and what the completely incomprehensible words across the airwaves giving me so much pleasure might mean.

Music was, on the one hand, a dissatisfying and boring drill of piano exercises in which Burgmüller, Czerny, and Hanon were the books I was chained to in mindless repetitions that did not seem to improve my keyboard prowess sufficiently, and on the other hand, an enormously rich and haphazardly organized world of magnificent sounds and sights comprising not only what I listened to but also embellished versions of the snapshots and portraits in Gustav Kobbé's *Complete Opera Book* and Ernest Newman's *Opera Nights,* both of which were in my parents' library, combined with imagined scenes generated out of sounds made by the orchestra's preperformance tune-up, which I learned to cherish on radio broadcasts. Without a clear rationale or system, the family record collection provided me with a strange hodgepodge of Jeanette MacDonald and Nelson Eddy, Richard Strauss, Paderewski, Paul Robeson, and Bach, plus oddities like Deanna Durbin singing Mozart's *Alleluia.* As I devoted myself to the private experience of music, I saw and heard a vast theater, with lots of black ties and bare-shouldered women (my father had taken to wearing his tuxedo on those nights he went to his top-secret Masonic lodge meetings; my mother took to wearing evening clothes that emphasized her ample bosom and white shoulders when they began attending regular subscription nights during the Cairo opera and ballet season). All this suggested to my erratically nourished imagination a gala of wonderfully ornate sexual exhibition and impossibly brilliant musical performance, sometimes orchestral in the manner of an MGM film (this, after all, was José Iturbi's heyday as maestro, a role he carried off with a gigantic baton topped with a gleaming red light, waved around with extremely lush results), sometimes operatic as only scantily indicated by sexually arousing portraits I ferreted out in Kobbé and Newman. One in particular, of Ljuba Welitsch as Salomé in a modified bathing suit, took hold of my fancy, caused it to make opera the embodiment of an erotic world whose incomprehensible languages, savage plots, unrestrained emotions, and dizzying music were extremely exciting.

Wagner remained the great mystery and the most enticing of all. An extremely enigmatic 78 rpm entitled "Hagen's Watch" on one side and "Hagen's Call" on the other introduced me at the age of about ten to the *Ring,* none of which I was able to see or hear until 1958, when I made my first visit to Bayreuth. Hagen was sung by an English performer—Albert Coates, I think—who bellowed, growled, and snarled in a suitably compelling manner sounds that represented a marvelously foggy world of spear-carrying villains, terrible oaths, bloody-minded action, all of it as remote as it was possible to be from the prim world of American children and parentally controlled life at home. I am convinced that were it not for the random and broad field provided by the miscellaneous collection of records, which never yielded up the underlying secret of what held it together or revealed to me the rationale of the history of Western music with its schools, periods, developing genres, and an occasional performance here and there, I would have been stifled completely by the sterile drills, "children's" piano pieces, and, alas, well-meaning teachers to whom I was officially subject.

While at CSAC I had become the pupil of a Miss Cheridjian (who had replaced my first teacher, the kind and patient Leila Birbary), whose weekly appearances for our lessons (first Jean's, then Rosy's, then mine) were unpleasant confrontations over my inability to follow her shouted instructions—count ta fa ti fi, forte, piano, staccato—punctuated by loud slurps of the coffee and energetic chomps on the cake brought to her dutifully by Ahmed, our ironic head *suffragi*. Cherry (as we called her) succeeded only in convincing me that I was a truant and a failed pianist, whereas alone with my records and books I was a kid who knew a great deal about opera plots and a few performers like Edwin Fischer, Wilhelm Kempff, and Bronislaw Huberman (I knew the latter through the recording he made with George Szell of the Beethoven Violin Concerto), and had my highly embroidered fantasies of concert life.

By the late forties I was finally able to attend opera performances—the *"saison lyrique italienne,"* as it was called—at Cairo's Opera House, originally built by Khedive Ismail for the Suez Canal opening in 1869. My parents' subscription also included the French Ballet des Champs-Elysées, led memorably by Jean Babilée and Nathalie Phillipart, who to this day represent for me the touchstone of a dazzling, glamorous kind of dancing, a genre in which I placed the stunning Cyd Charisse, all of whose films I saw: to me dance was a spectacular kind of sexual experience only to be had vicariously and surreptitiously. Cairo was then an international city dominated in its cultural life, so far as I could tell, by Europeans, some of whom my father knew through his business. I always felt that I was at several removes from what was most exciting about it, though I was eagerly grateful to have what I could of it, mostly under the rubric of "art." CSAC, where I stayed through the academic year 1948–49, got smaller and less challenging as I moved up through the ninth grade, less stimulating intellectually and more and more cloistered, straightlaced, gray, sedate, unexciting. Going to the opera in the winter months represented a great increase in my knowledge of music—of composers, repertory, performers, traditions. I can date to those years my exasperated impatience with books by Sigmund Spaeth, the American "tune-detective," and his tacky "stories behind the world's greatest music," as well as with children's books, of which we had many, on the "great composers." Only Wagner remained just out of reach: a performance I attended of *Lohengrin* in Italian during the *"saison lyrique"* I remember mystified and disappointed me, for its incomprehensible action, the literal obscurity of an interminable second act, and its general air of despondency and lostness. The pudgy Neapolitan Lohengrin struck me as the very antithesis of what I had expected in nobility and chivalric stature.

The first opera I saw (and never saw again) was Giordano's *André Chenier,* when I was twelve. I remember asking my father whether "they" sang all the way through, or if there were breaks for speaking (as in the Nelson Eddy–Jeanette MacDonald films and records I was accustomed to). "All the time," was his brusque reply, but his answer came a few weeks after an excruciating evening at the Diana Cinema attending a concert by the singer Om Kulthum that did not begin until nine-thirty and ended well past midnight, with no breaks at all in a style of singing that I found horrendously monotonous in its interminable unison melancholy and desperate mournfulness, like the unending moans and wailing of someone enduring an extremely long bout of colic. Not only did I comprehend nothing of what she sang but I could not discern any shape or form in her outpourings, which with a large orchestra playing along with her in jangling monophony I thought was both painful and boring. By comparison, *André Chenier* had the dramatic animation and the plot line to keep me absorbed. One of our 78s was *"Nemico della patria,"* so I waited rather expectantly for the aria to occur as the drama unfolded, but was unable to spot it. Gino Bechi, a regular in the visiting company assembled from Rome and Naples's San Carlo, played Gerard with a panache and intensity I tried to recreate later by bounding and sliding about in the privacy of my room. I had no idea why characters should sing at all, but was compelled by this mystery from the moment I first encountered it on the Cairo stage.

I can date my most important musical discoveries, however, almost to the minute: all of them occurred in private, away from the hectoring demands of the piano as construed by my mother and teachers like Cherry. This disjuncture between what I felt about and what I actually did in music seems to have sharpened my memory considerably, allowing me first to retain, then to play over in my mind's ear, a sizeable number of orchestral, instrumental, and vocal compositions without much understanding of period or style. I was always tormented by the rarity, the unseizable preciousness, of a "live" musical experience, and therefore was always looking for ways to hold on to it. When I saw *The Barber of Seville* for the first time at age thirteen, I was riveted by the performance, and curiously forlorn at the same time; I knew that what I was witnessing—Rossini's fecund gaiety and irreverence, Tito Gobbi's wit and authority, Ettore Bastianini's mock-solemn *"La Calunnia"*—

would not soon recur in any form, although I could hope that "Nights at the Opera" might broadcast an aria here or there, which for some time the program did not. Yet, exactly a year later, ever the alert, not to say snoopy, loiterer around my parents' room at Christmastime, I suspected that I would be getting a present of records. At about four on Christmas morning I crept into our darkened drawing room, felt my way to the unnaturally green, artificial tree that my mother recovered from the attic, decorated, and restored to its niche year after year, and discovered an eight-record album of selections from the *Barber* sitting at its base. Its cast included Riccardo Stracciari, Dino Borgioli, Mercedes Capsir, Salvatore Baccaloni. Carefully opening the package, I played through the records immediately, doors closed, volume turned down very low, the somber room gradually lightening as the morning dawned. To have had the staged performance as I remembered it confirmed in so private and exclusive a setting was the highest of pleasures, yet I also found myself semiconsciously trapped by that very special quality in a realm of silence and an impossible subjectivity which I had inadequate power to sustain.

More than any other composer, it was Beethoven who informed my musical self-education most consistently. I wasn't deemed fit for his sonatas as a pianist (Mozart was my bane), although I made repeated covert attempts to play the "Pathétique" Sonata and in the process developed a sight-reading appetite way beyond my digital capacities. Scolded for not practicing my assigned Hanon and Czerny exercises, despite my mother's ever-watchful presence, I fled into records and illicitly deciphered "grown-up" pieces at the piano by Mendelssohn, Fauré, Handel, who seemed to me programmatically neglected for the trash I was required to persist with for hours on end.

I was once taken to the Ewart Hall (part of the American University of Cairo, the auditorium was the largest of its kind and was used then—as it still is now—for important concerts) to attend a concert given by the Musica Viva orchestra conducted by one Hans Hickman, a careful time beater who buried his head in the score as if in his pillow. The soloist in, I think, either the First or Second Beethoven Piano Concerto was Muriel Howard, wife of AUC's dean, mother of Kathy, a schoolmate of mine at CSAC. My father was close to Dean Worth (a name whose solid ring for me had the power of the American continent) Howard, and insisted on taking me and my mother up to him and his, I thought, strangely retiring wife who had just completed a breath-lessly rapid rendering of the concerto. "Bravo," said my father, and then immediately turned to my mother for back-up help. "Wonderful," she added before turning brusquely to look at me admonishingly. I of course was totally tongue-tied and stood there looking, as well as feel-ing, deeply embarrassed. "You see," my mother said triumphantly to me, although it was also Muriel that she was addressing, "you see how important it is to practice your scales, Edward. Scales and Hanon. Isn't that so, Mrs. Howard?" She nodded agreement with a clear sense that practicing scales was the last thing she wished to talk about at that moment.

By comparison the Stokowski recording of Beethoven's Ninth (the chorus sang Schiller's *"An die Freude"* in English—"Joy, thou daughter of Elysium") elated me in its explanation of freedom and the eerie mys-tery of the open fifths with which it began, and what I heard jealously as the orchestra's routine ease in getting flawlessly through scales and difficult figurations, which I unconsciously tried to transpose to mental finger positions that my inexpert fingers denied me on the piano. I reveled in *"Salomes Tanz,"* as the brown record label advertised it, or in Paderewski's recording of Chopin's F-sharp Nocturne and the C-sharp-minor Waltz, which I considered the ultimate in, and the opposite of, my miserably inadequate pianism.

The greatest musical experiences of my adolescent Cairo years were visits in 1950 and 1951 by Clemens Krauss and Wilhelm Furtwängler with the Vienna and Berlin philharmonics, respectively. Although in both cases I was taken to the Sunday afternoon performances, stuffed in Krauss's case with lollipops like the *Donna Diana* overture and Strauss's Pizzicato Polka, I was liberated from every pedestrian consideration by the gorgeous sound, the authoritative presence on the podium, and even the magic of the German names (Wiener Philharmoniker, for instance). Never having heard anything on this scale of such direct opu-lent virtuosity before, I remember how exhilarated I felt and how I tried by every means available to prolong and extend the experience beyond the measly two hours I had been given at the Rivoli Cinema (I have never understood why the Rivoli, an extravagantly ornate movie palace, complete with a vibrato-rich, throbbingly sugary neon-lit the-ater organ and English organist—Gerald Peal, a pink-faced showman whose acrobatic leaps onto and off the majestically ascending and

descending instrument amused me more than his endless Ketelby ren-
ditions and tame-Latin dance rhythms—was chosen for Krauss and
Furtwängler over the more appropriately serious Ewart). Mostly this
meant trying to keep the music in my ear, conducting an imaginary
orchestra, looking unsuccessfully for records that were far too expensive for my means that featured the same pieces by the same orchestra
and conductor. I was depressed, indeed, often quite sad, at how fast
such rare pleasure came and went, and how I spent so much of my time
later trying not only to reexperience them but also to confirm them by
seeking out books, articles, people who would tell me about them,
affirm their truth and pleasure, revive in me what seemed to be on the
verge of total disappearance.

A year after Krauss, Furtwängler also stood on the Rivoli podium
on a Sunday afternoon. This was *the* overpowering musical performance of my first twenty-two years of life, approached only when in
1958 I heard the opening measures of *Das Rheingold* rising out of the
black Bayreuth pit. I knew nothing at all about Furtwängler, except for
his name as it appeared on the red HMV labels in his recording of
Beethoven's Fifth: for at least five years that recording was my favorite,
the touchstone by which I judged all other musical performances, the
summit of an indescribable force that seemed to travel out of our
Stewart-Warner stand-up radio-gramophone to address me directly. At
first it was Furtwängler's name that was the source of that power: I
repeated it often to myself (I had no knowledge of German) and imagined Furtwängler to be a wonderfully built, super-refined being for
whom Beethoven's music had been written expressly. I remember how
with considerable impatience I once dismissed a cousin's amateurish
speculation that the Fifth's motto was "Fate's knocking at the door."
What I discerned in the piece, thanks to Furtwängler, was something
I believed instinctively to be without any such concept. "Music is
music," I remember responding, partly out of impatience, partly out of
my inability to articulate what it was about the music that moved me
so specifically and wordlessly.

We always sat in the same balcony seats—in those days the balcony
seemed to be reserved for what my father called "a better class of
people"—as for Krauss, who seemed in retrospect to be a stodgy busi-
nessmanlike figure. Besides, Furtwängler's program, like his appear-

ance, was more challenging: the Schubert "Unfinished," the Mozart G-minor, Beethoven's Fifth. On his other program, to which I was not taken, was Tchaikovsky's Sixth, plus Bruckner's Seventh: my parents had drawn the obvious conclusion that only Program 1 was suitable for me, and it may have been the unknown "Bruckner" that put them off. Furtwängler's gaunt, angularly tall and ungainly figure crowned with a majestically bald pate made just the right impression on me: here was an ascetic other-worldly musician whose figure symbolized to me the transfiguration that music such as Beethoven's necessarily required. I was struck that unlike the fluent Krauss, Furtwängler did not so much conduct (with an unusually small baton, as I remember) as actually move the music with his shoulders and awkwardly long arms. He did not use a score, and consequently there was no page turning and pedantic time beating à la Hans Hickman, the local classical orchestra leader. Instead I had the impression of music as unfolding with an inexorable, totally absorbing and fulfilling logic, unfolding before me as I had never before experienced, without any "mistakes" of the kind that crippled me with Cherry, without the need to pause for a record change, without any sound but that of Beethoven. I also sensed that this was better, and therefore rarer, than any experience a record might have produced, although of course I felt a kind of delicious regret after it was over and could never again be recovered except through the approximations available to me either mechanically or in flawed memory. When I played Furtwängler's recording of the Fifth it gave me pleasure, but not the satisfaction I had enjoyed in the theater; the replica was displaced once and for all by the real thing. Yet I still cherished the work as a particularly favored item to be played and replayed.

My later efforts to find out more about Furtwängler were utterly frustrated by the Cairo of my adolescence. There was no German circle in postwar Cairo to rival the cultural institutions of the triumphant British, French, or Americans. I ransacked the papers—the *Ahram, Egyptian Gazette, Progrès Egyptien,* as well as periodicals like *Rose el Yousef* and *al-Hilal*—for information on him, but there was none to be had. The city was beginning to be flooded with American movie-fan magazines like *Photoplay* and *Silver Screen,* and whereas you could find out all about Janet Leigh and Tony Curtis, there was nothing comparable about the strange (to my friends) figures who interested me. The war was over, of course, but any documentation of what had happened *inside* Germany (where Furtwängler figured so prominently) was unavailable. On my fifteenth birthday, in 1950, my parents had given me Percy Scholes's *Oxford Companion to Music,* which I still own, and which had a tiny entry for Furtwängler ("German conductor born in 1886; see 'Germany and Austria'") that elaborated upon a bit in a general but very oblique discussion of music under the Third Reich, and Furtwängler's role in the *Mathis der Maler* case. This gave no sense of why he was so controversial a figure after the war, or that the question of morality and collaboration had so powerful a bearing on him.

One of the main reasons for the relatively limited way in which I experienced Furtwängler was my sense of time as something essentially primitive and constricting. Time seemed forever against me, and except for a brief period in the morning when I sensed the day ahead as a possibility, I was boxed in by schedules, chores, assignments, with not a moment for leisurely enjoyment or reflection. I was given my first watch, an insipid-looking Tissot, at age eleven or twelve; for several days I spent hours staring at it obsessively, mystified by my inability to see its movement, constantly worried whether it had stopped or not. I suspected at first that it was not entirely new, since there seemed to be something suspiciously worn about it, but was assured by my parents that it was indeed new, and that its slightly yellowed (tinged with orange) face was characteristic of the model. There the discussion ended. But the watch obsessed me. I compared it first with what my CSAC schoolmates wore, which, except for the Mickey Mouse and Popeye models that symbolized the America I didn't belong to, struck me as inferior to mine. There was an early period of experimenting with different ways of wearing it: the face turned inward; on the sleeve; underneath it; fastened tightly; fastened loosely; pushed forward onto my wrist; and on the right hand. I ended up with it on my left wrist, where for a long time it gave me the decidedly positive feeling of being dressed up.

But the watch never failed to impress me with its unimpeded forward movement, which in nearly every way added to my feeling of being behind and at odds with my duties and commitments. I do not recall ever being much of a sleeper, but I do remember the faultless punctuality of early-morning reveille and the immediate sense of anxious urgency I felt the moment I got out of bed. There was never any time to dawdle or loiter, though I was inclined to both. I began a life-long habit then of simultaneously experiencing time as a wasting, and of resisting it by subjectively trying to prolong the time I had by doing more and more (reading furtively, staring out the window, looking for a superfluous object like a penknife or yesterday's shirt) in the few moments left to me before the inexorable deadline. My watch was sometimes of help, when it showed me that there was time left, but most often it guarded my life like a sentinel, on the side of an external order imposed by parents, teachers, and inflexible appointments.

In my early adolescence I was completely in the grip, at once ambiguously pleasant and unpleasant, of time passing as a series of dead-lines—an experience that has remained with me ever since. The day's milestones were set relatively early in that period and have not varied. Six-thirty (or in cases of great pressure six; I still use the phrase "I'll get up at six to finish this") was time to get up; seven-thirty started the meter running, at which point I entered the strict regime of hours and half-hours governed by classes, church, private lessons, homework, piano practice, and sports, until bedtime. This sense of the day divided into periods of appointed labor has never left me, has indeed inten-sified. Eleven a.m. still imbues me with a guilty awareness that the morning has passed without enough being accomplished it is eleven-twenty as I write these very words—and nine p.m. still represents "late-ness," that moment which connotes the end of the day, the hastening need to begin thinking about bed, the time beyond which to do work means to do it at the wrong time, fatigue and a sense of having failed all creeping up on one, time slowly getting past its proper period, late-ness in fact in all the word's senses.

My watch furnished the basic motif underlying all this, a kind of impersonal discipline that somehow kept the system in order. Leisure was unavailable. I recall with stunning clarity my father's early injunc-tion against remaining in pajamas and dressing gown past the early-morning hours; slippers in particular were objects of contempt. I still cannot spend any time at all lounging in a dressing gown: the combined feeling of time-wasting guilt and lazy impropriety simply overwhelms me. As a way of getting around the discipline, illness (sometimes feigned, sometimes exaggerated) made life away from school positively acceptable. I became the family joke for being especially gratified by, even soliciting, an unnecessary bandage on my finger, knee, or arm. And now by some devilish irony I find myself with an intransigent, treacherous leukemia, which ostrichlike I try to banish from my mind entirely, attempting with reasonable success to live in my system of time, working, sensing lateness and deadlines and that feeling of insufficient accomplishment I learned fifty years ago and have so remarkably internalized. But, in another odd reversal, I secretly wonder to myself whether the system of duties and deadlines may now save me, although of course I know that my illness creeps invisibly on, more secretly and insidiously than the time announced by my first watch, which I carried with so little awareness then of how it numbered my mortality, divided it up into perfect, unchanging intervals of unfulfilled time forever and ever.

VI

ON NOVEMBER 1, 1947—MY TWELFTH BIRTHDAY—I RECALL
the puzzling vehemence with which my oldest Jerusalem cousins,
Yousif and George, bewailed the day, the eve of the Balfour Declaration, as "the blackest day in our history." I had no idea what they were
referring to but realized it must be something of overwhelming importance. Perhaps they and my parents, sitting around the table with my
birthday cake, assumed that I shouldn't be informed about something
as complex as our conflict with the Zionists and the British.

My parents, sisters, and I spent most of 1947 in Palestine, which we
left for the very last time in December of that year. As a consequence I
missed several months of CSAC and was enrolled at St. George's
School in Jerusalem.

The signs of impending crisis were all round us. The city had been
divided into zones maintained by British Army and police checkpoints,
through which cars, pedestrians, and cyclists had to pass. The adults in
my family all carried passes marked with the zone or zones for which
they were valid. My father and Yousif had multizone passes (A, B, C,
D); the rest were restricted to one or perhaps two zones. Until I turned
twelve I did not need a pass and so had been allowed to wander about
freely with my cousins Albert and Robert. Gray and sober Jerusalem
was a city tense with the politics of the time as well as the religious

competition between the various Christian communities, and between Christians, Jews, and Muslims. My aunt Nabiha once gave us a big scolding for going to the Regent, a Jewish cinema ("Why not stick to the Arabs? Isn't the Rex good enough?" she asked rather shrilly. "After all, they don't come to our cinemas!"), and even though we were sorely tempted to go back to the Regent we never did so again. Our daily conversation in school and home was uniformly in Arabic; unlike in Cairo, where English was encouraged, our family in Jerusalem "belonged" and our native language prevailed everywhere, even when talking about Hollywood films: Tarzan became "Tarazan" and Laurel and Hardy *"al Buns wal rafi*ᶜ*"* ("Fatso and the Thin Man").

I went to St. George's School each morning, usually with my twin cousins Robert and Albert. Always the leader, Albert was a captain and a star at the school, and a year ahead of Robert, who was not athletic, and gregariously one of the boys. I was a junior figure, enrolled in the seventh primary, part of the lower school, across the street from the more elevated senior place where my two cousins studied. St. George's was the first all-male school I went to, and the first with which I had a deeper connection than with the ones in Cairo, where I was just a fees-paying stranger. My father and, I think, my grandfather had gone there, as had most male members of my family except Uncle Asaad (Al), who had been at Bishop Gobat's. For a couple of days I felt that the absence of girls and women teachers gave the school a slightly harsher atmosphere, rougher, more physical, far less genteel than the establishments I had known in Cairo. But very quickly I felt totally at home; for the first and last time in my school life I was among boys who were like me. Nearly every member of my class was known to my family; for weeks after I started school my parents, aunts, and Yousif either asked me questions about "the Saffoury boy in your class" or made casual, well-informed comments about a Dajani or Jamal classmate whose 107 parents or uncles and aunts were their friends.

The teachers were mostly British, although I had two, Michel Marmoura, an older contemporary of Albert's and son of the Anglican pastor, and Mr. Boyagian, a Jerusalem Armenian and a young boy during my father's time, who weren't. The one woman on the premises was Miss Fenton, who occasionally sat in for the regular English teacher. Black-haired, sandal-shod Miss Fenton, a slim figure in her white blouse and navy skirt, struck me as dashingly attractive. I had far too little interaction with her, too little occasion for time away from the rough-and-tumble boys' and masters' world I inhabited. And so she remained a romantic figure, someone whose graceful presence gave me private pleasure as she floated through the primary school's arcades, or as I glimpsed her through a window in the staff tearoom. Many years later, I discovered she was the aunt of the poet James Fenton. At the opposite extreme was Mr. Sugg, a seriously lame Englishman whose name when pronounced brought forth peals of sadistic laughter for his appearance and his stutter. One of the first British academic misfits I met, he was a man who seemed disconnected from the (perhaps too) complicated realities of the school he served and the students he tried on the whole unsuccessfully to teach. Neither the class nor I was attentive to, much less taken by, the droning lessons on geography that he offered; in his stiff collar and eternally beige suit, he was a creature from another world, full of Danubes, Thameses, Apennines, and Antarctic wastes, none of which made any impression on the indifferent and resolutely self-involved boys.

My class was divided equally between mainly Christians and Muslims, boarders and day students. Michel Marmoura, who taught mathematics, belonged to a world that was very soon to face dissolution and exile in the cataclysms of 1948. He was a gentle and acutely intelligent teacher who despite his nervousness at being a family friend of most of the students (and son of the cathedral dean who had baptized me) taught us the rudiments of fractions with considerable skill. I have seen him over the years in Madison, Wisconsin, and Princeton, and later in Toronto, where he now lives; the pathos of his shattered past has never left him. The rest of St. George's academic offering made no mark on me: it combined indifferent teaching, a volatile atmosphere, and, as I look back on it fifty years later, a general sense of purposeless routine trying to maintain itself as the country's identity was undergoing irrevocable change. Already too tall and developed to look my age, when I turned twelve and needed a pass just to go to school, nervous Tommies at the barbed-wire barricade peered into my satchel, and examined my zone pass suspiciously, their unfriendly foreign eyes looking me over as a possible source of trouble.

Though this pass restricted me to the area where my school was located, my aunt's family had a light-green Studebaker which Albert and Robert were allowed to drive, and so the three of us tooled around

Talbiyah, idly dropping in and out of their friends' houses. On my own, I rode a bicycle around the little square just west of the house. Two blocks up the hill behind the house, a British army bugle corps would rehearse in the unyielding midday sun; on weekends I remember crouching behind the rocks to look at them, transfixed by their unintelligible shouted cries, their large black cleated boots pounding on the black asphalt, almost melting in the heat, and their weirdly savage bugle calls. Albert had a knack for English poetry, which he declaimed with a great deal of eye rolling, a caricature of both the English teacher and the actor in full flight: "'Half a league, half a league, / Half a league onward, / All in the valley of death / Rode the six hundred,'" he would orate, his right hand slowly rising along with his voice. "'Theirs not to make reply, / Theirs not to reason why, / Theirs but to do and die. / Into the valley of death / Rode the six hundred.'" I took it that we too were supposed to be noble soldiers plunging forward, with no thought in mind but our duty. Albert's voice rose still higher: "'All the world wondered. / Honour the charge they made. / Honour the Light Brigade. / Noble six hundred.'" Until much later, I never knew anything about the Light Brigade, but gradually learned the poem, and as I declaimed it with my cousin I remember thinking that words could blot out all thought and feeling. "Theirs not to reason why" was an eerily apt forecast of an attitude I had not directly encountered but would recognize and be gripped by twenty years later as I watched the vast Egyptian crowds that cheered and clapped for Gamal Abdel Nasser in the Cairo heat.

My aunt Nabiha's family would be driven out of Jerusalem in stages, so that by early spring of 1948, only my oldest cousin, Yousif, remained; he had abandoned the Talbiyah house because the whole quarter had fallen to the Hagganah, and moved to a small apartment in Upper Baqaᶜa, an adjoining district in West Jerusalem. He left even that last foothold in March, also never to return. My distinct recollection of Talbiyah, Katamon, and Upper and Lower Baqaᶜa from my earliest days there until my last was that they seemed to be populated exclusively by Palestinians, most of whom my family knew and whose names still ring familiarly in my ears—Salameh, Dajani, Awad, Khidr, Badour, David, Jamal, Baramki, Shammas, Tannous, Qobein—all of whom became refugees. I saw none of the newly resident Jewish immigrants except elsewhere in West Jerusalem, so when I hear references today to West Jerusalem they always connote the Arab sections of my childhood haunts. It is still hard for me to accept the fact that the very quarters of the city in which I was born, lived, and felt at home were taken over by Polish, German, and American immigrants who conquered the city and have made it the unique symbol of their sovereignty, with no place for Palestinian life, which seems to have been confined to the eastern city, which I hardly knew. West Jerusalem has now become entirely Jewish, its former inhabitants expelled for all time by mid-1948.

The Jerusalem my family and I knew in those days was a good deal smaller, simpler, and superficially more orderly than Cairo. The British were the holders of the mandate, which they terminated suddenly in 1948 about six months after my own family had left Jerusalem for the last time. There were British soldiers everywhere—most of them had already disappeared from Cairo—and the general impression was of an extremely English place with neat houses, disciplined traffic, and a great deal of tea drinking, a place whose residents were, in the case of my family and its friends, English-educated Arabs; I had no idea what either the mandate or the Palestine government—whose name was featured on currency and stamps—really meant. Compared to Cairo, Jerusalem was a cooler place, without the grandeur and wealth—opulent houses, expensive shops, big cars, and large, noisy crowds—that surrounded us in Cairo. Jerusalem, moreover, seemed to have a more homogeneous population, made up mainly of Palestinians, although I do recall the briefest glimpses of Orthodox Jews and one visit to or very near Mea Sharim, where I felt a combination of curiosity and distance, without assimilating or understanding the startlingly different presence of the black-suited, -hatted, and -coated Orthodox Jews.

One boy in my class has remained clearly in my memory. I think David Ezra, whose father was a plumber, was the only Jew (there were several in the school) in Seventh Primary, and the thought of him still grips and puzzles me in light of the subsequent changes in my life and Palestine's. He was strongly built, dark-haired, and spoke to me in English. He seemed to stand apart from the rest of the class, to be more self-sufficient, less transparent, less connected than anyone else: all that attracted me to him. Although he did not resemble the Levantine Jews I had known at GPS or at the club in Cairo, I also had very little idea what his Jewishness meant for us, except that I recall distinctly not feeling anything peculiar about his presence among us. He was an excellent athlete who impressed me with his powerful shoulders and thighs, as well as his aggressive play. Ezra never joined us as we walked away together in small groups from school after classes were over in the afternoon, a way of traversing checkpoints in the security of numbers. The last time I saw Ezra, he was standing at the top of the road looking in my direction, while three or four of us ambled off together toward Talbiyah. When my family suddenly determined just before Christmas that we had better return to Cairo, my ruptured connection to Ezra soon came to symbolize both the unbridgeable gap, repressed for want of words or concepts to discuss it, between Palestinian Arabs and Jews, and the terrible silence forced on our joint history from that moment on.

As the autumn wore on in Jerusalem we were thrust more and more on our family, a narrow circle of cousins and uncles and aunts. We paid one visit to my uncle Munir Musa's new house in Jaffa, where he had gone after Safad; it was on a bleak sandy street and had none of the charm and mystery of the cavernous Safad residence I had found so entertaining, and as recent arrivals he and his family seemed to have no friends nearby. In Jerusalem we saw a great deal of Uncle Shafeec Mansour, my father's second cousin, and Auntie Lore, a handsome Stuttgartian who spoke an alarmingly fluent Arabic with a strong German inflection, together with their children, Nabeel and Erica Randa, roughly my age and Rosy's. Shafeec was director of the YMCA's Boys' Department, and Lore worked as his assistant: he was always full of enthusiasm for what he did, for the Y, which was a few blocks from our house, and for his work running sports, handicraft, language, and home economics programs.

More than the church, which I really disliked for its somber and incomprehensible services, the Y represented the great social institution of my last years in Jerusalem. It had an indoor pool, tennis courts, and a magnificent carillon in the tower, all of which I unconsciously assumed belonged to "us." Everyone in my family had had some connection with the Y, either as participants in its programs, users of its facilities (I can still see my cousin George playing tennis there one sunny afternoon), or members of its board. But the Y became part of Israeli Jerusalem and Uncle Shafeec and his family, who had gone to the States on a YMCA fellowship in early 1948, were never able to return.

They were marooned first in Chicago and then in rural Wisconsin in depressing circumstances. For a while the energetic, voluble head of the Boys' Department worked as a coat-check attendant in the Chicago Y, then took to the road in northern Wisconsin as an organizer of Lions Clubs. His anger at what had taken place in Palestine and his early days in America scarcely diminished with the years, although more than any of my relatives he was able to derive some satisfaction and even joy from his later American years. Nevertheless he could never reconcile the two halves of his life.

There was one very colorful character in those early Jerusalem years who fascinated me, even though I had little idea until much later who he really was. My father's unappeasable appetite for playing *tawlah* was often satisfied it seemed by an elderly, heavily mustachioed man who always wore a dark suit and tarbush, smoked cigarettes incessantly through an ivory holder, and with an alarming frequency coughed his way through the smoke that circled his head. He was Khalil Beidas, my father's cousin, and the senior Arabic teacher at St. George's; I never saw him at school, however, and did not know about his professional connection to it until four decades later, when my cousin Yousif told me that Beidas had been *his* Arabic instructor. The other fact that I later acquired about Beidas was that he was the father of Yousif Beidas, a man who had once worked for the Palestine Educational Company, had been my father's best man, and after a short stint in the Arab Bank had come to Beirut as a refugee and in a matter of ten years or so had become Lebanon's premier tycoon. He was the owner of the Intra Bank, which had enormous holdings in airlines, shipyards, commercial properties (including a building in Rockefeller Center), who exercised a powerful influence in Lebanon until he was ruined, and Intra collapsed in 1966. He died of cancer a few years later in Lucerne, destitute, nursed at the end by Aunt Nabiha, who had herself moved to Switzerland a short time earlier. Beidas's astounding rise and fall was considered by some to presage the terrible Lebanese-Palestinian disputes of the seventies, but it seemed to me to symbolize the broken trajectory imposed on so many of us by the events of 1948.

Yet what I discovered much later about Khalil Beidas was that far from just being an Arabic teacher, he had been educated first in Jerusalem's Russian Colony School (al-Mascowbia, now an Israeli interrogation and detention center mainly for Palestinians), then in Russia itself as a ward of the Russian Orthodox church there. When he returned to Palestine early in the century he became a participant in the literary *nadwa,* or ongoing seminar, held in Nazareth at its al-Mascowbia, now *that* town's Israeli police station. When he returned to Jerusalem, full of ideas from the nineteenth-century Russian Christian cultural nationalists, from Dostoyevsky to Berdayev, he began to achieve recognition and even fame as a novelist and literary critic. During the twenties and thirties, he contributed to the construction of a Palestinian national identity, particularly in its encounter with the incoming Zionist settlers. It is a sign of how overprotected and ignorant I was as a boy of our political situation that I hadn't any comprehension of Beidas's real stature in Palestine, that I only thought of him as a quaint old man with racking cigarette cough and—when he played *tawlah* with my father—a rollicking, very jovial manner, all of which, I discovered a few years later, did not survive the loss of his country. Unlike his children, he was spared the fate of refugee.

What overcomes me now is the scale of dislocation our family and friends experienced and of which I was a scarcely conscious, essentially unknowing witness in 1948. As a boy of twelve and a half in Cairo, I often saw the sadness and destitution in the faces and lives of people I had formerly known as ordinary middle-class people in Palestine, but I couldn't really comprehend the tragedy that had befallen them nor could I piece together all the different narrative fragments to understand what had really happened in Palestine. My cousin Evelyn, Yousif's twin, once spoke passionately at our Cairo dinner table about her faith in Kawoukji, a name that meant nothing to me when I first heard it; "Kawoukji will come in and rout them," she said with definitive force, although my father (to whom I had turned for information) described the man with some skepticism and even disrespect as "an Arab general." Aunt Nabiha's tone was often plaintive and scandalized as she described the horrors of events like Deir Yassin—"naked girls taken through *their* camps on the backs of trucks." I assumed she was expressing the shame of women being exposed to male eyes, not only the horror of a horrendous cold-blooded massacre of innocent civilians. I did not, could not, at the time imagine whose eyes they were.

Later, in Cairo, a certain formality kept the extended family's relationships as they had always been, but I remember detecting fault lines, little inconsistencies and lapses that had not been there before. All of us seemed to have given up on Palestine as a place, never to be returned to, barely mentioned, missed silently and pathetically. I was old enough to notice that my father's cousin Sbeer Shammas, a patriarchal figure of authority and prosperity in Jerusalem, now appeared in Cairo as a much older and frailer man, always wearing the same suit and green sweater, his bent cane bearing his large slow bulk as he lowered it painfully and slowly into the chair where he sat in silence. His two unmarried daughters, Alice and Tina, were attractive young women, one of whom worked as a secretary in the Suez Canal Zone, the other in Cairo. I liked his two loud and fractious sons, whose new insecurity expressed itself in blustery attacks on Egyptians, Britishers, Greeks, Jews, and Armenians. Their mother, Olga, became a tremendous complainer, her high-pitched voice shrill with the difficulties of paying bills, finding a decent house, and looking for work. We visited them in a many-storied, dingy Heliopolis apartment building, with peeling walls and no elevator. I remember being alarmed at the emptiness of the flat, and the air of forlornness it seemed to convey.

My mother never mentioned what had happened to all of them. I did not ask my father; I had no available vocabulary for the question, although I was able to sense that something was radically wrong. Only once in a typically sweeping way did my father elucidate the general Palestinian condition, when he remarked about Sbeer and his family that "they had lost everything"; a moment later he added, "We lost everything too." When I expressed my confusion as to what he meant, since his business, the house, our style of life in Cairo, seemed to have remained the same, "Palestine" was all he said. It is true that he had never much liked the place, but this peculiarly rapid monosyllabic acknowledgment and equally quick burial of the past was idiosyncratic to him. "What is past is past and irrevocable; the wise man has enough to do with what is present and to come," he often said, quickly adding "Lord Bacon" as an authoritative seal to close a subject he didn't want to discuss. I never failed to be impressed by this unblinkingly stoic turning of his back on the past, even when its effects remained in the present. He never cried or showed the emotions he must have felt in extreme situations. I recall virtually imploring my mother to tell me whether he cried at his brother Asaad's funeral in Jaffa. "No," my mother said implacably, "he put on his dark glasses, and his face looked very red. But he didn't cry." As weepiness was one of my failings, I saw this as an enviable strength.

Two of my mother's brothers appeared in Egypt shortly after the middle of December 1947. Emile, the youngest one, worked in Tanta, the dusty but large provincial city in the Delta, employed at a glass factory owned by my grandmother's distant relative Malvina Fares, who disconcerted us all with her black eye patch and semicrazed demeanor. Alif, the other brother, was a few years older than my mother and was married with four children. He was a gentle, somewhat passive soul who loved nothing more than doing gigantic jigsaw puzzles, cataloguing and recataloguing his little private library, and listening to music. In Nablus, he had been an Arab Bank employee, but in Cairo, and then Alexandria, he worked for UNESCO. After moving from Baghdad to Beirut, he now lives at the age of eighty-five in Seattle, a victim of 1948, the Iraqi and Egyptian revolutions, and the final blow, the Lebanese Civil War. In Cairo, Alif and Salwa, his wife, exuded a combination of paralyzed indignation and supplicatory passivity that I had never seen before.

Emile's disorderly life, his many moves, homes, and complaints about harsh work conditions, and difficulties jarred our Olympian detachment and seemingly stable and comfortable way of life. Emile seemed a somewhat forlorn bachelor trying to make his way in Egypt after the fall of Palestine. Many years later I learned that he had an Egyptian Muslim wife and two daughters, all kept hidden from us as we were growing up. The subject of Palestine was rarely talked about openly, although stray comments by my father suggested the catastrophic collapse of a society and a country's disappearance. Once he said of the Shammases that they used to consume ten barrels of olive oil a year—"a sign of wealth in our country," he said, since where there was ample oil there were olive trees and land. Now all that had gone.

Then there were the Halabys, Mira and Sami, neighbors in Zamalek whose tiny apartment and extremely straitened circumstances were discussed in stark contrast to their former wealth in Jaffa. I gathered that Mira was an especially favored child of prosperous, prominent parents; she spoke French (unusual in our circles, but a sign of privileged schooling and much travel in France) and had a natural dignity that impressed us all with its Job-like calm, even though my parents routinely spoke of her now as miserable, distressed, under constant pressure. There were other families too, not least those whose fathers and mothers ended up working for us either at home or in my father's business. Marika, a simple Christian refugee woman, was induced by my aunt to attend Arabic services at All Saints Cathedral, an extremely English establishment that we as Anglicans frequented. She became my mother's personal maid.

But it was mainly my aunt Nabiha who would not let us forget the misery of Palestine. She would have lunch with us every Friday—her dynamic presence overshadowed the older and by now considerably diminished Auntie Melia—and describe the rigors of a week spent visiting refugee families in Shubra, badgering callous government authorities about work and residence permits for her refugee families, and tirelessly going from one charitable agency to another in search of funds.

It seems inexplicable to me now that having dominated our lives for generations, the problem of Palestine and its tragic loss, which affected virtually everyone we knew, deeply changing our world, should have been so relatively repressed, undiscussed, or even remarked on by my parents. Palestine was where they were born and grew up, even though their life in Egypt (and more frequently in Lebanon) provided a new setting for them. As children, my sisters and I were cloistered away from "bad people" as well as from anything that might disturb our "little heads," as my mother frequently put it. But the repression of Palestine in our lives occurred as part of a larger depoliticization on the part of my parents, who hated and distrusted politics, feeling too precarious in Egypt for participation or even open discussion. Politics always seemed to involve other people, not us. When I began to be involved in politics twenty years later, both my parents strongly disapproved. "It will ruin you," said my mother. "You're a literature professor," said my father: "stick to that." His last words to me a few hours before his death were: "I'm worried about what the Zionists will do to you. Be careful." My father and we children were all protected from the politics of Palestine by our talismanic U.S. passports, as we slipped by customs and immigration officials with what appeared to be risible ease compared to the difficulties faced by the less-privileged and fortunate in those war and postwar years. My mother, however, did not have a U.S. passport.

After the fall of Palestine my father set about in earnest—right until the end of his life—to get my mother a U.S. document of some kind, but failed to do so. As his widow, she tried and also failed until the end of hers. Stuck with a Palestine passport that was soon replaced with a Laissez-Passer, my mother traveled with us as a gently comic embarrassment. My father would routinely tell the story (echoed by her) of how her document would be placed underneath our stack of smart green U.S. passports in the futile hope that the official would allow her through as one of us. That never happened. There was always a summoning of a higher-ranked official, who with grave looks and cautious accents drew my parents aside for explanations, short sermons, even warnings, while my sisters and I stood around, uncomprehending and bored. When we did finally pass through, the meaning of her anomalous existence as represented by an embarrassing document was never explained to me as being a consequence of a shattering collective experience of dispossession. And in a matter of hours, once inside Lebanon, or Greece, or the United States itself, the question of my mother's nationality would be forgotten, and everyday life resumed.

After 1948 my aunt Nabiha, who had established herself in Zamalek about three blocks from where we lived, began her lonely, exasperating charity work on behalf of the Palestinian refugees in Egypt. She started by approaching the English-speaking charities and missions connected to the Protestant churches, which included the Church Mission Society (CMS) and the Anglican and Presbyterian missions. Children and medical problems were the most urgent issues for her; later, she tried to get the men, and in some cases the women, jobs in the homes or businesses of friends. My strongest memory of Aunt Nabiha is of her weary face and complainingly pathetic voice recounting the miseries of "her" refugees (as we all used to call them) and the even greater miseries of prying concessions out of the Egyptian government, which refused to grant residence permits for more than one month. This calculated harassment of defenseless, dispossessed, and usually very poor Palestinians became my aunt's obsession; she narrated it endlessly, and wove into it heart-rending reports of malnutrition, childhood dysenteries and leukemias, families of ten living in one room, women separated from their men, children destitute and begging (which angered her beyond reason), men stricken with incurable hepatitis, bilharzia, liver, and lung disorders. She told us of all this week after week over a period of at least ten years.

My father, her brother, was her most intimate confidant and friend. Between her and my mother there was always civility if not love ("She was jealous of me when we were first married," said my mother). The two women who played an essential role in my father's life apparently made a pact after his marriage that allowed cooperation, hospitality, sharing, but not closeness. She and I had a special bond—she was also my godmother—which manifested itself in an almost embarrassing display of affection on her part, and on mine, in a feeling that seeing her, listening to her talk, watching her operate was an experience to be sought out and cherished.

It was through Aunt Nabiha that I first experienced Palestine as history and cause in the anger and consternation I felt over the suffering of the refugees, those Others, whom she brought into my life. It was also she who communicated to me the desolations of being without a country or a place to return to, of being unprotected by any national authority or institutions, of no longer being able to make sense of the past except as bitter, helpless regret nor of the present with its daily queuing, anxiety-filled searches for jobs, and poverty, hunger, and humiliations. I got a very vivid sense of all this from her conversation, and by observing her frenetic daily schedule. She was well-off enough to have a car and an exceptionally forbearing driver—Osta Ibrahim, smartly dressed in a dark suit, white shirt, and somber tie, plus a red fez, the tarbush worn by respectable middle-class Egyptian men until the revolution of 1952 discouraged the practice—who began the day with her at eight, brought her home for lunch at two, picked her up again at four, and stayed with her until eight or nine. Homes, clinics, schools, government offices were her quotidian destinations.

On Fridays she would stay at home and receive people who had only heard about her as a source of help and sustenance. It was a powerful shock to me, when I visited her one Friday, that I could barely make it in the door. She lived on the second floor of an apartment house on Fuad al-Awwal Street at one of its most congested, noise-filled intersections; on one corner was a Shell station, and beneath her flat a well-known Greek grocer, Vasilakis, who occupied the whole ground floor. He was always crowded with customers whose waiting cars blocked traffic and produced an almost constant racket of angry, cacophonous honking, overlaid with the sounds of raucous yelling and expostulation. For some reason my aunt was not bothered by this unholy din, and she conducted herself during rare free moments at home as if she were at a resort. "Like a casino," she would say of the evening racket; for her a "casino" was not a gambling casino but, inexplicably, a hilltop café of the imagination where it was always calm and cool. Added to the deafening street noise as I tried to enter her building were the cries, even the wails, of dozens and dozens of Palestinians crowded onto the staircase all the way to her flat's door, the elevator having been angrily switched off by her sulky, scandalized Sudanese doorman. There was the barest semblance of order in this pitching, heaving sea of people: she refused to let in more than one petitioner at a time, with the result that the crowd scarcely diminished in size or impatience in the course of a very long day.

When I finally entered her drawing room I found her calmly sitting on a straight-backed chair without a table or any sort of paper in evidence, listening to a middle-aged woman whose tear-streaked face told a miserable story of poverty and sickness which seemed to spur my aunt to greater efficiency and purpose. "I told you to stop taking those pills," she said testily; "all they do is to make you drowsy. Do what I say, and I'll get you another five pounds from the church, if you promise to keep off the pills and start to take in washing on a regular basis." The woman began to remonstrate, but she was cut off imperiously. "That's it. Go home and don't forget to tell your husband to go see Dr. Haddad again this week. I'll take care of what he prescribes. But tell him to do it." The woman was waved out, and another one, with two children in tow, entered.

I sat there silently for about two hours as the sad parade continued its relentless course. My aunt occasionally went to the kitchen for some water, but otherwise she sat, imperturbably passing from one desperate case to another dispensing money, medical, and bureaucratic advice, helping to find places for children in schools that she had managed to cajole into accepting these destitute, uncomprehending waifs, jobs for women as personal maids or office helpers, and for men as porters, messengers, nightwatchmen, factory workers, hospital orderlies. I was thirteen and a half at the time and still recall dozens of details, faces, pathetic little speeches, my aunt's executive tones, but I do not recall ever clearly thinking that all this woeful spectacle was the direct result of a politics and a war that had also affected my aunt and my own family. It was my first experience of trying to allay the travails of Palestinian identity as mediated by my aunt and informed by the misery and powerlessness of those Palestinian refugees whose situation demanded help, concern, money, and anger.

The overall impression I've retained of that time is of an ongoing state of medical emergency. With no visible office or institution to back her, my aunt's presence to the people whom she voluntarily took on as her charges seemed to me nothing less than Hippocratic; she was a physician alone with her patients, equipped with amazing discipline and a moral mission to help the sick. And so many of these Palestinian refugees seemed to have lost their health along with their country. For them the new Egyptian environment, far from nurturing them, depleted them further, even as both the pre- and postrevolutionary governments proclaimed their support for Palestine, vowing to eliminate the Zionist enemy. I can still hear the radio broadcasts, see the defiant newspaper headlines in Arabic, French, and English declaiming these things to an essentially deaf populace. It was the detail, the lived unhappiness of unhealthy, disoriented people, that counted more to me then, and for that the only remedy was personal commitment and the kind of independence of thought that allowed a tiny middle-aged woman to battle through all sorts of obstacles without losing her will or her certainty. Whatever political ideas she may have had were hardly ever uttered in my presence: they did not seem necessary at the time. What was of central importance was the raw, almost brutal core of Palestinian suffering, which she made it her business to address every morning, noon, and night. She never preached or tried to convert others to her cause: she simply worked unaided and alone, out of her head and directly from her will. Three or four years after she had started her ministrations a shadowy young man appeared as a personal secretary, but he was soon dropped, and she was alone again. No one seemed able to keep up with her.

Her medical partners were Dr. Wadie Baz Haddad, our family doctor, a short, powerfully built, silver-haired man who was originally from Jerusalem but had lived in Shubra, one of Cairo's poorest sections, ever since he got his medical degree in Beirut. Following his death in August 1948, his place was immediately taken by his son Farid. She also relied on Wadie's younger brother, Kamil, who owned a pharmacy across the street and seemed to be able to supply Aunt Nabiha's Palestinian wards with a considerable amount of free or almost free medicine. Dr. Wadie has never been mentioned in any history of the period, but he played a remarkable role among Cairo's poor for his astoundingly profound but unsung charitable mission and, according to my mother and Aunt Nabiha, his genius as a diagnostician. He had an affiliation with the CMS Hospital (it was then on the road to Maadi, just past Qasr al Aini, the great medical school and hospital complex operated by the state) and I gathered that through him my aunt was able to get patients admitted for little or no charge. I can still remember his no-nonsense manner as he boiled steel needles and glass hypodermics in a little metal box over a tiny collapsible spirit lamp he carried in his pocket; he always called on us at home when one of us was ill, always dispensed medicine and advice with great speed, leaving without taking even one sip of the coffee or lemonade that was offered him, and always, according to my father, refusing or "forgetting" to submit his bills for payment.

Dr. Haddad was peripatetic and ubiquitous. He could rarely be reached by telephone but, like my aunt, was known to be at home two or three afternoons a week, and since home and clinic were basically one, dozens of people—all of them poor Egyptians—would gather outside his door without appointments, waiting to see him. A rather taciturn man, he never engaged in small talk and made sure that he was never in a place long enough for this to be necessary. His wife, Ida, a gaunt Swedish-German woman, was an early avatar of today's Jesus freaks, and would use the presence of her husband's mostly indigent patients as they anxiously waited for their turn inside, as an opportunity to try to talk to them about Mary and Joseph, and their infant son. Frida Kurban, an elderly Lebanese expatriate known to everyone either as Auntie or Miss Frida, who worked as a girl's matron at a local school, knew Mrs. Haddad quite well, and never tired of telling us about the dotty old Swede's attempt to convert a lot of poor Shubra (entirely Muslim) residents. She had invited them off the street into the living room, turned out all the lights, and regaled them with a slide show, droning on and on about the Holy Family, salvation, and Christian virtue. Meanwhile the bored and puzzled strangers, grasping the fact that the elderly foreigner was oblivious to them, each lifted a piece of movable furniture—a vase, a rug, a box—and exited Dr. Haddad's modest living room. In about an hour, the room was stripped while the good doctor was on his rounds and his wife was giving an inspired sermon.

We were on our first visit to the United States in the late summer of 1948 when my father received a cable informing him of the kind doctor's death, and asking for money to have him buried. He had left his family totally penniless, Ida was of course ravingly incompetent, and Farid, the eldest son, was in jail at the time for being a Communist. He had just completed medical school when he was picked up, although he was released a few months later. The moment he was able to he became my aunt's medical adjutant, living in the same unself-consciously committed way as his father, caring not a whit for money or advancement—except that, unlike his father, he was, and remained till his death in prison in late 1959, a profoundly political man. His affinity with my aunt was perfect. She referred Palestinians to him, he treated them without charge, and seemed unshaken and indeed strengthened by the daily sorrow he confronted. Forty years later I discovered that even his Communist party friends considered him to be a saint, as much for his extraordinary service as for his unfailingly even, kind temperament.

During the last of my college years in the mid-1950s I saw quite a lot of Farid (like me a graduate of British colonial schools), but he was aggravatingly parsimonious in speaking about either his politics or his extramedical activities. Palestine never came up in all our conversations over at least a decade. He was perhaps twelve to fifteen years older than I, and had married Ada at a young age, had had two (or perhaps three) sons, and somehow managed to divide his life between domesticity in Heliopolis, where he established his family and a middle-class clinic; his charitable work in the old clinic in Shubra and the CMS Hospital; and his increasingly clandestine politics. When I was about eighteen and a Princeton freshman, oddly combining the appearance of a crew-cut American undergraduate and an upper-bourgeois colonial Arab interested in the Palestinian poor, I recall his pleasant smile when I tried to question him about what his work and political life "meant." "We must have a cup of coffee together to discuss that," he said as he headed for the door. We never did meet socially, although as I educated myself gradually in Arab history and politics I constructed a rationale for what happened to him as a casualty of the prevailing unrest and roiling nationalism of the early Nasser years. He was an activist, committed Communist party man, a doctor carrying on his father's work, and a partisan for a social and national cause he and I weren't able to discuss or, except for the facts of our birth, even pronounce.

I had no idea that in 1958, he was increasingly under pressure from his family and mine to give up the Party, which was applying equal pressure on him to do more for the cause, no matter the personal consequences. I was away at graduate school on that late December day in 1959 when he was summoned from his Heliopolis flat for questioning at State Security. Two weeks later, his wife, Ada—disheveled and barely dressed—came screaming into the Heliopolis Anglican Church, breaking up the weekly Arabic service. "They came to the door and told me to pick up Farid at the local police station. I thought they were letting him out, but when I got to the place a man at the desk said that I should come back with three or four men. When I asked why he only said that I needed the men to carry Farid's coffin." Too distraught to say more, she was escorted home by a parishioner, while my cousin Yousif, along with three companions, drove to the police station. From there they were led to a desolate graveyard in Abassiya where they were met by an officer with two shirtsleeved soldiers in attendance guarding an open hole with a crude wooden box perched at one end. "You can put the coffin in the ground, but one of you must sign a receipt first. You aren't allowed to open the box or to ask any questions." Farid's bewildered, grieving Palestinian friends did as they were told, whereupon the soldiers quickly shoveled some earth into the hole. "Now you must leave," the officer curtly said, expressly denying them again the right to open their friend's coffin.

Farid's life and death have been an underground motif in my life for four decades now, not all of them periods of awareness or of active political struggle. Since I lived in the United States totally outside social and political circles that might have had any contact with Farid's, I felt I had to spend years if necessary trying to discover exactly what happened to him after his arrest. In 1973, when I was in Paris, a Palestinian political representative there introduced me to two Egyptian Communists of the period, who said that Farid had been killed while being beaten in the jail. But they hadn't actually seen the crime, although they were sure of "their sources," a phrase that was full of that moment's idiotic Third World posturing, secrecy, and air of furtive self-importance. Twenty years later, when I was in Cairo and first working on this memoir, my friend Mona Anis introduced me to an elderly Coptic man, Abu Seif, and his wife, "Tante Alice," who were close personal friends of Farid, although it later transpired during our visit that Abu Seif had in fact been Farid's direct superior in the Party hierarchy. Mona and I went to see the elderly couple, now retired and marooned in a depressing ground-floor flat up the Nile from Bulaq, in a large, Rumanian-style apartment complex, as if they too should not be remembered. It was dark, dusty, and hot, despite the carefully arranged furniture and Tante Alice's tea and cakes.

I asked them whether they knew if Farid's wife and boys, after emigrating to Australia, had left behind any address or been in touch with their old friends. Both of them said no—sadly, as if to signify that the chapter had been closed when Farid died. Alice brought out a carefully preserved marriage portrait of the young couple—Farid sporting a smart suit; plump, pretty Ada in a white taffeta dress—so that we might together muse on the fleeting moment of connubial repose they had once enjoyed. Later I was given the photograph to keep in acknowledgment perhaps of my continuing interest in the cause, effectively buried for so many years. "He was taken directly to prison—I heard this—and stripped of his clothing, as were we all. Surrounded by a circle of guards, we were then beaten with clubs and canes. Everyone called this the welcoming ceremony. Farid was directly taken off for interrogation, though he had already been severely hurt and seemed stunned and very shaky; he was asked whether he was a Russian doctor—we were all leftists and members of various Communist groups; his and mine was Workers and Peasants—and he replied, 'No, I am an Arab doctor.' The officer cursed him and flailed at Farid's head for about ten seconds, then it was over. Farid rolled over dead."

Only after we left the Abu Seifs did it occur to me to ask them whether they knew that Farid's father was a Palestinian—but it was too late. I surmised that to them he was mainly a comrade, a member (like them) of a Christian minority; perhaps also they thought of him as a Shami. I also speculated that given the substantial Jewish membership in the Egyptian Communist movement, Farid never made much of his potentially divisive origins. That I had never been able to discuss the question of Palestine with Farid during his lifetime is another example of its suppression as a political issue in my early life.

But where Palestine played an even more problematic, though equally mysterious, role by virtue of silence and, in my case, partial ignorance was in the slowly developing conflict between my father and his business partners—my cousins and my aunt Nabiha. George, her second son, and his wife, Huda, had come to Cairo just a few months before Palestine fell in mid-1948. When Yousif and his wife, Aida, came a short time afterward via Amman, there was considerable tension in the air between the two younger men and my father. As a family we were thrust together even more, now that there was no Jerusalem to return to. But the big question was, who was in charge, and that question rested on a narrative and its interpretation that differed strongly between their branch of the family and ours. For me, my mother played the role of chief historian and of course loyal interpreter. True, she said, Uncle Boulos (my father's first cousin and his sister's husband) founded the business in Jerusalem around 1910. But it was a small, mainly book-selling and stationery shop until Wadie came back from the United States around 1920. He put some money—no one knew exactly how much, since, my mother always said, he never kept records—into his cousin's Palestine Educational Company and they soon became equal partners. According to my mother, Wadie brought in a lot of new American ideas, galvanizing the business into venturesome routes and unexpected prosperity.

A few years later he went to Egypt, Palestine seeming to him to be too small and restricted a place, and in Cairo he established Standard Stationery, acquiring the agencies for companies like Royal typewriters, Sheaffer pens, Art Metal furniture, Monroe calculators, which were familiar to me from childhood. Soon Cairo outstripped Palestine in sales. During this period (1929–40), the claim was later made by my older cousins and, I gathered, Aunt Nabiha, that Boulos was always in charge. They had preserved hundreds of pages of Boulos's handwritten letters to my father in Cairo to prove it. I recall seeing only one of these letters, since my father, intent on his work, was oblivious of the need for keeping records, in contrast to his cousin's almost Jesuitical mania for writing down and keeping everything in pitiless detail. My cousins evidently had the carbon copies of these long, haranguing letters, and with these in the overheated atmosphere of the post-1948 period the younger men were able to demonstrate to their satisfaction that my father had always been regarded as a second-rate manager, a partner who needed to be kept in check by an older, wiser executive who was really in charge and knew how to run a business properly, even from a great distance.

George and Yousif, perhaps urged on in this deeply awful struggle by my aunt, who somehow managed to remain extremely close to her brother, seemed to provoke crisis after crisis in my father's office. We were afforded only the merest glimpse of these through my mother's often allusive and deliberately incomplete retellings. With his quasi-Baconian, quasi-evasive, quasi-inarticulate unwillingness to deal with the past as something to be recounted, analyzed, evaluated, my father was probably able to express his shocked, and very angry, reactions to his nephews' provocations only to his wife. It seems he was regularly held accountable for such things as overextending the firm's credit, for being too much of a "salesman"—the word taking on a nasty, demeaning aspect as it was applied to him—and for being unwilling to let the two younger men assume more responsibility. I remember my father's asking me once, undoubtedly alluding to his executive-minded nephews' denigration of salesmen, what the hell were we all about if not selling, using salesmen with salesmanship to get it done. Shortly after his arrival in Cairo, Yousif was given the Alexandria business to manage, but came back to the capital after a few unhappy months in what he considered to be the provinces. In the meantime, as a result of the whole family's peculiar tight-lipped and formalistic social attitudes, we used to have regular family get-togethers, lunches, dinners, and picnics, at our house or under my father's aegis without so much as the slightest trace of tension being apparent to us children.

By the time I departed Cairo in 1951 for what I felt was my American banishment, the whole relationship between the Cairo and Jerusalem branches of our family was, from a business point of view, irreparably damaged. I felt then that the disappearance of Palestine itself was at the bottom of this, but neither I nor any other member of my family could say exactly how or why. There was a fundamental dissonance that we all experienced, as foreigners in Egypt without recourse to our real point of origin. The frequency of references to passports, residence or identity cards, citizenship, and nationality increased at the same rate as our vulnerability to the changing political situation in Egypt and the Arab world. During 1948, 1949, and 1950 the British presence in Egypt diminished, as did the power and prestige of the monarchy. In July 1952 the Free Officers' Revolution occurred, directly threatening our interests as a well-off family of foreigners, with little support inside Egyptian society for our kind. I have the impression that my cousins—by virtue of their youth, better knowledge of Arabic, willingness (at first) to manage with the status quo—initially were not as alienated in Egypt as my father. This increased the tension considerably. My father told his own children almost literally nothing, but I was once informed by my mother that George—who had always seemed to me a benign, bespectacled, somewhat professorial type when he came for dinner and played Chopin's E-flat Grande Valse Brilliante and the Schubert Marche Militaire on the piano—and my father had actually come to blows. This was tremendously exciting and I was torn between the satisfaction that someone else besides me had endured my father's blows and the unrealistic hope that perhaps my father was at last the victim of a stronger antagonist.

Always, the issue was the dispute over decision-making, which, because authority seemed not totally to derive from Jerusalem and the past (as Yousif's did), made my father seem more and more embattled, at the same time that as a group (my aunt, her children, and the seven of us) with an anomalous national status we seemed to be thrust closer and closer. I was conscious how my father's past, his money (since by now I was hopelessly tongue-tied by guilty shame and inhibition when it came to talking to him about money), Palestine, the simmering interfamilial disagreements were—like sex—off limits to me, a set of issues I couldn't raise or in any way allude to.

My mother spoke repeatedly of how regrettable it was that "your father" or "Daddy" never replied to Boulos's hectoring letters from Jerusalem, and that being so decent a man he never even kept the letters, so that it was always Yousif who would badger him with a text, leaving my father always at a loss, the atmosphere heavy with allusion and unspoken charges and countercharges, so much so that we were cautioned about what to say in front of my aunt, and not to accept lunch invitations. Then suddenly, in the late spring of 1948, with the family battles intensifying and the political situation worsening, my father announced to us that except for my two youngest sisters, Joyce, five, and Grace, two, we were going to America. I did not fully grasp the extraordinary step we were taking.

That spring I had been thrown even more intensely together with American fellow students at the CSAC because of a musical play the school had put on in which I was, surprisingly, given a part (largely because of my swarthy appearance, I suspected). It was called *Enchanted Isle,* a heavily sentimental Americanization of Chopin's sojourn on Mallorca with George Sand, a story whose love interest was highlighted by the presence of a Spanish family—I played Papa Gomez, and Margaret Osborn, a tenth-grader, played Mama Gomez—whose young daughter falls temporarily in love with the worldly and enviably brilliant Chopin, who was acted by Bob Fawcett, a pimply American with a pleasant tenor voice.

The whole idea of a play as a "school activity" was new to me; at GPS, which also put on theater pieces, most of the physical work was done by servants, the acting tightly controlled by one teacher, the students (even the gifted Micheline Lindell) treated as pawns by one overweening pedagogue-director. For *Enchanted Isle* even the younger children were given something to do, from being stagehands to acting as supernumeraries; there were student carpenters, and painters, and prompters, and chorus members. All of us were supervised (the word is a shade too strong) by Miss Ketchum, an energetic, toothy twenty-six-year old, who was an English teacher and all-purpose activities director. I recall with embarrassment once shattering the quiet of the "study hall" (a division of the schoolday unknown to English schools) by asking her in a rather loud voice what the word "rape" meant. Miss Ketchum—occasionally abetted by the older, extremely high-strung Miss Guille—guided us through the inanities of *Enchanted Isle,* in which my role as elderly father of the simpering Conchita was to redirect her attention away from Chopin to Juan, a semimoronic village boy who was deemed to be her equal. Every brief exchange between the characters was succeeded by a "number" based in (to me) annoyingly simplified, four-square and hymnlike adaptations of Chopin's Berceuse, the "Military" Polonaise, the E-flat Valse Brilliante, and the D-flat melody from the Funeral March, which reemerged in *Enchanted Isle* as a spirited if somewhat bizarre love duet.

I found the proceedings extremely discomfiting: as a twelve-and-a-half-year-old impersonating a late-middle-aged man, a father, husband, Spaniard, against a background of mutilated, jazzed-up Chopin, to say nothing of the American group feeling that left me even more alienated and improbable than I had been before *Enchanted Isle*. It was in the middle of all this that our impending trip was announced, and I in turn sheepishly reported it to my indifferent fellow-actors. There were to be two performances of the play, to the second of which my parents came, my father in particular being impressed with the fact, he said, that I already had acquired a wife. My mother hugged me with her characteristically enveloping warmth, whereas I felt both irritated and embarrassed by what my father said. We stood around with the other parents and actors, drinking punch, chatting amiably to various skittish teachers. Only the redoubtable Miss Clark maintained her ponderous gravity, smoking and drinking at a distance from the rest, her auburn hair done up in a threatening, top-heavy bun. My father spent much time vainly looking for "the American minister," who was in charge of "the American legation," a favorite subject of his lunchtime conversation (it had not yet become an embassy: the British were still the grander, albeit steadily diminishing, Cairo presence).

All of this preceded our embarkation from Alexandria by one day. Rosemarie, Jean, and I were quickly shepherded by our mother onto the Italian liner *Saturnia* from a sun-baked, teeming Alexandria pier, where my father followed us handing out tips and tersely uttered commands to the small army of local porters who were carrying our many leather suitcases. Although I had heard about the Italian liners from school friends, I had never encountered something so foreign, so vast, so utterly unfamiliar. Everything about it, from the language to the shiny white uniforms of steward and officer alike to the shimmering table settings and the unlimited, non-Arabic food to the ingeniously arranged cabins with their neat little portholes and politely purring overhead fans, fascinated me. No sooner had we reemerged on deck to watch the ship's majestically slow departure than my father (using the half-affectionate, half-mocking "Eddy boy" he used after I started at CSAC) announced to me that "your wife is on board." There was mischief in his eyes as he told me the good news, knowing how embarrassed I'd be. Beyond the sort of standard companionship I witnessed between my parents, and also among their friends, I had no idea at all what a wife was, although I sensed an undercurrent of naughty behavior in the word, as it applied to me, a risible Papa Gomez whose stage wife, Margaret Osborn, happened also to be on the *Saturnia*.

I saw her only once as she bounced past me down a staircase, but we exchanged no greetings or even a gesture of recognition. My father often asked me about her, and this increased the distance between us. My sisters and I were barely conscious that our trip was really undertaken because my father was in need of medical attention; he never mentioned anything about any illness, although my mother, in her usual "this really isn't something you ought to worry your little head with" manner, had made a mystifying allusion to some great American doctor whom they were planning to see. The reason for the journey was never brought up again on the *Saturnia*. My father played a great deal of bridge, joining us for dinner or lunch in the spacious first-class dining room, or much less frequently for consommé at eleven on the main deck. Once on board I alternated between moments of anxiety about my father's health (which took me back to the troubling Ramallah days of the summer of 1942), compounded by his sudden jibes and lectures on the dangers of self-abuse, my worsening posture, and my habits as a spendthrift, and longer moments of self-forgetting delights in the luxury of shipboard life. I participated in shuffleboard, Ping-Pong, and almost nightly games of bingo, and allowed myself great long exploratory trips all over the generously endowed ship, which I experienced rather strangely as a welcoming, totally benign female presence.

To my delight I discovered that I was impervious to the ravages of heavy weather. While everyone else in my family was miserable and confined to their quarters as we crossed the straits of Messina pitching and heaving mercilessly, I luxuriated in the solitude of the empty lounges, bars, recreation areas, and decks. There were plenty of American magazines, nightly films, a miniature dance band playing to deserted ballrooms, and dozens of white-suited Italian attendants whose anonymity, I thought, matched mine perfectly as they kept me amused and very well fed.

The *Saturnia* made stops in Athens, Naples, Genoa, Marseilles, and

Gibraltar. Except for Gibraltar, we were driven around each drab, war-ravaged city for a few hours, followed by a nondescript lunch at a local restaurant, before returning to the ship and our voyage. Naples alone felt like a treat, because after a hasty visit to Pompeii, where we were forbidden to look at the "not-for-children" mosaics, we had a spaghetti lunch near the harbor; there we could see and hear a boatman sing "Santa Lucia," Caruso's recording of which was one of my father's favorites. But what I most remember about all our day trips was the sense of us as a self-enclosed little group, a sort of dirigible suspended above new strange places, making our way through foreign cities but remaining untouched by them.

When we first arrived in New York the question of my mother's status as a nonperson after the fall of Palestine once again became urgent. The main difficulty was that in order for her to have a more durable U.S. passport she would have to reside there, and this she refused to do. Every government or lawyer's office we visited in New York told her that residency was required. Both my parents were understandably opposed to this, and for the next seven or eight years the search for some device to circumvent the two-year residency requirement was carried on with undiminished zeal.

The irony of my mother's fruitless search for citizenship is that after 1956, through the intervention of the Lebanese ambassador in Egypt, she successfully applied for Lebanese citizenship, and until her death in 1990 traveled on a Lebanese passport, on which, mystifyingly, her birthplace was changed from Nazareth to Cairo. Even in the fifties, the seeds of the Lebanese Civil War having already been planted twenty years early, I speculated that it was apparently deemed less objectionable to be of Egyptian than of Palestinian origin. All was well until the late seventies, almost a decade after my father's death, when being the holder of a Lebanese passport exposed her to great difficulties both in getting visas to Europe or the United States and in going through immigration lines: being Lebanese had suddenly become synonymous with having a potential for terrorism, and so, incongruously, my fastidiously proud mother felt herself to be re-stigmatized. Once again we made inquiries about citizenship—after all, as the widow of a First World War veteran and the mother of five citizens, she seemed roundly eligible for the honor—and once again she was told she had to reside in the United States. And again she refused, preferring the rigors of life in Beirut without phones, electricity, and water to the comforts of New York or Washington. Then she was stricken with a recurrence of her breast cancer, originally operated on in January 1983 by a Beirut surgeon. She knew perhaps that the end was near, even though she also refused chemotherapy, for fear, she said to me, of the side effects. She bought herself a condominium in Chevy Chase, Maryland, in 1987 and—with her visitor's visa—stayed on for longer and longer periods of time, regularly seeing her doctor, whom she liked but whose counsel she stubbornly refused. One of those visas ran out as she lost consciousness in March 1990, and my sister Grace, who was living with and selflessly caring for her, found herself involved in deportation hearings as my mother approached her very last days. The case was ultimately thrown out of court by an irate judge who scolded the Immigration and Naturalization Service lawyer for trying to deport a comatose woman in her mid-seventies.

Having refused a short period of residency, my mother ended up dying and ultimately being buried in the America she had always tried to avoid, had always basically disliked, but to which, first through her husband, then through her children, and through her last illness, she was ineluctably bound. All this had begun when we entered New York harbor on the *Saturnia* in early July 1948. Palestine had fallen, unbeknownst to us our lives were turning us toward the United States, and both my mother and I were starting the process of life and cancer that would end our lives in the New World. I have no clear picture at all of our arrival at the Italian Line pier in New York, nor any idea what I first felt about the skyline of the totally foreign new space we were entering for the first time. I recall only the wistful sadness of the vast first-class lounge turned into a shabby space for desks and chairs for customs inspectors and the quite sizable group of passengers—now seen bunched together for the first and last time—making entry there.

By contrast, I retain a strong impression of how unforecast and, I gathered from something my father said, how anticlimactic our first view of North America was, owing to the wind and fog that pushed us unexpectedly far north: it was early in the morning two or three days before the New York landfall that the two of us went up on deck as we entered Halifax harbor. The fog was very dense, we could barely see a few yards ahead of the ship's prow, and a bell was tolling mournfully in the distance. A map of our crossing route had been pinned up near the bridge. There I could see our curving line into Nova Scotia, which appeared at a considerable tangent to our original southward course. We were entering the West, something I had dreamed about, although it was neither Hollywood nor the mythic canyons of New York City: a small, utterly silent and unpopulated little town whose character it was impossible that morning to make out from the *Saturnia*'s deck.

Our address in the city was to be the well-run and modern Commodore Hotel on East Forty-second Street. My father had stayed there in 1946, since it was close to the Royal Typewriter offices at 2 Park Avenue and Thirty-fourth Street. We were all struck by the white gloves worn by the elevator operators, and of course by the tremendous speed at which we hurtled up and down to and from the thirty-fifth floor. The ice-water tap came in for a lot of marveling. ("Wadie," my mother said, "why can't we put those in in Cairo? They make life so much easier." As was his life-long custom with my mother and me, he didn't answer if he felt that the question was a stupid one.) The line-straight streets, the forest of tall buildings, the noisy but speedy subways, the general indifference and sometimes rude quality of New York pedestrians: all this contrasted starkly with Cairo's meandering, leisurely, much more disorganized and yet unthreatening style. In New York no one paid any attention to us, or, if they did, my mother said that they patronized us as somewhat handicapped by our accents and generally overdressed appearance. I felt this when, on our fifth visit to the Forty-second Street Horn and Hardart Automat, I made repeated trips to the milk spigot, twice forgot to put a glass underneath (making a spectacle of myself as I watched the milk pour itself into the trough), twice mistook "buttermilk" for ordinary milk, and twice left the glass I had paid for sitting rather pointlessly on the counter.

For a week we made the tourist rounds: Metropolitan Museum, Hayden Planetarium, St. Patrick's Cathedral, Central Park. Only Radio City Music Hall made an impression on me, less because of the overwhelming stage show than because of the film *A Date with Judy,* starring Jane Powell, George Brent, Carmen Miranda, and Lauritz Melchior. This lush Technicolor world was what I had expected from America; as it rushed by, me on my deep velvet seat buried in a seductive darkness, I quickly forgot the America outside, now made problematic by news of my father's need of an operation in September and by the impending necessity of doing something with the children during the intervening month or five weeks. I remember a long visit to the *Parents* magazine office on Vanderbilt Avenue during which my mother looked through two sets of camp catalogues, one for boys, the other girls: two were chosen (Maranacook in Maine for me, Moymadayo, also in Maine, for Rosy and Jean), phone applications were quickly made, a shopping visit to Best and Co. outfitted us with the requisite camping essentials, and a day later we took the Boston & Maine sleeper from Grand Central bound for Portland.

My memory of our arrival there early the next morning is a muted one: all I recall is a certain numbness, a feeling of dull powerlessness. This was the first time in my life I was to be separated from both my parents for any length of time. I compared their reassuring dress, accent, and gesture with the jovial but wholly alienating A. B. Dole (known as A.B., the camp's second in command) and Mr. Heilman, both wearing seersuckers and white shoes, who met us in Portland to take me away toward the town of Winthrop, a few miles from the camp. I was handed over with dispatch—a kiss from my mother, a brief hug, my father's bearlike embrace accompanying his "Good luck, son"—and the exchange was complete. We drove off in total silence, me in the backseat of the station wagon, the two of them in front.

I was at Maranacook for a month with perhaps two letters and a postcard (from Chicago) from my parents. Housed in a cabin with six other twelve-year-olds and a counselor, Jim Murray, seventeen, I found myself carried along pleasantly by the daily routine of crafts, riding, swimming, horseshoes, softball, canoeing—the unceasing succession of events seeming to replicate my pell-mell life in Cairo. As I was bigger and stronger than most of the other "middle" campers, I quickly acquired a reputation as a force on the swimming and softball teams. I was "Ed Said, the Cairo wonder." Of my cabin mates only two, a kindly New Yorker named John Page and the histrionic, nervous, and voluble Tom Messer, who wet his bed every night and accordingly had a special sheet service, made any long-term impression on me. There was a kind of flatness to the experience until one brief exchange reminded me of my alien, insecure, and highly provisional identity once again.

On a few evenings we boated over to an island in the middle of Lake Maranacook for picnics, storytelling, and campfire singing. That particular night was a gloomy, overcast one, chilly and humid, unwelcoming. We stood around waiting for fires to be lit and the marshmallows and hot dogs to be prepared for roasting, and for me there was a sense of lonely purposelessness. Where was I? What was I doing here in an American setting that had no connection at all to what I was, or even with what I had become after three years at an American school in Cairo? The meal was a meager one: one hot dog, four marshmallows, a dollop of potato salad. After the food had been doled out, the group wandered off closer to the shore; there was some desultory singing, then one of the older counselors—a bulky middle-aged man with streaks of silver running through his hair, which reminded me of villainous American Indians in Hollywood Westerns—began to tell a story about a colony of red ants first entering a sleeping man's ear, then destroying his brain.

I restlessly wandered away from the unpleasantly eerie confines of the circle gathered around the storyteller, toward the quietly glimmering coals of the dinner fire. There were still a few hot dogs left on the table, I was hungry, and couldn't see the harm in quickly wolfing down one of them, although I did so furtively, not wishing to be seen. When we had rowed back across to camp, Murray beckoned to me to follow him outside the cabin toward the lake. "Look, I saw you take that hot dog," he began, as I stood transfixed in shame and wordless embarrassment. "That was very sneaky. All of us only had one hot dog. What makes you think you can get away with stealing one like that?" He paused for a few seconds. I couldn't see his face in the dark, but I was sure that it was angry, disapproving, perhaps even full of hate. "If you don't shape up, and act like the rest of the fellows, I'm going to tell Dole and Heilman to send you home. We don't want any of this sort of thing here."

I found myself figuratively teetering over the edge, and therefore blubbering apologies, idiotic excuses, pleas not to be sent away, as it would land me in awful trouble. I imagined my mother's tears and, typically, her cutting anger; I saw my father beckon me into his room for a beating. At that moment I had no idea where my parents were, but imagined several days of terrible anguish as they made their way back to Portland to take me away, more disgrace, stricter punishment, greater feelings of guilt and anxiety.

But that was the last I heard of it from Murray, who turned away into the night, leaving me to make my way back to my damp, uncomfortable bed. It was only years later, when I read Stendhal, that I recognized much the same kind of deformation in Julien Sorel, who when he is suddenly confronted with a priest's direct gaze swoons away. I felt myself to be a shameful outsider to the world that Miss Clark and Murray wished to exclude me from. Nationality, background, real origins, and past actions all seemed to be sources of my problem; I could not in any convenient way lay the ghosts that continued to haunt me from school to school, group to group, situation to situation.

So beginning in America I resolved to live as if I were a simple, transparent soul and not to speak about my family or origins except as required, and then very sparingly. To become, in other words, like the others, as anonymous as possible. The split between "Edward" (or, as I was soon to become, "Said"), my public, outer self, and the loose, irresponsible fantasy-ridden churning metamorphoses of my private, inner life was very marked. Later the eruptions from my inner self grew not only more frequent but also less possible to control.

The rest of the time in Maranacook was quite routine, as I had stopped deriving any pleasure from the place, and none at all from my fellow-campers. Murray hardly spoke to me again, nor I to him. One later experience emblematized the peculiarity of a camp summer that had lost its pleasure or point for me and had become either empty or onerous. There was an overnight canoe trip laid on for my age group that involved portage from one lake to another in the blank Maine forests, as well as long trajectories when we rowed across vast blazing hot tracts of brown-water lakes. My canoe was manned by me in the stern and another camper in the bow. Comfortably stretched out in the space between us was a counselor, Andy, with a long Czech name, who in his shiny red bathing suit, moccasins, and smoking pipe sat for hours reading a book whose title and contents I could not decipher. The odd thing was that after quickly going down a page with his left index finger he would methodically detach the page from the book, roll it up into a ball, and toss it casually into the lake. For one moment I looked back at the line of bobbing paper casualties of Andy's destructive reading habit, wondering what it all could mean. Discovering no sensible or at least plausible answer (except that he did not want anyone to read the book after him), I put it down to an aspect of American life that was inscrutable. In any event I remember reflecting afterward that the experience took its significance from the desire to leave no traces, to live without history or the possibility of return. Twenty-two years later I drove to where the camp I thought had once been: all that was left of any habitation were the deserted cabins, which had become a motel, then a retirement colony of some sort, then nothing, as the elderly Down East caretaker told me. He had never heard of Camp Maranacook.

We spent the last half of August and the first two weeks of September in New York. During the time my father was in the Harkness Pavilion at Columbia-Presbyterian Hospital, my mother and I were in a nearby rented bed and breakfast establishment. My two sisters were quartered with my uncle Al's widow, Emily, and her three children, Abe (Abie), Charlie, and Dorothy, all of them several years older than I, all of them commuters from Queens to various jobs in Manhattan, Abie at a bank, Charlie at Foster's Forty-second Street pen shop, and Dorothy at the Donnelley Company (phone-book printers) in the Wall Street area. My father's kidney operation was what our entire U.S. trip was built around, though it was not until the evening before it took place that the risk of what was being embarked upon began terrifyingly to dawn on me. This was the second crisis in his health during my early life, yet it was the first time I sensed the likelihood of his death and a life without him. The third crisis thirteen years later was by far the worst, but this one in 1948 disoriented me greatly, filled me with apprehension and vicarious pain, gripped me with its potential for future despair and loneliness.

My parents had invited Fouad Sabra, then a gifted young Lebanese resident specializing in neurology at Columbia-Presbyterian, to dinner at the Cedars of Lebanon Restaurant on Twenty-ninth Street. It was two nights before the operation, so after dinner Fouad had arranged for my parents to meet a fellow resident, an Australian called Fred, as I remember, who was working in urology under the celebrated John Latimer, who was to perform the surgery. With the zeal of the fledgling expert, Fred took it upon himself to lay before us all the things that could go wrong—infections, heart complications, blood deficiencies, the lot. This had a terrifying effect on my father, who, true to his character, saw the coming ordeal as something to be very worried about but necessary, whereas my mother and I believed it to be something to be avoided or postponed at all costs. Poor Fouad tried desperately to turn his friend off, or at least to temper and deflect the man's unstoppable wish to make an impression, but to no avail. For years later, after Fouad came back to Lebanon, married Ellen Badr, my mother's young cousin, and himself became an important professor and neurological expert at the American University of Beirut, the evening with Fred became a proverbial instance of what not to do just before an operation, an incident referred to by my father and Fouad together with uproarious laughter and insouciant banter.

Yet the operation was a success. There was only a cyst and no tumor in the kidney, but the whole organ had to come out leaving an enormous wound running back to front across my father's midsection. For the two weeks he was at the Harkness Pavilion, my mother hired a little English male nurse; I would accompany him and my father on their wheelchair walks. Otherwise I was reduced to silent observation, spending long hours in an adjoining waiting room as my mother sat next to my father's bed. What had briefly been for me a dramatic approach to something really serious was deferred and, like the fall of Palestine, transmuted into the new postoperative circumstances of great attention paid to my father's health and healing, then within a short time absorbed in the rhythms of our lives. I soon became a marginal spectator to the nurse and my father, walking alongside the wheelchair while the two of them chatted monosyllabically; then later when we moved for a month into a suite at the luxurious Essex House for Wadie's "recuperation" (a new word for me: my father seemed to me to say it with considerable relish) and he began to receive his Monroe, Royal Typewriter, and Sheaffer Pen visitors, insisting that I should be "there," even though I had nothing to contribute to his meetings, I found myself to be daydreaming and distracted, with little that was interesting or profitable to do.

A solicitous doorman warned us against strolling in Central Park, so when I could escape parental requirements, I took refuge on the orderly

and yet (after Maranacook) lively New York streets, among the pedestrians, the enormous proliferation of shops everywhere, the theaters and
cinema marquees, the tiny newsreel theaters, the overwhelming number of new cars and buses, the remarkable hustle of subways, the steam
pouring through manhole covers, the efficient and helpful policemen
(in Cairo they were farm boys, my parents said, which explained why
they didn't know the names of the streets on which they were stationed). And New York's tremendous scale, its toweringly silent, anonymous buildings reduced one to an inconsequential atom, making me
question what I was to all this, my totally unimportant existence giving me an eerie but momentary sense of liberation for the first time in
my life.

Allusively, almost imperceptibly, Palestine would appear and then
quickly disappear in our New York lives. I first heard about President
Truman's support for Zionism that summer, as my father rifled through
the newspapers early one morning in the Essex House. From then on
Truman's name took on an evil talismanic force, which I still feel today,
since I, like every Palestinian for the last three generations, blames him
for his crucial part in handing Palestine over to the Zionists. Within an
hour after we had returned to Cairo, one of my older refugee relatives
told me with a hint of accusation trembling in his voice, "How do you
like that Torman of yours? How can you stand him? He destroyed us!"
(In Arabic, *tor* is the word for "bull," used to derogate a person as both
obdurate and malign.) One of my uncles recounted to me that
teenagers at the Rockefeller Center collected money under signs that
proclaimed: "Give a dollar and kill an Arab." He had never been to
New York, but wanted me to confirm the story, which I couldn't.

As I returned to the United States a few years later and have lived
there ever since, I feel a much sharper sense of dissociation about its
relationship with Israel than my Palestinian contemporaries, who see it
as a Zionist power pure and simple, but do not acknowledge any contradiction in the fact that they also send their children to college here,
or do business with U.S. corporations. Until 1967 I succeeded in mentally dividing U.S. support for Israel from the fact of my being an
American pursuing a career there and having Jewish friends and colleagues. The remoteness of the Palestine I grew up in, my family's
silence over its role, and then its long disappearance from our lives, my

mother's open discomfort with the subject and later aggressive dislike of both Palestine and politics, my lack of contact with Palestinians during the eleven years of my American education: all this allowed me to live my early American life at a great distance from the Palestine of remote memory, unresolved sorrow, and uncomprehending anger. I always disliked Truman, but this was balanced by my surprised admiration for Eisenhower's resolute position against Israel in 1956. Eleanor Roosevelt revolted me in her avid support for the Jewish state; despite her much-vaunted, even advertised, humanity I could never forgive her for her inability to spare the tiniest bit of it for our refugees. The same was true later for Martin Luther King, whom I had genuinely admired but was also unable to fathom (or forgive) for the warmth of his passion for Israel's victory during the 1967 war.

I think it must have been the result of that 1948 trip that a sort of political landscape of the United States opened up in our Cairo lives, to which my parents made regular reference. Dorothy Thompson became an important writer for us, in part because she appeared in Cairo for some event attended by my parents, in part because my mother subscribed to the *Ladies' Home Journal* and read her occasionally pro-Arab pieces there. I never read her but well remember the positive valence attached to her name. Also to Elmer Berger's name and, a little later, Alfred Lilienthal's—both were outspoken anti-Zionist Jews. But it was all distant and intermittent. Much more lively and immediate was my recollection of the Davega stores that dotted the Midtown area, where you could buy Van Heusen shirts and baseballs; or the grand halls of Best and Co. on Fifth Avenue, where my sisters and I had been outfitted for camp; or the various Schrafft's coffee shops preferred by my mother for lunch or afternoon coffee.

We returned to Egypt by the American Export Line's one-class *Excalibur,* a smaller, less well appointed boat than the *Saturnia.* The staterooms seemed austere, barren, divided into upper and lower berths, without much light, and hardly any place to sit. No sooner had we left New York in late September than we were hit by a vicious tropical storm that confined my father, his wound scarcely healed, to his bunk, and my mother and sisters to theirs, with acute moaning and seasickness the common condition. I was virtually alone for about three and a half days; once again the pitching had no effect at all on my stomach or frame of mind, though being alone at such a time on a more rigorously run ship than the *Saturnia* meant that I was forbidden to leave the library or lounge for the howling decks, and was obliged to take my meals of sandwiches and milk in the bar alone with a sadly depressed-looking barman. The final days of our trip into Alexandria harbor were placidly uneventful, a period in which the United States seemed to drop away from us like a way station we had stopped at for a while before we resumed our main journey, which was in Cairo and, more and more, Lebanon.

As a country lost, Palestine was rarely mentioned again except once, during my last year at CSAC, when, just after an animated debate about Joe Louis and Jersey Joe Walcott, I suddenly grasped what my friend Albert Coronel was referring to when he spoke contemptuously of "six against one." The phrase jolted me, as it seemed to contradict what I implicitly believed: that Palestine was taken from us by Europeans who, coming with (as well as after) the British, were incomparably more powerful, organized, and modern than we. I was dumbfounded that to someone like Albert—a close friend of mine who, with his older sister Colette, had been with me for a while at GPS and was now at CSAC because his family (Jewish with Spanish passports) had sensed the post-1948 danger to the children in a hostile Arab environment—the fall of Palestine should seem like another anti-Jewish episode. I recall to this day the abrupt sense of mystified estrangement I felt from him, along-side the puzzled (and contradictory) feeling I shared with him at how unsporting and bullying those six were. I was suffering a dissociation myself about Palestine, which I was never able to resolve or fully grasp until quite recently, when I gave up trying. Even now the unreconciled duality I feel about the place, its intricate wrenching, tearing, sorrow-ful loss as exemplified in so many distorted lives, including mine, and its status as an admirable country for *them* (but of course not for us), always gives me pain and a discouraging sense of being solitary, unde-fended, open to the assaults of trivial things that seem important and threatening, against which I have no weapons.

My last year at CSAC, 1948–49 as a ninth-grader, was sadly limited both academically and socially. I had about four classmates and only one main teacher, Miss Breeze, an elderly woman given to frightening tremors when upset. She taught us biology, math, English, and history, while French and Arabic were given by nondescript local teachers whose place in the curriculum resembled recreation time more than instruction. There was no tenth grade, so it was decided that the next year I should go to a school in which, as Miss Breeze put it in a letter to my parents, I would be "challenged." This meant I had to sit the entrance exam to the English School in Heliopolis. The questions were uninteresting but nonetheless reminded me how much my knowledge of England's pastures green lagged considerably behind the expected level: the years at CSAC weren't too useful to this other environment. Better the rowdier, all-male precincts of Victoria College (which accepted me without much fuss) than what seemed to me the precious, inhospitable outpost of the English School. My foreignness and difference barred me from the privileged exclusivity of the English School, in contrast to my sisters who were shining examples of assiduous students, well-liked, with lots of friends who would often turn up at home for tea and birthday parties.

I was more done than ever that last spring at CSAC, which seemed less and less like a real institution and more like a one-room schoolhouse fussily run by the ubiquitous and erratic Miss Breeze. All of the older students—Stan Henry, Dutch von Schilling and his sister, Bob Simha, Margaret Osborn, Jeanne Badeau—had left, as had many of the teachers except for obviously overage and unhirable creatures like Blow, as we called her.

At the same time, my moral and spiritual character was being attended to by weekly catechism classes at All Saints' Cathedral on Sharia Maspero. The church itself was part of a grand compound facing the Nile a little to the north of the British Army's Kasr el Nil barracks (now the site of the Nile Hilton). An impressive plaza with ceremonial driveway allowed cars entry to the cathedral's main doors, the whole of the place communicating that sense of monumental power and absolute confidence which was so much the hallmark of the British presence in Egypt. On both sides of the cathedral stood annexes that housed offices and homes for the resident staff, which included a bishop, an archdeacon, and various padres, all of them British. All this completely disappeared in the late 1980s when a traffic flyover was constructed across the Nile.

But it was especially from Padre Fedden, whom my parents represented to me as a saintly man much envied by the others, and from Bishop Allen, who was nominally in charge, that I learned to love (and have still managed to hold in my memory) both the Book of Common Prayer and the spirited parts of the Gospels, John in particular. Fedden seemed more approachable and human than the others, but I always felt the rift between white man and Arab as separating us in the end, maybe because he was in a position of authority and it was *his* language, not mine. I remember nothing of the weekly catechism classes in terms of what we discussed, none at all. But I do remember the earnestly sincere look on Fedden's face when he intoned, "in the beginning was the Word," for example, or when he explained the Apostles' Creed, "On the third day he rose from the dead, ascended into heaven, and sitteth on the right hand of God, the Father Almighty," or aspects of the Trinity. I still have my Book of Common Prayer from that time, even though I read it only as a way of regretting the pedestrianism of the New Standard Revised Edition, or whatever it is now called.

My fellow catechist was an American university student eight or nine years my senior, a bespectacled Copt called Jimmy Beshai, whose interest in psychology had somehow delivered him to seek the embrace of the Anglican church. Occasionally he and Fedden would engage contentiously on points that Beshai thought could be made more "experiential" (a word I did not know then but that he patiently explained to me one day as we left the class) and less dependent on either faith or vision, Fedden always and in the end impatiently holding out for mystery, drama, inexplicability. I admired Fedden's belief without completely accepting it, since the whole business seemed to be important because my family was set on this confirmation ritual, not because God had moved me.

Bishop Allen's rare appearances were somber and dispiriting. He had apparently been an Oxford don or religious figure of some estimable sort, and over time had risen in rank to become Archbishop Geoffrey Allen, head of the Egyptian, Sudanese, and one other I've missed here (perhaps Ethiopian), Diocese, a man of considerable power and administrative stature. He was always in at least some of his scarlet-robed uniforms whenever I saw him, communicating a sense of haughty distance, even indifference, together with a sense of powerful connections to the embassy and more worldly affairs. He had an intensely executive air totally at odds with Fedden's enthusiasm for religious substance. When I saw the two of them together, it was clear that Allen regarded his junior deacon as barely to be taken notice of; when he examined us ("Let's take a look at the meaning of the sacraments," he might begin) his eyes flitted impatiently and curiously while he busied himself with his tea, though it was evident he had the religious material down pat and could reel off concrete facts and features about James I and Hooker that Fedden's expostulations did not contain. All this took place in a country whose own astonishingly long and dense history, from the Pharaohs to King Farouk, was simply never mentioned.

I was confirmed and took my first Communion on a Sunday in early July 1949 with my godmother, Aunt Nabiha, standing next to me in the imposing transept of the cathedral. Fedden was there but was relegated to a minor role, while Bishop Allen presided over the ceremony with almost Oriental opulence—candles, intoned prayers, crosses, crooks, antiphonal choruses, the organ and choir, procession, recession, and several orders of lesser clergy—all for me and Jimmy Beshai. Having been received in Communion with the company both of saints and ordinary participants, I found myself trying to feel different, but only experienced a feeling of incongruence. My hope that I might gain insight into the nature of things or a better apprehension of the Anglican God proved fanciful. The hot and cloudless Cairo sky, my aunt Nabiha's disproportionately large hat perched on her small head and body, the placidly flowing Nile immediately in front of us in its undisturbed immensity as we stood on the cathedral esplanade: all these were as I was, exactly the same. I suppose I had been vaguely looking for something to lift me out of the strange limbo into which I had fallen, with CSAC ending and Victoria College about to begin in October, but confirmation was not it.

I was now even more in a disconcerting orbit between my mother and my father (who seemed increasingly distant and demanding at the same time); Cairo in that period was full of reports of assassinations and disappearances, and as I neared my fifteenth birthday the following year, there was yet more apprehension in my mother's voice as she warned me not to come home late, not to eat anything off the vendors' carts, not to sit too close to people on the tram or bus—in short, to spend most of my time at home—whereas an awakened sexual hunger stimulated me to wilder and wilder dreams of what I wanted to do in Cairo. A kind of steady but receding motif in our lives was Aunt

Nabiha's Palestinian work. Despite the tension between her sons and her brother (my father), she still came for Friday lunch, and her interest in my catechism continued, as symbolized by the gold ring inscribed "ES," which she presented to me on that hot and cloudless day after the service and which I still wear.

VII

BEGINNING IN 1943, THE SUMMER AFTER MY FATHER'S
nervous breakdown, and for the next twenty-seven summers, we
would spend most of July, August, and September in the Lebanese
mountain village of Dhour el Shweir (which means "on the outskirts of
Shweir"), a village my father loved and my mother claimed to hate,
even though her mother's family, the Badrs, came from there. Dhour
was a summer resort whose houses and hotels were strung along a narrow ascending road that meandered along the backs of three small
mountains in central Lebanon. Shweir itself was a little town, strung
along a steeply descending road, going in the opposite direction, that
began in Dhour's only significant public space, the main square, or *saha,*
dipped sharply to the left next to the Greek Orthodox church, and
wound its way down to the valley, to its very heart, ᶜAyn al Qassis, the
"priest's spring." A totally Christian village, Shweir produced the shopkeepers and functionaries who serviced Dhour during the season. As a
child I had assumed they simply sat home during the long, dark, and
snowy winter. Except for my mother's extremely aged great-uncle Faris
Badr, a rosy-faced, heavily mustachioed gentleman who always wore
dark glasses and a black suit and tie with a red tarbush, carried a very
ancient black umbrella, and was resident there all year, my mother's
Lebanese relatives lived and worked in Beirut, only visiting Dhour in
the summer season.

We spent our first summer of 1943 in Dhour's only "grand" hotel, the Kassouf, which sat rather haughtily and pretentiously on a promontory near the end of the road leading due east for two miles out of the *saha* toward Bois de Boulogne, the next village; the Kassouf was clearly modeled after a château, its long sweeping staircase, balustrades, and massive stony assertiveness dominating the village and valley. I first learned about red wine and red vinegar in the Kassouf's formal dining room, and I also caught my first glimpse of a roulette and baccarat room. The hotel seemed to be full of wealthy Syro-Lebanese tourists from Egypt (Shawam), people from our class, I suppose, for whom in comparison with Cairo's oppressive summer heat, Dhour's sunny and relatively dry warm days and cool, foggy afternoons and evenings were a bracing contrast. These people, like us, spent a good deal of time walking the Kassouf's terraces, occasionally venturing onto the only road, which had no pavements and a steep fall on either side, at the risk of being run over by a speeding car or bus. There were no shops between the Kassouf and the *saha,* and the hotel was just far enough to make a casual stroll into town out of the question; so we stayed on the grounds with the other children, their nannies, and parents. My mother was pregnant that summer with Joyce and seemed to spend most of her time in the room, while my father—by now a confirmed bridge addict—stayed in one or another card room most of the morning, afternoon, and, at least three times a week, evening.

Not until 1944 did I begin very tentatively to make out the broad lines of my parents' plan for each summer, which began after school finished in the early spring. By late May I could sense the impending departure date without being told. New shorts and sandals would have to be purchased, there would be an agonizingly long and maddeningly finicky family photo session with a pair of elderly spinster sisters, both of whom were totally dumb and therefore limited in communication to excited grunts and agitated nods, in their extremely hot third-floor studio around the corner from Shepheard's Hotel. Dr. Haddad would call to give us our round of typhoid shots, and one day all the living room and smaller salons' furniture would suddenly be draped in pink, white, or pale-green sheets. Until 1948 we would gather, on the appointed day, in the lobby of 1 Sharia Aziz Osman for a caravan of two or (later, as our number increased) three cars to take us, one or two maids, and the cook, to Bab-el-Hadid Station, where we would board the wagon-lit bound for the Suez Canal towns of either Ismailia or al-Kantarah. From there we crossed into Sinai for the long overnight ride to Haifa, which we would reach at about noon the next day.

The train journey was indescribably romantic and pleasurable. I loved the polished wood walls, the handsome seat I could pull down and sit on by the window, the blue shaded lamps coming on at twilight, the Greek waiters and vaguely French conductor, who sat at the end of the corridor along which our three or four compartments lay and, after dinner, came by to pull down the upper beds and do up the lower ones. I used to look forward to going to the resplendently gaudy dining car, with its table silver and beady lampshades tinkling as the train lurched from side to side, making the white-robed *suffragis* and the tuxedo-clad Italian or Armenian maître d'hôtel do the same. The menu always contained a rice first course, followed by a second course of lamblike meat with gravy, and finally a small bowl of oversweet crème caramel, all of them foods banned from my parents' rigorously healthy table of spinach, carrots, celery, and peas enlivened only slightly by broiled chicken or grilled veal and the bland pastas that seemed so important to what we called my father's "regime." When I crawled into the fresh sheets of my tightly made up upper-deck bed I would switch on my special reading light and extricate my book from the odd little net strung up along the wall where I could store my possessions with a rare sense of privacy, safe from sudden parental invasion. Sleep would come very late and the desert dawn very early. The melancholy of the half-lit desert wastes brought with them an additional sense of calm, and in the scene's monotony, and my utter solitude as everyone else slept, I was relieved of pressure and the continual anxiety of not getting anything right.

In Haifa we would be met by two seven-seater taxis operated by the el-Alamein company, which took us either to Jerusalem for a week or, more frequently, along the northwest road out of Palestine via Acre to Naqura, the Lebanese border village, and from there a few more kilometers to the fishing village of al-Sarafand. There we stopped at the waterside restaurant where it always seemed like hours before the fish was slowly grilled to my father's satisfaction and duly eaten, and we were able to proceed north along deserted roads to Tyre and Sidon.

Bypassing Beirut we would take the Dhour–Bikfaya road, which with a sudden hoist took us up above Antelias and the dark-blue Mediterranean spread out in all its shimmering mystery beneath us.

In the early days, there was often a decrease in the number of cars as we climbed the dramatically hairpinned road to Bikfaya, the large town just below Dhour that I knew for its famous peaches and a fantastic red-and-tinsel-colored toy shop, "Kaiser Amer." It was only later, in the 1970s, that I knew it as the family seat of the Gemayel family. Pierre Gemayel, impressed with the German blackshirts he saw at the 1936 Olympics, was the founder of the extreme-right Maronite party, the Phalanges Libanaises, and was father of two Lebanese presidents—Bashir, whose assassination in September 1982 unleashed the massacres at the Sabra and Shatila Palestinian refugee camps perpetuated by his pro-Israel henchmen, and Amin, who ran a regime drenched in corruption and incompetence. Bikfaya then acquired a sinister reputation as rabidly anti-Palestinian, and I have avoided it and Dhour for almost two decades.

Above Bikfaya the road became steeper and more treacherous, with still fewer cars and the views were usually obscured by the great washes of afternoon fog sweeping across the peaks through which we chugged, the two heavily loaded cars struggling against the dramatically steep inclines. When we finally entered Dhour, through the little suburb of Douar, I would feel the combination of mournfulness and impending dread that the place always induced.

For our summers we lived in an unfurnished rented Dhour house, since despite his wealth my father told me many times that he did not trust real estate, and consequently spent his life outside Palestine in rented residences. This was an important part of my parents' plan for summer living and the houses were as plain, unadorned, and free of ornament or luxury as they could find. In 1944 a truckload of wooden furniture was being moved in just as we arrived that June. In stark contrast to the comfort and plushness of what we had left behind in Cairo, I saw a collection of rather rickety, splinter-filled, badly finished wooden cupboards, tables, and chairs that my father had ordered from Beirut. This ugly spartan furniture followed us around the various houses we rented in Dhour, until 1946, when we took the second floor of a big square house in an impressive terrace which would be our summer abode for the next twenty-four years. The seven beds had identical metal frames hastily painted in a white that never stopped peeling, as well as formidable springs that looked like something out of a medieval torture chamber. The living-room furniture was confected out of a couple of low daybeds that my mother covered with something she had brought from Cairo, in addition to a few cushions slung across the wall behind them. There were no pictures anywhere.

The idea was that we would lead an austere, rustic, minimally comfortable existence stripped of any amenities that my father considered to be either too urban or too luxurious. We were not allowed to have a radio in the house until 1949. I vividly recall how on the cool August 1949 afternoon when I first had the little radio to myself I heard the BBC announce Richard Strauss's death, then crackle and fade gently off the air, and how when we returned to Cairo I wrote in the date next to his name in my one-volume music encyclopedia. A telephone was allowed in around 1954, and a car in 1956. Except for our maids Ensaf and later her sister Souad, our cook Hassan (in the village he was always referred to demeaningly by the natives as *al-ʿabd,* "black slave") had to endure about five years of Dhour before my father allowed my mother some local help: an aged and wrinkled crone known as Um Najm who did the washing and bread baking, and a different younger woman each year for general housecleaning and kitchen help. The electricity and hot water were highly unreliable, and a bath required several hours of wood burning in the mammoth *qazan,* or stove. In 1953, at my mother's importuning, a spinet piano was rented for me to play, but it was installed in my room for fear that it might create too civilized an impression in the main room. What books we had in the house were brought in strictly limited quantities from Cairo, since weight and space were important considerations. In Dhour, the only bookshop was a branch of Stematazky's installed in an unrefurbished garage and staffed by an erudite-looking, vaguely clerical man in open sandals and massive black-rimmed spectacles who carried an extensive line of comics and movie magazines, plus a few paperback murder mysteries for which I never developed a taste. I would forage for books at the houses of my mother's relatives, and was later able to purchase them in Beirut. Dhour drove me further into the world of print, which because I had so little time to read in Cairo became for me a precious respite from the abysmal vacancy of my life there.

For my father the idea of Dhour was to be as far away as possible, in every sense, from his Cairo business world and all that it entailed: cars, employees, phones, business suits, papers, and the city. Rest, rest, rest. For him this meant hours and hours spent either at the bridge table at the Hotel Salwa in the morning or the Cirque Café in the afternoons, or playing backgammon on the terrace with a local friend or a visitor from Beirut, Jerusalem, or even Cairo. Had it not been for my mother's insistence he would never have changed the green or maroon sport shirt, baggy beige trousers, scruffy brown shoes, hat, and cane that made up his uniform every day from earliest morning to bedtime. There were no morning newspapers to read, and so he began the day by sauntering off to town to visit Nicola Touma, an attractive and suave middle-aged fellow from Shweir whose clan was the largest one there. Touma's grocery shop was amply stocked with everything from fruit and vegetables to toilet paper, soap, oil, and spices. Mysteriously to me, we never paid cash but said instead, "Put it on the account." When the bill turned up in my mother's hands every two weeks it would elicit cries of "What a rascal he is; I don't remember any of these expenses."

To my father, normally a very hardbitten businessman, it did not matter what Nicola put on his bill; their relationship was engagingly social. Sitting at Nicola's desk at the back of the shop, holding a cup of Turkish coffee in his hand, my father would nonchalantly survey the merchandise, ordering five kilos of this or that, two watermelons, five jars of jam, a kilo of figs (rarely available), and three pounds of cheese, which would be delivered by a slim boy on a tricycle who would have to push rather than ride the overladen vehicle up the very steep hill to the house. After his visit to Nicola my father would saunter down to Edmund Halabi's ABC three doors down, and proceed to order masses of toilet articles needed by none of us. Next would be the butcher, then the coffee merchant, and then the pharmacy: for each of them, my father's profligate orders must have been the sale of the day. Finally he would plant himself at a bridge table until it was time to amble home for lunch. In the meantime my mother, left with her children, without a phone or transport, would have to receive the seemingly endless succession of delivery boys, each one inducing greater cries of frustration and chagrin. Much of the merchandise would be sent back, and when my father finally turned up for his midday meal he would be greeted with a highly repetitious daily scolding delivered by my mother in a relentlessly querulous voice, his only occasionally raised in monosyllabic response as he ate his stringy chicken or tough grilled meat, apparently indifferent to her fury. After a siesta he would wander out again in search of more bridge, this time without the leisurely shopping stops, which would resume as inevitably as the sun rose the next morning.

My father regarded Dhour as his opportunity to desert the strenuous post he held as parent, disciplinarian, and imperious master in Cairo. In Dhour my mother became my companion, with only very occasional breaks when I would strike up short-lived and temporary summer friendships with boys of my generation staying nearby. She was left the daily responsibility of running the house, which without the kind of help she had in Cairo was a stressful affair. The absence, in the beginning, of a telephone and a car with a driver isolated us and imposed a kind of powerlessness on her that she resented deeply. But knowing only how to comply with her designated role as head of household, she did not know how to protest and ask my father to improve her situation. My youngest sister, Grace, was born in March 1946, when Joyce was only two and a half years old, so she had two babies to care for in addition to her older children.

The year 1946 was particularly trying for my mother. My father decided that his business required him to make his first American trip since he had left the States in 1920 to return to Palestine. Two weeks after we arrived in Dhour and quickly installed ourselves in the cavernous and inhospitable house, he took the laborious overland route back to Egypt, via Jerusalem, and embarked for the United States on the first direct commercial air service from Cairo to New York, TWA.

His two-month absence—during which he sent occasional letters and (mainly) postcards—left my mother in a hyperenergized panic. The main purpose of her day seemed to be to get me out of the house and away from my volatile sisters for as long as possible. In order to do this my mother devised a continuous series of "errands," as we both called them, which I, ten and a half years old, dreaded. At roughly eight-thirty I was sent off to Nicola's, the butcher shop, and the bakery. There was nothing going on at that hour; even Abu Bahbouha, a grizzled, rough man missing several fingers who wore a filthy apron over his plaid shirt and sold hot peanuts off a little cart with a tiny smoky chimney, just outside the church, hadn't appeared yet, and old Bou Fares, always wearing the darkest of dark glasses and his perdurable khakis, standing alongside the church, was just beginning to polish and then line up the ancient bicycles he rented out. It would be another year before I was allowed to rent one, though even then my father never thought it a "wise" practice anyway. The morning commuters to Beirut had already been to the *saha* to catch their taxis, so with the exception of Najib Farfar's 1936 Ford, which still saw service as a local Dhour taxi, there were no cars about. Just a few shopkeepers, me, and clumps of buzzing flies and bees that went from the apricots in one store to the raw meat hanging in the doorway of another.

A few loaves of bread were the only things I carried home about an hour later. Immediately after my arrival my mother would ask me to chase off after the tinker (*sankary*) and ask him to repair a leaking kitchen faucet. Then when the groceries had been delivered there were always two tomatoes, three eggplants, four lemons, and ten plums that had to be returned and replaced with better ones. "Your father has spoiled the man so much that he thinks he can get away with sending us his worst produce. Edward, tell him that I'm very angry!" It took me even longer for this third errand into town, mainly because I was extremely anxious about saying anything disapproving to the benevolent Nicola, who seemed to have reserved all his cordiality and good cheer for my father, his best client. When I deposited the offending stuff on his desk he barely looked up from one of his account books: "What's the matter with these?" he would ask me coldly. I tried to pull the words out but would only sputter something incoherent that included the phrase "my mother," to which he coldly replied: "Leave them there. I'll look at them later," meaning something that fell short of replacing them right away. I was faced either with the choice of returning home empty-handed and being sent back or facing down the sharp-eyed grocer myself, with little confidence in the demand. I settled on a complete evasion, which amazes me to this day for its unforeseen brilliance. "Could I have a cheese and pickle sandwich please?" I said firmly to Nicola, who languidly waved to one of his helpers to make the thing for me. "And put it on the account," I added smartly as I wandered off with the delicious object in my hand.

Later in the day Nicola would replace the offending items, and several additional errands were devised for me, until by sundown I was exhausted and incapable of much more than a tired slump with a novel before I went off to bed. The state of fatigue itself was not as unsettling as the alarming remoteness I felt in my mother. Our relationship of intimacy had soon been attached to one whose essence I now think was expressed in a scene I remember with unhappy clarity. One hot weekday morning she had sent me all the way to the Hotel Kassouf to take an electric iron wrapped in brown paper to a visiting friend from Cairo, Eugenie Farajallah. I returned home an hour and a half later, dead tired, thirsty, from the long walk through a most unappealing landscape. There were no side roads to consider, no shady spots, no springs, no other pedestrians, not a café or restaurant as I trudged along the endless narrow road heading east, all of it steep and barren. I remember also that this was the year my father had bought for me and insisted I wear a heavy khaki pith helmet; a salesman at Avierino's, a men's shop in Cairo's Esbekiah district, had recommended it to him for me while my father was buying a handsome Panama for himself. The helmet's inside band was disgustingly soggy with sweat as the ridiculous thing bore down on me, too cumbersome to take off and carry, hence fated to remain on me as I trudged along. As I wearily climbed the long dusty stairs that led from Dhour's only road back to our house, I saw my mother standing on the balcony, dressed in a shapeless gray housedress, without makeup, her hair wrapped in the turban she wore in those years, waving to me with what I had hoped was a greeting on my return but in fact was a hail to attract my attention, to intercept me before I too securely began to climb the final set of stairs onto the terrace. In her right hand she was holding a black electrical cord: "Darling," she said to me in English, not always a good sign, "I forgot to give you the cord for the iron. What must Eugenie be thinking? Please take this back up to the Kassouf right away." A terrible feeling of fatigue and despondency overcame me.

What had been a sustaining intimacy with my mother, during our Shakespeare readings, for instance, seemed suddenly to grow into something else, though here and there during the Dhour months she would give me a sign that some of our former life remained. In addition to a tattered Arabic hymnbook the Dhour house contained something called *A Family Songbook,* a mostly English collection we must have brought with us from Jerusalem or Cairo. Since I could read music well enough to sing some of the songs, I would often softly either hum or sing "The Minstrel Boy" or "John Peel" from the book to myself; overhearing me from her room my mother would call out a sentence of loving approbation, which quickly lifted a humdrum or merely uninteresting day into momentary happiness. My room, the only one on the kitchen side of the immense high-ceilinged living room and its dining room, heightened my sense of unfruitful isolation and always remained for me a symbol of Dhour's underlyingly negative aura, despite the small downstairs garden amenities of a Ping-Pong table, a croquet set, a creaky swing that my father reluctantly accepted as part of our rustication.

As I look back over those years, I can see the real anxiety induced in me by my mother's withdrawal, where the need to reconnect with her was kept alive paradoxically by the obstacles she placed before me. She had become a taskmaster whose injunctions I had to fulfill. Yet the emptiness into which I fell during and after my errands when she gave little warmth or thanks genuinely bewildered me. The intelligence of our relationship was temporarily gone, in Dhour replaced by the series of drills set for me to keep me out of everyone's way. Years later she would tell stories of my capacity for troublemaking as a child, and how she devised stupid, only occasionally useful, errands for me.

It must also have been part of my parents' plan to get me out of Cairo's putative (because never actually seen or experienced) fleshpots during the summer, and deposit me in a place where there weren't and could never have been any temptations. The only girls from these early Dhour days were one or two of my sisters' friends, none of whom took any notice of me. Toward the end of July 1946 my mother's youngest brother showed up from Palestine, and being of a more adventurous nature than his sister, offered to take us all out one night to see a *numéro,* as cabaret acts were called in those days, at Café Nasr, one of two far-stretching places—the other being Café Hawie—opposite each other about a hundred yards beyond the *saha;* they were both family enterprises, Nasr run by Elias Nasr and his sister, an attractive middle-aged spinster with an enormous phlebitic leg, and Hawie's by the brothers Iskandar and Nicola Hawie. The two establishments seemed engaged in mortal commercial combat.

Nasr had upped the stakes by bringing in what were advertised as "international" variety performers, mostly acrobats and dancers whose main attraction, looking back on them now, was that the women wore skimpy costumes. That night we were crowded around a small table one back from the dance floor, and the main act was a pair of acrobats, George and Adele, whose last name seemed Hungarian. He was a short, muscular man in his mid-forties, and she was an only slightly younger blonde in a modified bikini that reminded me of Kalita, especially since she bent her body in similarly unnatural ways. Advertised as a nine p.m. "soirée," the show didn't start until a little past eleven, with lots of false starts and moments of fake urgency engineered by waiters who were obviously under strict orders to prod the customers into buying more food and drink "before we begin the *numéro*." A tiresome wait for all of us, until a sustained snare drumroll brought out the two stars, complete with long silver cloaks, and flashy overly wide gold-toothed smiles. I remember being disappointed with how little beyond a few distinctly unadventurous poses they attempted—he lifts her over his head, she does a back bend, he swings her under his arms—until the final trick, which the Armenian bandmaster warned us was extremely dangerous and required absolute silence. A short pole was brought out, on which George hoisted Adele; then as he slowly twirled it around him Adele held on to one end, like a flag, and was gradually swung with her body at a ninety-degree angle to the pole, all this with what I recall was a superfluous commentary by the Armenian maestro on what was plainly taking place before our eyes. We trudged home at about midnight full of admiration for the intrepid duo's last feat, though I recall that my mother was disapprovingly silent throughout. Bare flesh always caused her to frown and then "tsk" exasperatedly with unconcealed distaste.

I realize now that so innately trivial an episode as the battle of *"numéros"* between Hawie and Nasr, who competed with each other in weekly entertainments, seemed much more interesting than it was because of the total uneventfulness of our Dhour summers during the early years. I recall the indifference I felt when my mother would receive guests for morning coffee or afternoon tea, during which I would be summoned from my room for a perfunctory handshake, and then sent either back or on an errand. There was a ritualized formality to the whole business of these visits. Usually a messenger would be dispatched a day before to announce one of the occasions, although they could also occur without warning. The idea was that each family was entitled to one such social call per summer from a family with which it had some connection—the dentist, a cousin's cousin, local notables, the Protestant minister, and so on. The morning time was always around eleven, as they—no one ever came alone—trooped up the rocky path, then the single flight of stone stairs to our house, in a single file led by the man or men, the women following silently behind. Soon there would be coffee, followed by chocolate or, after my mother had learned the practice from Marie Nassar, a piece of Turkish Delight wedged between two plain biscuits. This was considered a special treat. A little later came glasses of tamarind or mulberry syrup in water and a box of cigarettes. An hour later the guests stood up ready to leave, though it was considered the polite thing to say, "So soon? It's still quite early," which my mother always did. Afternoon visitors came at four-thirty and were supplied with tea; on those occasions the men were commuters who had returned from Beirut after the workday.

There was something needlessly rigid about these visits, not just because it was understood that my mother should be at home to receive guests day in, day out, but also because she would have to make similar visits herself. One had the impression that a careful record was being kept somewhere, that Mrs. Haddad had *not* been visited, whereas we had had *her* visit. For all its bustle, our life in Cairo was a good deal more private in those years, though I did sense the stirrings in my mother of a sense of social obligation with regard to one or two families like the Dirliks and the Gindys. In Dhour, however, my mother seemed obsessed with what was done and not done, what "the people" said or might say, how things would look. As she grew older, these matters became more important, making it less possible to do what she liked and imperative that she conform to an outside standard, which in the case of Dhour she patently detested but doggedly held on to nonetheless.

That summer she felt especially imprisoned, since when my father returned from his long trip it was only to play bridge. My mother's distaste for his daytime bridge partners—who never made an appearance at our house and included taxi drivers, dry-cleaning clerks, and the like from the various cafés in town—spurred him a little to find respectable men for bridge evenings at home. Of this group, Emile Nassar and Faiz, his cousin, were regulars, in addition to new friends like Anis Nassif and Salim Kurban, Aunt Frida's Beirut cousin. Occasionally the austere Anis

Makdisi, a professor of Arabic at the American University of Beirut, would join; his house was just above ours on the hill, which is where I first met Samir, his youngest son and a contemporary of Alfred Nassar, who was later to marry my sister Jean. My mother made sporadic efforts to join in by learning canasta and even a card game called *concain,* but not until after my father's death did she herself become a serious, if not entirely robust bridge player.

The day of my father's arrival from the United States at the end of August 1946 was an unpleasant one for the most trivial of reasons. He had written my mother to send him our measurements in inches so that he could buy us clothes from Best's; in due course two gigantic trunks were dispatched to Cairo while he came overland from there to Beirut. My mother and I met him in the early afternoon at the Alamein terminal in central Beirut, and then we rode up to Dhour all together. His first words to me after he hugged me were "You've really gotten very fat, haven't you?" When I expressed surprise, he added "Your waist is thirty-four inches. The people at Best's were very surprised." My mother's tape measure was a metric one, and the conversion to inches had been at best an improvised one. When two months later the trunks were unpacked in Cairo I recall no less than six pairs of heavy brown wool shorts—unwearable in the Cairo heat—that my mother had to throw out because they were vastly too big for me; as it turned out most of what he had bought for us, evidently in the same way he ordered groceries and produce at Nicola's without paying very close attention either to quantity or quality, also had to be jettisoned. "Is that one of the things I got you from Best's?" he would ask me for the next year, and I would nod affirmatively, though of course I never wore what he had bought.

"Go play in the forest," I remember my parents telling me, as if the scraggly pines and thorn-filled bushes were a natural playground full of delightful and even instructive amusements. The landscape struck me as an inhospitable and hot wasteland, swarming with giant horseflies and menacing bumblebees. The overwhelming natural fact about Dhour and its bosky environs was the total absence of water: the dryness without a pond, lake, stream, or even swimming pool to relieve it meant that the place gave off a pungent sense of discomfort that the occasionally cool mountain air and the absence of urban pollution did little to offset.

There was but one break in the dryness of the summer. A blissfully long day, on which we would escape to Beirut and the sea on our annual late July excursion, which always began with an hour's taxi ride to Saint-Simon and Saint-Michel, two adjacent sandy beaches just south of the city, where we swam all morning in a surfy but rather shallow sea, and were occasionally permitted a ride on a rented *périssoire*— a kind of elongated surf board with a hull and a kayak paddle—which always overturned in the exciting, churning water. I always felt I could not get enough of the Mediterranean, whose sheer abundance and cool drenching effervescence would have to last in my memory for the rest of the year. Neither of my parents swam, but they seemed content to spend the day under the thatched awning of the beach café, where we had our lunch. Occasionally our Cairo friends the Dirliks would be prevailed upon by telegram to join us from Bharudoun, their summer town, for the day, so at least my parents had company till the early afternoon. During one lunch at Saint-Simon, my father suddenly leapt up from his chair as if he were about to assault a young man sitting at a nearby table. "No Wadie, please no," wailed my mother as she held on to her husband's powerful white shirtsleeved arms, preventing him from going after the man who had provoked him. "I'll tear your eyes out," my father called to the man as he sat down. Then, turning to me he added, "I won't let anyone look at your sister that way." Finding this illogical I remarked that "there's nothing wrong with looking," to which Loris Dirlik sagely rejoindered, "There are ways and ways of looking," since clearly to everyone but me the person in question had crossed an imaginary line.

My sister Jean, the source of this turmoil, appeared oblivious, but I certainly felt at the time that I could not emulate my father's possessiveness: I was far too reticent to start a fight, too ill equipped in vocabulary and sentiments of outraged honor to carry through any such action, and, finally, too indifferent to anybody's mere looking at my sister. The incident passed quickly enough but I remember thinking at the time that it afforded me more insight into my father's powerful virility, from which I shrank in consternation. What if his eye turned on me— who knows what he might have found in my feelings about my mother or in my secret lasciviousness about one or another female relative. Without the insulation of school and Cairo's daily routine there was nowhere for me to hide my vulnerability from this man who could erupt with such frightening volcanic force.

At about three-thirty we would be showered and dressed, and on our way to Ras Beirut to visit a Badr cousin for tea and cakes; and then we made our final stop in town at the Patisserie Suisse, a small cake shop and café in Bab Edriss in the heart of the city, where we were allowed to gorge ourselves on *chocolat mou* and heaping plates of ice cream and whipped cream. Overexposed to the sun, overfed at lunch and tea and with afternoon sweets, tired out by the one rare day when we could leave Dhour's confines and be exposed to the Mediterranean's glamour and salty, surfy expansive blueness, we made our dreary way back to the village for several more weeks of uninterrupted vacancy. On very rare occasions, perhaps once or twice more per summer, my father would go to Beirut to change money (Dhour, in this service, being as ill endowed as with other modern amenities: the place did not even have a bank) and took me along on an excursion entirely restricted to the garish, sweaty, smelly, and noisily crowded downtown area, as far from the beaches as it was possible to be. Our destination was the Banque de Syrie et du Liban, and a strangely hairless, eunuch-like young man whose high-pitched female voice belied the drab gray trousers and white shirt he wore with studied nonchalance. These were the days of gigantically large letters of credit from which this clerk would clip several little boxes with scissors, make half a dozen trips to various desks for signatures, and return finally with a thick wad of Lebanese pounds, which he would first count with his rubber-coated thumb, then pass portentously under the steel window to my father, who would recount the whole pile to make sure he got the exact amount.

After an hour and a half of the bank the two of us would go shopping for heavy goods unobtainable in Dhour—wicker baskets, plates and cups, sheets and towels, 20-kilo bags of sugar and rice—and hire one of the numerous barefoot, *sharwal*-suited porters idling on the main tramline to carry them for us. Normally about 120 kilos of these goods were loaded carefully into the porter's long basket, which he strapped to his padded back, with one of the bands going across his forehead; I was afraid it might split open from the pressure. We usually stopped at the Café Automatique, with its bustling seemingly all-male clientele, gaily colored tile floor teeming with shop clerks, shoppers, bank employees and the like, for me to have a quick ice-cream cone, my father a small cup of coffee, before we made our way, the porter slowly plodding at our side in his barefeet, to the Dhour el Shweir taxi stand at the bottom of Place des Canons for our ride back up to the mountains. I remember these occasions for the uncomfortable sticky heat of the day, the absence of air, and the stifling boredom punctuated by the small pleasures of the many hours at my father's side, with nothing to do except to "be there" and only the most meager conversation to enliven the silence between us.

In our terrace house we acquired neighbors, the Nassar family, who lived on the ground floor. The Nassars were everything we were not. The patriarch was Emile Nassar, also known behind his back as Lord Gresham because as the local representative of the London-based Gresham Assurance Company he spoke incessantly of the company he worked for, always trying to interest his bridge partners, or a fellow taxi passenger, or a visitor in purchasing a Gresham policy. He left for his Beirut office at the crack of dawn, returning home in midafternoon for a late lunch, siesta, and bridge; unlike my father he always wore a suit and furnished his house like a replica of his customary city residence. The Nassars had real furniture, a phone, a record player and radio (referred to as "a pickup"), curtains at the windows, rugs on the floor, and an extremely ornate heavy dining table covered with dishes of real cooked food twice a day, in contrast to our solitary evening meal on the floor above of "Protestant supper," which was always cold, and somehow medicinal—cheeses, olives, tea, a few fruits and raw vegetables, and the dried cakes called *irshalleh*—much like the rest of the puritanical summer life instituted by my father. The Nassar life was more interestingly advanced.

The three Nassar boys, Raja, Alfred, and Munir, were about ten, six, and three years older, respectively, than I. Their "real" mother had died quite young, and their father had become remarried to a cheery francophone woman, Marie, whose relationship to the boys I could never fathom. This was the first broken, or at least divided, family I had ever had contact with. It had never occurred to me that a family could be unlike ours in terms of its basic structure, and divorce I had associated (as did my two older sisters) with glamour and crime (the "divorced woman" we could see on our Cairo street being the perfect example, with her cigarette and red hair). Raja and Alfred referred to Marie as Tante, but for Munir, who was a very young child when his father remarried, she was Mama. In addition there was young Wadad, Marie's child with Emile, who acted like and was treated by Munir as a younger sister, but by the two older boys as a niece.

Much as I liked and was drawn to them I never felt truly comfortable with the Nassars, partly because they were so different but also because of my parents' nagging insistence that I should not spend so much time in the place for fear, my mother said, that I might become an unwelcome presence there. So I always felt that I was intruding, though they never gave any hint that I might have been a nuisance; only later did I recognize that such fearful parental injunctions were intended to keep us psychologically enclosed within our own tight family circle. The thrill I felt when Marie Nassar or Munir asked me to join them for a delicious dinner was always accompanied by a sense of unease and a feeling that I shouldn't be there at all. A dinner might include lots of salads, bits of leftover cooking like kibbe or white bean stew, mountains of rice, lavish desserts, all of which I wolfed down with avid pleasure. My mother routinely put on a disapproving look when I mounted the stairs from the Nassars' to our house after such an occasion. "It's bad to eat such heavy food at night," she might say, "you'll have trouble sleeping." And of course I did.

To my disappointment during the forties and early fifties Munir and his brothers were rarely there during the week, either because they had jobs or, in Munir's case, because he was enjoying the freedom of Beirut and the family house with his parents away. They did give me generous access to their books, however. During my high school years I became more friendly with Munir Nassar, whose expansively positive feeling about his Beirut school and university was an emotion I never could have had as an outsider in my school. The elevated subjects proposed by Munir for our rather ponderous discussions—the meaning of life, art, and music, for example—rounded me intellectually but kept us away from any real intimacy. This suited us both, I think. What we spoke of together was self-consciously deliberate and serious, but at least, since he and his closest friend, Nicola Saab, were hard-working medical students, our discussions had the virtue of keeping me aware of complexities that in almost every other way life in Dhour seemed designed to suppress. "Philosophy" was our main subject, of which I knew nothing, but Munir had been influenced by two Americans, Dick Yorkey and Richard Scott, both products not of missionary piety but of the secular liberal arts, and this opened new intellectual doors for me that I first reacted to defensively, then entered with surprising enthusiasm. I first learned about Kant, Hegel, and Plato during those discussions, and, as when I heard Furtwängler and then rushed to his recordings for confirmation, I started borrowing Munir's book of extracts from the great Western philosophers.

Such relatively modest, even imperceptible breaks in the dullness and enforced monotony of our "relaxation" in Dhour provided me with a gradually emerging sense of complexity, complexity for its own sake, unresolved, unreconciled, perhaps finally unassimilated. One of the themes of my life as conceived by my parents was that everything should be pushed into the preordained molds favored by my father and embodied in his favorite adages: "Play cricket"; "Neither a borrower nor a lender be"; "Take care of your mother"; "Protect your sisters"; "Do your best." All this was what "Edward" was supposed to be, although my mother held out some inducements for straying further beyond these boundaries, which with typical contradictoriness she herself never explicitly renounced. My father's prescriptions may not have been her style, but she would often endorse them with phrases like "Your father and I think." And yet there survived an unspoken compact between us that encouraged me in music, literature, art, and experience, despite the silly errands and reductive clichés. I recall talking to her about *The Idiot* when I was fifteen, after I had heard about the book from Munir and his friends: she had read it and was much taken with the blank goodness of Myshkin, and urged me to read *Crime and Punishment,* which I subsequently did—a book I also borrowed from Munir.

The sense of complexity beyond Dhour's appalling limitations continued to grow in me after my departure to the United States in 1951; but the seeds had been planted paradoxically at a time of my greatest deprivation, while I wandered the summer resort's bleak streets with only the heat and a generalized dissatisfaction to preoccupy me on the surface. Slowly I found ways to borrow books from various acquaintances, and by my middle teens I was aware of myself making connections between disparate books and ideas with considerable ease, wondering about, for example, the role of the great city in Dostoyevsky and Balzac, drawing analogies between various characters (money lenders, criminals, students) that I encountered in books that I liked and comparing them with individuals I had met or known about in Dhour or Cairo. My greatest gift was memory, which allowed me to recall visually whole passages in books, to see them again on the page, and then to manipulate scenes, characters, giving them an imaginary life beyond the pages of the book. I would have moments of exultant recollection that enabled me to look out over a sea of details, spotting patterns, phrases, word clusters, which I imagined as stretching out interconnectedly without limit. I did not know as a teenager what the whole texture was or what it really meant, only that it was there and I could sense its complex workings and vividly grasp relationships between, say, Colonel Faiz Nassar and his nephew Hani, the Badr family and a certain kind of furniture, me and my sisters and our schools, teachers, friends, enemies, clothes, pencils, pens, papers, and books.

What I wove and rewove in my mind took place between the trivial surface reality and a deeper level of awareness of another life of beautiful, interrelated parts—parts of ideas, passages of literature and music, history, personal memory, daily observation—nourished not by the "Edward" whose making my family, teachers, and mentors contributed to, but by my inner, far less compliant and private self, who could read, think, and even write independent of "Edward." By "complexity" I mean a kind of reflection and self-reflection that had a coherence of its own, despite my inability for some years to articulate this process. It was something private and apart that gave me strength when "Edward" seemed to be failing. My mother would often speak about the Badr "coldness," a sort of reserve and distance radiated by some of her cousins, uncles, and aunts. There was much talk of inherited traits ("You have the Badr hunchback," she would say, or "Like my brothers, you're not a good businessman, you're not clever that way"). I connected this sense of distance, apartness in myself with the need to erect a kind of defense of that other non-Edward self. For most of my life I have in an ambivalent way cherished and disparaged this core of icy detachment that has seemed impervious to the tribulations of loss, sadness, instability, or failure I have lived through.

One summer two new friends who fit the increasingly but unacknowledged sophistication of my inner life came into my existence at Dhour. John Racy, my mother's classmate's oldest son, like me was unusually fluent in English, liked music, and was a gifted game player and craftsman. The Racy family was spending the summer of 1947 in a house beyond the Medawar Hotel, off to the left of the main square, a good mile from our house. I was impressed with John's deliberate, meticulously shaped English sentences (he must have been four or five years older than I) and his extraordinary self-possession. He used to talk to me about books, music—he introduced me to Beethoven's E-flat Piano Sonata, "La Chasse," played by Claudio Arrau—and about the finer points of chess, a game I neither mastered nor particularly enjoyed, except when Johnny talked about it and about Stefan Zweig's *The Royal Game*. I don't recall ever saying more than yes or no and asking Johnny questions to get him to say more, as I listened to him entranced. Years later his mother, Soumaya, would remind me of how after they stopped coming to Dhour—he had become a psychiatrist, had married an American nurse, lived first in Rochester (where I visited him at Strong Memorial Hospital in 1956), then in Arizona, after which I never saw him again—she would remind me that in 1949 or 1950 I had said to her plaintively, "But where is Johnny; I miss him." Perhaps it was not quite a friendship because it was so one-sided, but he opened up a rich world to be found nowhere else in Dhour.

My other friend, also from our early days in Dhour, was Ramzy Zeine, whose father, Zeine Zeine, professor of history at American University of Beirut, was a Bahai whom we would see not so much in Dhour but on his twice yearly visits to Cairo. A gifted storyteller, Professor Zeine went with me on my first museum visit, to Cairo's Wax Museum, where in the funereally still, empty rooms framed by elaborate wax scenes from modern Egyptian history, Zeine would speak grippingly about Muhammad Ali, Bonaparte, Ismail Pasha, the Orabi rebellion, and the Denshawi incident. I rarely saw him after I was about sixteen but I know that during the Lebanese Civil War of 1975–90 he was outspokenly anti-Muslim and anti-Palestinian, and during the 1980s refused to leave his house until his solitary death at the age of ninety.

Ramzy was, like me, a lonely child, but his family had constructed a small rustic green wooden bungalow for him in a vineyard a few dozen meters from our heavy stone house. I had never seen such a place, but with his pet rabbits, his unerring little slingshot, which he had made himself out of an oak branch lying just outside his door, Ramzy struck me as what I might have liked to be, a child of nature, happy and at ease in Dhour's arid environment. He provided an unwonted contemplative dimension to the place's inhospitableness. Like Johnny, Ramzy's Dhour presence was extremely brief and, as the summers wore on and I looked back on it wistfully, very precious. I did not sustain a relationship with either Johnny or Ramzy past my late childhood, and both disappeared from my life thereafter.

As if to make up for his absence, my father, when he returned from the United States in mid-summer 1946, organized a series of family trips throughout Lebanon. He had made the acquaintance of Jamil Yared, who owned a pink seven-seater taxi; and with this very long eye-catching car we went to the Hamana waterfalls, the heights of Suneen, the rather disappointing cedar forest in the north, to Ein Zhalta, Kasrwan, the Qadisha cave, Beiteddine. Certainly these trips offered a welcome opportunity to leave Dhour for the day, but spending anywhere from three to six hours each way on the road, arriving and having lunch in a restaurant picked by Yared, then returning to Dhour scarcely qualified as a real picnic. My six-year-old sister Jean was discovered to be very prone to car sickness, so her discomfort managed to overtake and somewhat spoil the journey for us all, except for my father, who maintained his composed indifference. The food was almost always the same, with local variations providing entertaining relief: in Ein Zhalta, the springwater was so cold it would burst open a watermelon. In Bsherye, where we went on a desultory fifteen-minute tour of Khalil Gibran's house "as he left it," with the bed unmade and the waste baskets unemptied, the local restaurant specialized in grilled chicken. What I took for granted as we traveled about was that no one consulted a map, and in fact there seemed to be no maps available; most of the time Jamil steered by his nose, which often occasioned numerous stops for information. Lebanon then had no advertisements, road signs, or tourist services; arriving in Raifoon was like suddenly entering a new country where the people stared at us, and tried to make sense of my father's quixotic mixture of Egyptian and Palestinian dialects, my mother gently mocking his linguistic clumsiness from the back seat: "Why does he think these people understand words like *halqait* ["now" in Palestinian] or *badri* ["early" in Egyptian]?" As we unloaded ourselves out of the long pink car we must have seemed like a family of odd bedraggled strangers from across the oceans, so exaggeratedly guarded and reserved were the reactions to us. It was from those excursions that I have derived, and later nurtured, the habit of always being dressed differently from the natives, any natives.

I still find myself surprised at not only the assiduous frequency of these journeys, but at how little we learned about Lebanon generally or the places we visited in particular. A great deal depended on our driver, whose knowledge, as far as it went, was spotty and essentially folkloric and gastronomic: "The grapes here are exceptionally good" or "You really ought to order their green walnuts here." There seemed to be little history to impart to us, and we were content with geographical "facts" such as that Ein Zhalta isn't as high in its elevation as Dhour. Very occasionally I would glean from something that passed between my parents and a waiter or maître d'hôtel that a particular village was Maronite or Orthodox or Druse; but the inflamed sectarian sentiment about Lebanon that I would first become aware of in the mid-fifties was still submerged.

The particular status attached to my mother's Protestant relatives, the Badrs, came to seem a very distinctive one, but the strange later affiliations with Roman Catholicism became fully apparent only over the course of the latter part of the fifties through the seventies. Originally from Khinshara, a mid-size town in the northeast, the Badrs had migrated to Shweir about two hundred years earlier; my great-grandfather Yusef Badr was the Protestant Evangelical minister, first in Marjeyoun, in the south (now under Israeli occupation), later in Beirut. In the American missionary Henry Jessup's memoir, *Fifty-three Years in Syria,* he is described as the first "native" Protestant minister of Lebanon, in 1880 or thereabouts. With their Protestant counterparts in Palestine, the Badrs continued their affiliation with the American Protestant mission in Lebanon but also had an embattled, even belligerent, sense of what it meant to be Christian in a Muslim part of the world. My mother's first cousins and her uncles were educated at the American University (formerly the Syrian Protestant College), and all had been or were still avidly religious, and further developed these affiliations through frequent trips to the United States and graduate studies there, plus, in my later view, too close an identification with American views on Islam as a depraved and unregenerate religion.

But there were early signs of this hostility toward Islam, which I caught glimpses of beneath the merry atmosphere of familial gatherings in Dhour. They seemed to emerge as expressions of unquestioning enthusiasm for Christianity, unusual even within Jerusalem's pious confines. As "Edward Said," I found myself counted as a Christian in Lebanon, though even today after years of internecine civil conflict there I must confess I am unable to feel any identification at all with Christianity as threatened by Islam. But when Eva and Lily, my mother's first cousins, who were close friends and former classmates of hers, seemed slightly skeptical of the Arabs collectively and Arabism as a creed I was nonplussed because their language, culture, and education, their love of the music, their closeness to family tradition, their way of doing things struck me as much more unequivocally Arab than ours. Later I thought this aggressively Christian ideology was very paradoxical and difficult to accept, so little did I, or anyone in my immediate family, have any sense of primarily *religious* hostility toward Muslims.

And yet in the 1940s and early '50s there was a nice conviviality about our relationships with my mother's Lebanese relatives. Uncle Habib, Teta Munira's and Aunt Melia's brother, was a mild-mannered, ever so lightly ironic gentleman who had spent several years with his wife and children working as a member of the British civil bureaucracy in Sudan; his wife, Hannah, was a supremely capable and quick woman who, like her husband, was much admired and liked. Their only son, Fouad, my mother's first cousin, was our family common favorite. Fouad was much too old really to be my friend, but he and I had a close relationship nevertheless: we played doubles together in the 1950s, and I was always impressed by his dashing manner, his chivalry with women, his friendliness, and his wry, self-deprecating humor. The three other Badr children of my mother's generation we would see intermittently as summer residents in Dhour: Lily and her husband, Albert (also a cousin of my mother's); Ellen, the youngest, and her husband, Fouad Sabra, Wadad's brother and our friend from the Columbia-Presbyterian Hospital experience; then Eva, the eldest, and her husband, the philosopher and diplomat Charles Malik, who was to play quite an important role in my life and the development of my ideas in Dhour.

The easy and friendly association we enjoyed with the Badrs in Lebanon was soon to be eroded by illnesses, deaths, voyages, disagreements, and long gaps, but while it lasted, in the forties and fifties, it lightened the austerity and general barrenness of our daily life in Dhour. An occasional visit to my aging great-uncle Habib meant a chocolate and a glass of lemonade, plus an interesting account of life in Khartoum just after World War I. And when some of them came to us for lunch or dinner, the table would be spread with delicious grown-up food, and a kind of festive abundance and sense of barriers being let down that gave vitality to the summer's lifeless atmosphere. In 1947, when my mother, having undergone a biopsy to determine the possible presence of breast cancer, discovered she did not have the disease, the good news was celebrated at a lavish family lunch put on by my father at ᶜAin al Naᶜas, a famous spring with an excellent restaurant situated near Bikfaya. All the Badrs young and old were invited. This was perhaps the last harmonious family occasion of its kind before 1948 and the various subsequent Lebanese eruptions. Everyone drank ᶜarak, a few smoked *argeelas* (water pipes), and my father was able to get up a table of bridge in the corner. For us the swings in the Naᶜas garden were particularly thrilling, with longer hanging chains, deeper seats to sit in, greater heights to achieve than anything we had in Dhour.

That very year, I believe, my father decided to take up bird hunting because someone at the bridge table had said what a salutary effect it would have on him. He came home one evening from bridge with a slim black French rifle in his hand, a box of cartridges and a belt in the other. "They said it would be relaxing," I recall his saying with considerable enthusiasm. Right after our very early breakfast the next morning he slung the 9-millimeter rifle over his shoulder, strapped his belt on, and marched out of the house: he was headed for a fig-tree orchard a few hundred yards from where we lived, in search of a particularly large and fleshy bird that frequented such places and that was supposed to be wonderful to eat. He came back empty-handed an hour or two later, changed his bedraggled clothes for another equally shabby set, and went off to the *saha* to resume his normal routine: "One of the gardeners told me that I had to do two things. The first is to come at about six; the other was not to walk around looking for the birds, but to sit quietly under a tree and wait there." He left early the next morning with one of my mother's orange-colored living-room cushions and a book, since there was no use being uncomfortable or remaining idle during his vigil. He did this, I think, for about a week, always returning without birds, having fired his rifle quite rarely; for the first two or three days he would spend a few minutes cleaning the gun barrel with a long green-tufted brush dipped in gas, but stopped doing so when it appeared that infrequent firing scarcely demanded such an effort. Finally he came home ten days later carrying about six plump little birds and was summarily interrupted by my mother, whose scarcely concealed disgust seemed to propel her with the dead things into the kitchen faster than usual. We had them for lunch—tiny, tough creatures that were the size of a frog. My sisters, mother, and I then surrounded my father as if he were a hero, so elated were we all by his astonishing, albeit very sudden, success. As we pressed him for details of where and how he had accomplished this amazing feat his answers got shorter, he seemed befuddled by the insistence of our queries, and finally shook us all off by disappearing into his room. Later he admitted to my mother that he had bought the birds off a young hunter who had more use for some ready cash than for his six dead birds.

That episode effectively ended my father's brief hunting career, and the gun was passed on to me. For the first year that I ventured out into the woods behind our house my main problem was that I could not close one eye; my grandmother devised a wrap made out of a handkerchief that I would slip over my left eye as I readied my shot; invariably, this was such a cumbersome procedure that the bird had flown off by the time I was able to fix it in my gunsight. I recall spending hours practicing first the donning of my eye patch, then the raising of my left cheek to close my eye. I remained at the same rudimentary level for the four or five years I did it with my mother's grudging approval (she saw it as an extension of her time-consuming errands for me) and an occasional gesture of approbation from my father. I did not think of myself as a skilled hunter, although coming home with a couple of kills was a sign that I had done better than my father. I got to know the several patches of woods that were close to the house, but on the whole I found the experience unattractive and tedious. I was once able to persuade my sister Jean to come with me; she seemed to enjoy the foray more than I did.

The first opportunity for intellectual instruction during the summer came in 1949, when I was required to take a sort of catch-up tutorial in geometry as preparation for entering Victoria College in the fall. One of my father's bridge cronies was found for the job, and three mornings a week at nine I would hike to his house halfway down to ᶜAyn al-Qassis for a two-hour tutorial. Mr. Aziz Nasr was an amiable enough man, a retired engineer who had spent a long time working in Iraq before returning to his native village; he was, I think, a cousin of the café owner, which gave him appealing credentials for me. His precise little gestures fascinated me less for the soundness of the geometric logic they illustrated than for the incredible neatness of the diagrams and sketches he produced in the course of instructing me. My father had obtained a copy of the Oxford and Cambridge School Certificate geometry text—a thick gray book of appalling seriousness, unredeemed by any of the amiable pictures I had been accustomed to in CSAC manuals—and Mr. Nasr proceeded to take me through it, page after dreadful page. He had an inexplicable penchant during the biweekly tests he set of assigning me not the ordinary problems and questions provided by the authors, but the so-called "riders," those problems of exceptional difficulty that he presumed I should be able to figure out. I did so only very rarely. Most of the time I fumbled badly, waiting quietly as he went over my inadequate efforts, until, in a sudden gesture of impatience, he tore out the offending page from my exercise book and solved the problem, elegantly I thought, on a fresh one. He wrote a report of my erratic progress after about ten weeks of this, in which he stressed my intelligence but also my lack of concentration, unwillingness always to do my best, etc. This report (which, unfairly, did not mention the "riders" at all) earned me my father's by now familiar chiding comment, "You never do your best, Edward." My mother took a more dramatic and, I must say, apocalyptic view of my chances of success at the new, presumably more serious and demanding school I was about to enter. "What's going to become of you, Edward? Are you always going to fail and do badly? Remember Miss Clark: she understood you so well. When are you going to improve?"

During those summers in Dhour, I confess to some fairly obnoxious behavior, most of it the result of periods of enforced solitude in my cheerless little room after being told, "Take off your clothes and go straight to bed, and no reading." I recall distinctly that during the hours of lying in bed I once covered the wall with gobs of spit, peppering the invitingly empty white space to my side with little well-aimed missiles. And of course, it only further enraged my mother. There were not so many moments of tenderness during the long summer. My relationship to my two older sisters, Jean and Rosy, was usually a prickly, adversarial one, and I felt we slowly lost the habit of intimacy and even of accommodation with each other.

To her dying day my mother was a bilateralist; that is, she encouraged us to deal with each other through her. I was not conscious of either being in or trying to get entrance to her orbit, but I noticed that only one of us could be favored at a time. "Why can't you be more diligent, like Rosy," she might say; or, conversely, "None of your sisters has your musical talents." Jean had a better humor than Rosy; Rosy was stronger than Jean; Edward didn't behave around us. We lived in the element of my mother's myths, playing the roles assigned to us. I am still not sure how many of the earnest, often plaintive feelings that I confided to her she actually guarded, how many she passed on to my father or sisters. I needed to open myself to her but I knew it would make me vulnerable to her manipulations later. I kept trying to get close to her and direct her fondness toward me. She never let go of me in Dhour, and finally, I think, I seem to have absorbed her worries, her tireless concern with details, her inability ever to be calm, her way of constantly interrupting herself, preventing a continuous flow of attention or concentration on anything. My mother possessed a powerful, sensitive intelligence, which I was attracted to, but she tended to hide it to make herself seem like a helpless, much put upon adjunct to my father's strength. I remember admiring her fitful and incomplete efforts to complete her education in French and humanities as well as shorthand, but despite her years of grudging tolerance of my father's card-playing mania, only bridge did she study in earnest, becoming after his death a confirmed player too.

At its worst I'd describe this as the Dhour syndrome, formed because my mother felt herself to be unfairly left to fend for herself, an unfinished person who had to try frantically but also unsuccessfully to deal with everything she saw before her, like the circus performer who has to keep too many whirling plates from falling off too many rods. But I never doubted that she really understood me, despite her limitless capacity for manipulating us all the time. Instinctively I found myself drawn to persons in our acquaintance about whom she knew relatively little; finding other lives, other narratives, became my way of unconsciously seeking alternatives to my mother's dominance. Thus, Dr. Faiz Nassar and his second wife, Fina, a coquettish, lighthearted woman whom I found extremely engaging, soon became one of my favorite sources of exotic lore far removed from Dhour's humdrum horizons. We had originally met Fina and her two children in Cairo early in the forties; she was then married to an Egyptian, who later died. A widowed Shami woman in Cairo, she then met and married Faiz, who later brought her and her two children to Beirut. He was introduced to us by Emile Nassar, his cousin and our downstairs neighbor; I forged a bond with Faiz when he began to appear regularly for bridge and backgammon games with my father.

Like most of the Nassars, whose vast number by this time suggested to my puritanical Protestant gaze a great network of colorful and yet slightly *louche* tribe members consisting of divorcées and stepbrothers, Faiz was a small rather portly man with a neat brush mustache who moved and spoke with affecting gravity and slowness. We originally knew him as "Dr. Faiz," but soon after he and my father became regular partners it emerged that he had been a colonel in the Egyptian army in the Sudan; thereafter my father somewhat jovially started calling him "the Colonel" and soon everyone called him that too. Despite his serious mien and because he never talked down to me he was the only older man I knew in Dhour whom I actually considered a friend. His studious silences, his reserve, fascinated me. And the Colonel was often happy to delay an evening bridge game at home with some big-game hunting stories described in a stately English dotted with colonial words and phrases like "my native bearers" and "the old tusker," redolent of a mythological Africa that I had glimpsed in the Tarzan books and films I had always cherished. I think that as I grew older I speculated that some of his stories about "the big cats," for instance, were concocted for my pleasure rather than from specific experiences of his

own. But the solemnity never varied, and neither did his long, dignified pauses. During my younger years I had the impression that he told
the stories with so many lapses and such deliberation in order to set up
the tension of a real jungle chase, but as we both grew older I sadly realized that his memory and mind had been slowly failing him.

Later, one of his relatives told me—perhaps only with malice in
mind—that he had kept a black Sudanese woman as his own, and that
he was also a famous martinet. Sternness was undoubtedly a part of his
character, but for me it was part of his dignified mystery, which in a
garrulous society such as ours was very rare.

The Colonel's friendship was a kind of antidote to the atmosphere
created by my mother. There was order, knowledge, amusement in
what he offered. Yet as the years wore on our household seemed to get
busier and more populous, in part, I think, because more of my
mother's relatives got into the habit of taking houses in Dhour for the
entire season. As the Colonel himself grew older he could be seen
slowly inching his way forward along Dhour's unpaved and skimpy
sidewalks. His red tarbush, by then a complete anomaly, was never
abandoned; neither was the little green rosette stuck decorously into his
lapel buttonhole.

The Colonel seemed slowly to disappear from our lives, his place
taken for me not by anyone like him but by younger men, closer to me
in age, with whom I found myself in company as Dhour itself grew and
became more worldly. In my early teens, the old Cinema Florida right
next to the Café Cirque, whose single projector required a pause every
twenty minutes to change reels and whose films were full of cracks,
hisses, and overexposed frames, was superseded by the sleeker and more
comfortable City Cinema, which could actually project a relatively new
film without breaks. Three of us might go to the cinema and meet a
group of our cousins, or someone encountered that day on the tennis
court, or perhaps one of the Nassar boys in the company of a friend
from Beirut. The town began to change as one or two billiard halls, a
new tennis court, a few rehabilitated shops selling sports equipment and
shirts instead of fireworks and knitting wool, as well as more residents
with cars, appeared to brighten up its usual gloom.

But with every expansion in horizon came a chastening reminder of
my being an outsider, of not being at home in Dhour, nor indeed in

Lebanon. Thus one unusually bright afternoon Munir Nassar invited me to his place to meet a school friend of his from Beirut, Nicola Saab, the brightest boy in their class. (Ten years later, on the threshold of a brilliant medical career, he committed suicide.) Behind them were several years of close friendship and a kind of shared language full of deliberately arcane and precious phrases that excluded strangers such as me. I remember that the second time I met with the two of them we got into a heated discussion over the relative merits of Brahms, whom they both valued very highly, and Mozart, whom I preferred. I had just discovered Mozart's "Linz" Symphony and thought that its clarity of line and clean elegance were the ultimate in expression. I made the case as best I could but was put off by the two older boys, who dismissed Mozart as "light" and lacking in thought. The word I distinctly remember hearing to dignify Brahms was "profound," which I neither completely understood nor had ever used. Profound, deep, dark, troubling, stirring, significant: this was how the Brahms First Symphony was described, and when the record was played on the Nassar "pickup," there was a lot of nodding, glances exchanged, excited handshaking. I had no response to any of this. Brahms was the approved insider choice; Mozart and I, the slightly disdained, not quite serious enough aliens. At the end, as if to make up for their concerted, indeed orchestrated, polyphony, Saab turned to me in conciliation, saying, "But, you know, Mozart is in fact impeccable." Also an unusual word whose meaning I did not fully comprehend, "impeccable" made matters worse for me, as if being impeccable was a last resort of superficiality.

When I was nearly fifteen I was allowed to go to Beirut with Munir Nassar. He took me to the cement-covered and rather austere university beach, where your feet burned just trying to reach the water, and introduced me to his classmates, who greeted me cordially, but thereafter jovially exchanged jokes and anecdotes in an Arabic dialect that was clearly their language, and just as clearly not mine. It was one of the earliest moments when I experienced language as a barrier, even though I understood what was being said. Their accent was Lebanese, mine was Egyptian overlaying a thin remnant of Palestinian; their Beirut was mine only because I happened to be with Munir. I hung back as the others chatted busily with each other. When we went to a film matinee at the Cinema Capitol in central Beirut the cool darkness of the theater allowed me further invisibility as I asked myself whether

I could ever be on the same level as the two young men sitting beside me. I later told my mother of my feelings of isolation as I overheard them chatting with each other. "Did you ask them what they were talking about, and why didn't they include you?" she challenged me, simultaneously making me feel worse for my timidity, and better in that she had quickly come to my aid. Of course I hadn't, and couldn't imagine asking that sort of question.

By the mid-fifties, when we finally had a car and a telephone in Dhour, I was a Princeton undergraduate, and quite suddenly the sense of imprisonment and boredom so long associated with our summers there dropped away. Life in Dhour was no longer restricted to the *saha* and its environs but extended as far as the town of Brumana, ten kilometers below us to the south, and Mrouj, a few kilometers beyond the Hotel Kassouf.

The social center of our new activity was the tennis court. First there was the Halaby tennis court, which was open to anyone willing to pay the small sum required; the court was poorly maintained, but it was there that I made the acquaintance of Sami Sawaya (a distant relative of our grocer) and Shawqi Dammous, a massively built man in his forties who was also the sports master at International College, the American University prep school.

Sami was a tall, skinny young man about five years older than I who, because he spent what seemed to be all his time at the Halaby court and was naturally sociable and amiable, arranged a friendly set or two for me. Sami introduced me to the raucous atmosphere of the place, very far removed from the tedious loneliness I had been accustomed to. What I remember is the rowdiness of mornings spent at Halaby's: there were numerous verbal battles, always mediated by the indefatigable, uncondescending Shawqi, whose majestically sized pate was covered with perspiration as he noisily adjudicated between different claimants to the court; there were sometimes exciting, usually chastening baseline duels between me and the steady Sami, and occasionally, a random doubles match with young girls whom I had met there for the first time; and then there were gala occasions when Dhour, often represented by my cousin Fouad Badr, a gallant crowd-pleaser, would battle an IPC (Iraqi Petroleum Company) team from Tripoli, or a Brumana team, for a series of several singles and one, perhaps two, doubles.

Tennis finally gave me a life independent of my parents in Dhour, away from my mother's controlling gaze. There was an enormous improvement in our social life in 1954 when a large Muslim family, the Tabbarahs, bought a handsome house and built a tennis court next to it, which they then turned into a club whose presiding influence was once again Shawqi Dammous. As the club was almost a kilometer past the Kassouf, a car was indispensable, though passing passenger taxis (called *service*) or buses could usually be persuaded to drop us off for an afternoon of tennis, Ping-Pong, and socializing.

Soon after the Tabbarah Club came into being, I met the Emad sisters, Eva and Nelly, the youngest daughters of Naief Pasha Emad, originally from Ein al-Safsaf (a satellite town of Shweir) but now a notoriously wealthy soap manufacturer who lived and owned factories in the industrial city of Tanta, north of Cairo. The Emads lived across the road from the Tabbarah Club in an immense palacelike house with distinctive green shutters, encircled by a great stone wall. I never entered the house or met Emad Pasha, despite the closeness of my relationship with some of his children. Eva was slightly older than Nelly, and almost seven years older than I. Unmarried, wealthy, socially insulated from her surroundings, Eva was the first woman I really became close to, despite the fact that for a couple of summers we were never alone but part of the regular group that turned up in the mornings for tennis, went home for lunch, and reappeared in the afternoon for more tennis, noisy card playing, and Ping-Pong.

VIII

I HAD NO WAY OF KNOWING IT, BUT WHEN I ENTERED Victoria College in the autumn of 1949, aged almost fourteen, I was also nearing the last two years of my life in Cairo. For the first time I became "Said" exclusively, my first name either unknown or shortened to "E"; and as plain "Said" I entered a mongrel world made up of miscellaneous last names Zaki, Salama, Mutevellian, Shalom of very mixed provenance, all of them preceded by dangling, not to say irrelevant, first initials: Salama, C, and Salama, A, for instance, or Zaki, whose two first initials served as a mockingly reversed and cacophonous sobriquet for him, "Zaki A.A." or "Zaki Ack Ack."

Before school began I said to my mother that I was interested in becoming a doctor, to which she said that my father and she would be happy to buy me my first clinic. Both of us understood that the gift would be made in Cairo, although we both were also aware that Cairo couldn't in the long run be our home for "the future" as we imagined it. Reports of mysterious assassinations and abductions, mostly of well-known prominent men who had good-looking wives, testified to the influence of a corpulent, libidinous king whose nocturnal rampages and long European holidays had dislocated the country as much as the scandals of the 1948 Palestine war, in which faulty arms, incompetent generals, and a formidable enemy had not only routed the Egyptian army but brought the tottering, still not really independent Egyptian state to a new, low pass. The sudden prominence of the Muslim Brothers lent more anxious uncertainty to those of us Arabs who were neither Egyptian nor Muslim. A constant guerrilla struggle in the Suez Canal Zone, to which British forces had retreated, elevated the guerillas or *fedayin* (an Islamic epithet denoting warlike sacrifice) who fought the foreigners to the status of heroes, and also made our working relationships in Cairo with English doctors, nurses, teachers, bureaucrats far more tense than before.

I felt this the moment I set foot in Victoria College, later described to me by Mr. Hill, the geography master, as a school designed to be the Eton of the Middle East. Except for the teachers of Arabic and French, the faculty was entirely English, though unlike at GPS not a single English student was enrolled. My father drove me to school—located in temporary quarters at the former Italian School in Shubra, one of Cairo's most densely populated semislum areas, not far from Dr. Haddad's clinic—and on the first day left me at the front door with his usual cheery "Good luck, son" as he drove off with his driver. For the second time (after GPS) in my life I was dressed in a school blazer, gray trousers, blue-silver striped tie and cap: a uniform (bought at Avierino's) proclaiming me a VC boy, engendering a feeling of miserable solitude and profound uncertainty as I edged my way into the bustling corridors about five minutes before the school bell went off at eight-thirty. The office I timidly looked into in search of directions to the Middle Five classroom was the headmaster's, where an obliging servant (*farrash*) pointed me farther down the corridor and out into a teeming school yard, at one end of which stood a small two-roomed building. "That's it," he said. "Middle Five One is on the left." As I threaded my way hesitantly through a football game, several wrestling matches, an intense game of marbles, and a small crowd of guffawing older boys, I felt myself assaulted and dislocated by the uninhibited strangeness of the place in which I alone seemed to be new and different.

When I found the right classroom there was one rather small boy writing busily at his desk, a large reference book at his side; two others sitting side by side, reading silently; and three more comparing assignments. I shyly asked the assiduous writer (he introduced himself by his last name, "Shukry") what he was working at. "Reserve lines," he responded laconically. When I asked him what those were he explained that a standard punishment was to be made to copy out five hundred or a thousand lines from a particularly tedious book such as the telephone directory, dictionary, or encyclopedia; making some ready now and holding them in reserve would cut down on the burden later. I knew almost immediately that this school was a more serious place than any I had attended, the pressure greater, the teachers harsher, the students more competitive and sharp, the atmosphere bristling with challenges, punishments, bullies, and risks. Above all I felt that nothing from my home or family had prepared me for this: I was truly on my own, an unknown, strange quality about to be swallowed up in the minute workings of a dauntingly large place, ten times larger than any school I had ever been to before.

Each class in the Upper School was divided into a One and a Two section, the former for the relatively bright and hardworking types, the latter for slower, less-achieving boys generally regarded as Darwinian failures who deserved their lowly fate. The class divisions were in preparation for the Oxford and Cambridge School Certificate (high school diploma) or matriculation, undertaken by the boys of Lower Six; while the special young men of the Upper Sixth proceeded toward A levels, and university. These young men all seemed to me to be star athletes, prefects, geniuses, and were routinely addressed by us as "Captain," a title given added credibility by the silver piping on their blazers and caps. The two head boys, Captains Didi Bassano and Michel Shalhoub, were at first exceedingly remote figures, but over time Shalhoub in particular became an unpleasantly familiar presence, notorious for his stylish brilliance and his equally stylish and inventive coercive dealings with the smaller boys.

To impose coherence on the thousand or so boys of VC, the authorities had divided us all into "houses," which further inculcated and naturalized the ideology of empire. I was a member of Kitchener House; other houses were Cromer, Frobisher, and Drake. Cairo VC was an altogether less posh school than its Alexandria parent, which had been in existence for three decades and had a much more imposing roster of students (King Hussein of Jordan, among others) and masters, and a very handsome spread of buildings and playing fields in the great Mediterranean summer capital. Our Shubra campus was makeshift, originally rented during the war years to accommodate an overflow of students from Alexandria, which was principally a boarding institution. Most of the boys were day students from Cairo, less upper class and I supposed less accomplished than those from Alexandria. The classrooms and assembly hall were dingy and cramped. A permanent cloud of dust seemed settled over the place, even though four tennis courts and several football fields gave us outdoor facilities of a lavishness I had not before encountered.

As I stood around waiting for the class to begin that first day, the desks gradually filled with chattering boys, each carrying an immense briefcase filled with books, pencils, and copybooks. As the only new boy I assumed I would be an outsider for months, so dense was the web of associations and habits binding my twenty-five classmates together, yet by the end of that first day I felt quite at home. Mr. Keith Gatley, our form teacher, was white-haired and portly, with an enormous scar traversing his entire face diagonally. Like the other Britishers there, Gatley was an Oxbridgean who either had been marooned in Egypt by the war or had come there after the war in the absence of decent employment at home. Most of the staff were celibate and rumored among the students to be depraved pederasts who were able to indulge their illicit appetites among the vast corp of servants and perhaps even the school's younger boys. Gatley was referred to as *"al-Khawal,"* or "faggot," his dreadful scar (it was rumored) being the result of a fight with a pimp whom (according to the same scurrilous report) Gatley had tried to cheat. Obviously there was no way of knowing if any of this was true.

I discovered most of this "background" during the first English class, which was devoted to *Twelfth Night,* a highly inappropriate play for coarse teenagers for whom "the music of love" conjured only the rhythmic sound of a masturbating hand. Gatley asked us to read aloud and explain various lines in the first scene but achieved only raucous laughter, incomprehensible gibberish, and horrendous Arabic obscenities presented as "classical" equivalents of what the Duke of Illyria was saying. All the scene's "dying falls" and "entrances" and "abatement" were explicated with scarcely concealed lewdness, while Gatley, whose nearsighted gaze shielded him from most of the class's gestures, nodded lethargic approval of and vague assent to what he thought he was hearing.

In a matter of hours, years of earnestly solemn education fell away from me as I joined in the ceaseless back and forth between the boys united in group solidarity as "wogs" confronting our variously comic and/or maimed teachers as cruel, impersonal, and authoritarian Englishmen. It was generally believed that most of the masters were war casualties who, in our totally unsympathetic view of them, deserved their twitches, limps, and spastic reactions. Near the end of the class Gatley suddenly stood up, his great belly protruding out from his tight shirt and stained baggy trousers and, awakened from his torpor, lurched toward two chattering students whose insouciance prevented them from seeing the disaster looming near them. I had never seen anything like it before: a wide-armed heavy-set man flailing wildly at two pocket-size boys, he landing an occasional blow while trying to keep from falling, they nimbly dancing out of his way screeching "No sir, don't hit me sir" at the top of their voices, while the class gathered around the trouble zone, trying to divert his blows from the offending pair.

Gatley's class was immediately followed by an hour of mathematics drummed into us by one Marcus Hinds, as wiry and nervous as Gatley was lumbering and phlegmatic. Mr. Hinds thought of himself as something of a wit, the evident sharpness of his mind given support by a caustic tongue that brooked no laziness or sloppy reasoning. At least algebra and geometry had a precision to them lacking in Gatley's sentimental moonings about what to us was "foreign" poetry, so the class settled down to serious work in a matter of minutes. Yet Hinds's silence turned out to be literally more punishing than Gatley's lethargy. Equipped with a specially made extra-large blackboard eraser one of whose sides was lined with an inch-thick piece of wood, Hinds would descend on an offending student who may have been whispering to a neighbor or, an equally serious offense, was incapable of grasping an algebraic formula and start battering his head, shoulders, and hands with his painful weapon. It was my misfortune in the first class I had with Hinds to ask my neighbor George Kardouche which textbook of the three we carried we should be looking at: whereupon Hinds launched his eraser at me like a missile, a more efficient method than stalking to the back row and raining blows on me. My offense was relatively minor, and I was a new boy, hence the telegraphic punishment, which narrowly missed my left eye but raised an ugly purple welt on my cheek. Since no one had reacted to Hinds's abuse I choked back my response and simply rubbed my sore cheek. Thus were the lines drawn between us and them.

For the first time in my life I was part of an unruly school group insofar as I was neither English nor from Egypt, and certainly was Arab. Between us and them, the pupils and teachers, existed an unbridgeable gulf. To the imported English staff we were viewed as either a distasteful job or as a group of delinquents to be punished anew each day.

A little pamphlet entitled *The School Handbook* immediately turned us into "natives." Rule 1 stated categorically: "English is the language of the school. Anyone caught speaking other languages will be severely punished." So Arabic became our haven, a criminalized discourse where we took refuge from the world of masters and complicit prefects and anglicized older boys who lorded it over us as enforcers of the hierarchy and its rules. Because of Rule 1 we spoke more, rather than less, Arabic, as an act of defiance against what seemed then, and seems even more so now, an arbitrary, ludicrously gratuitous symbol of their power. What I had formerly hidden at CSAC became a proud insurrectionary gesture, the power to speak Arabic and not be caught, or, more riskily, the use of Arabic words in class as a way of answering an academic question and attacking the teacher at the same time. Certain masters were especially vulnerable to this technique, preeminently a Mr. Maundrell, the unfortunate and bedraggled history teacher who may have been a victim of shell shock. A tremor animated his gnomic lethargy as he muttered facts about Tudor kings and Elizabethan customs before a basically unreceptive and callous group. In answer to one of his questions a student would begin by suavely mouthing an Arabic imprecation ("*koss omak,* sir") immediately followed by a "loose" translation ("in other words, sir") that had nothing to do with the foul phrase ("your mother's c———t"). As the class roared their appreciation, Mr. Maundrell would jerk backward in fear and astonishment. We would also play *"akher kilma"* with him, repeating in unison the last word in every one of his sentences. "Elizabeth's reign was notable for culture and exploration," one of his typically torpid sentences, would draw a resounding chorus of the word "exploration" from us, which Maundrell would ignore for about six sentences, before exploding in a roar of shaking, spastic rage, which in turn drew delighted cheers from us. By the middle of the term he had given up trying to communicate, sitting sulkily in his chair mumbling about the regicide and Cromwell's revolution.

Teachers were therefore judged either as weak (Maundrell and Mr. Hill, the geography master) or strong (Hinds, and occasionally Gatley), never for their academic performance. A small staff of locals handled the Arabic classes, which were divided into advanced, medium, and beginners, but so far as I could determine all but one of these teachers were held in contempt by the students, as much, I think, because they were plainly second-class citizens within the school as because very few of us considered the study of Arabic poetry exemplified in dreadful patriotic encomia to King Farouk to be anything but the drivel it was. My teacher in the intermediate class was a Coptic gentleman known to us as Tewfik Effendi; his counterpart in the advanced group was Dab^c Effendi, the one teacher whose profound commitment to the sanctity of the language earned him the respect, if not the love, of his class. Tewfik Effendi was a smarmy gentleman badly in need of extra cash; early on he determined somehow that I might be a candidate for "private lessons" and succeeded in insinuating himself into my mother's good books, and thereby became a twice weekly visitor to our house as my tutor. After half a dozen inconsequential attempts to drill me in the complexities of grammar—resulting in more than twenty years of alienation from Arabic literature before I could return to it with some pleasure and enthusiasm—Tewfik Effendi and I spent our closeted hours chatting about, but never really studying, the books, the idea for him being to get his cash and his cup of coffee with biscuits served to him solemnly by Ahmed, our chief servant, and then leave for another doubtlessly as futile tutorial. Ahmed and I habitually made fun of Tewfik's ritual demurral when the coffee and biscuits were served—"No, thank you, I've already had my afternoon coffee with my friends at Groppi's," the fashionable downtown café whose habitué he pretended unsuccessfully to be—and his then ritual acceptance of the goodies, which he slurped down and chomped with great gusto.

There was a great distortion underlying the Victoria College life, which I was unaware of at the time. The students were seen as paying members of some putative colonial elite that was being schooled in the ways of a British imperialism that had already expired, though we did not fully know it. We learned about English life and letters, the monarchy and Parliament, India and Africa, habits and idioms that we could never use in Egypt or, for that matter, anywhere else. Being and speaking Arabic were delinquent activities at VC, and accordingly we were never given proper instruction in our own language, history, culture, and geography. We were tested as if we were English boys, trailing behind an ill-defined and always out-of-reach goal from class to class, year to year, with our parents worrying along with us. I knew in my heart that Victoria College had irreversibly severed my links with my old life, and that the screen devised by my parents, the pretense of being American, was over, and that we all felt that we were inferiors pitted against a wounded colonial power that was dangerous and capable of inflicting harm on us, even as we seemed compelled to study its language and its culture as the dominant one in Egypt.

The incarnation of declining colonial authority was the headmaster, Mr. J. G. E. Price, whose forest of initials symbolized an affectation of pedigree and self-importance I've always since associated with the British. I do not know where he and my father had become acquaintances, but that link had perhaps something to do with his initial cordiality toward me. A short, compactly built man with a black brush mustache and a mechanical stride as he took his black terrier for walks around the playing fields, Price was a remote figure, partly because so much authority was delegated to teachers, prefects, and house masters and partly because he seemed to grow dramatically weaker with ill health until, after remaining hidden in his study for many weeks, he finally resigned.

By the end of my first month at the school, I had risen to a kind of bad eminence as a rabble-rousing troublemaker, talking in class, hobnobbing with other ringleaders of rebellion and disrespect, perpetually ready with an ironic or noncommittal answer, an attitude I regarded as a form of resistance to the British. Paradoxically, though, I was also riven with all sorts of anxiety about failure, was insecure in my suddenly too-masculine body, sexually repressed, and above all in steady fear of exposure and failure. The school's bustle was formidable; with classes from eight-thirty until five-thirty or six, broken only by a lunch break and sports. This was followed by a long evening's homework, regulated by a small thick notebook, dutifully bought at the school's bookshop as a place to create a record of each day's assignments. The curriculum, consisting of nine subjects—English, French, Arabic, math, history, geography, physics, chemistry, and biology—was enormously pressured. I was soon in a state of anxiety, feeling totally unprepared to meet all the deadlines and exam requirements.

One day early in the term I was caught throwing stones during the lunch break and immediately taken by a prefect with clammy hands to Price's office for punishment. In a huge, indifferently furnished anteroom, Price's secretary, a burly local whom we knew only as Mr. Lagnado, sat behind one of the desks busily typing away. The prefect whispered something to him, and I quickly found myself with him in front of Price's oversize, empty desk in the next room. "What is it, Lagnado?" the ailing headmaster said sulkily, "what's this boy doing here?" I was left in place as Lagnado walked around the desk while, like the prefect before him, he said something confidential in Price's ear. "We can't have that," Price said firmly. "Come to the window, boy," he said coldly to me. "Bend over. That's it. All right, Lagnado." Out of the corner of my eye I saw Price give his man a long bamboo cane and, with Price holding me by the neck I saw Lagnado raise the vicious-looking whip and skillfully administer six of the best to my rear end.

Too physically weak to do the honors himself, Price subcontracted out to a local, who in turn did what he was told with neutral efficiency, the silent headmaster standing to one side nodding his head with each stroke. "That's all, Said," I was told by Price. "Get out and don't misbehave again" were his valedictory words, and as I left his inner sanctum I passed Lagnado, who had slipped out before me and was back at his desk, again typing as if nothing had happened. The pain was dreadful. Lagnado was a burly fellow, and—perhaps to please his master, perhaps to humiliate an "Arab" (I had once heard him say to an Armenian boy who was dipping his bread in his gravy, *"Ne mange pas comme les Arabes"*), Lagnado being a Europeanized Eastern Jew—the beating had been truly harsh. But I felt it as what was to be expected from a wartime situation. A ruthless fury took over as I vowed to make "their" lives miserable, without getting caught, without allowing myself ever to get close to any of them, taking from them what they had to offer entirely my own way.

Although I now had a virtual schoolful of accomplices and allies, my parents' rules and regimen still exercised their power. In part because of what was believed to be the salutary Dhour el Shweir experience of being tutored by Aziz Nasr in geometry the summer before, my parents decided that one way of getting me better adjusted to Victoria College's stiff academic routine was to increase the number and kind of tutorials ("extra lessons," we used to call them). Even though I did have a decent head for math and science, I was tutored in both math and physics, partly because my arithmetical skills were so far behind my father's and my oldest sister's. Huda Said, my older cousin George Said's stunningly beautiful wife, volunteered for math; and for physics, my father dragooned a bright young Palestinian refugee studying at the American University of Cairo, Fouad Etayim. Huda and I got on famously, mainly talking about music, doing very little in the way of algebra, which I understood rather quickly. Fouad was a journalism major, companion-in-arms of my cousin Robert (also at AUC), and he seemed to be learning the material more or less concurrently with me. I recall many drab hours struggling over the uses of British Thermal Units (BTUs) in calculations of heat, but for me the interest of the hours spent with Fouad were in discussing with him the villainous state of Arab journalism, listening to his caustic wit deconstructing the empty rhetoric and bankrupt ideology of writers for the newspapers *Ahram* and *Akhbar*.

It was to Auntie Melia that I finally confided my rising tide of woes, my sense of lostness and confusion at school, the overwhelming language and other requirements, the punishing atmosphere, the discordant uses of tutorials, sports, piano lessons that kept me fruitlessly, aridly busy from morning to night, seven days a week, in dramatic contrast to the illicit pleasures of delinquency. It was all too much for me, but Auntie Melia rose wonderfully to the occasion. "If you think of everything you must do as present before you, to be done all at once, you'll cripple yourself. Time obliges you to do them in sequence, one at a time, and this," she continued with the assurance of someone who had won the battle herself, "dissolves the burden almost entirely. You're very clever and you will manage." Her calm, almost affectless but somehow caring words have remained with me, surprisingly useful in times of sudden crisis and impending, albeit projected, disaster, as deadlines of all kinds have loomed before me. Her calmness and her authority had a positive effect, but unfortunately this was the last time that she and I talked together in confidence: her retirement from the American College was imminent, and after she left for her final move to Lebanon she was never again the same person.

It came only as a slight surprise that Auntie Melia was right, almost too much so. In a matter of two months I not only looked forward to school as an escape into a more manageable, less onerously demanding reality than the odd playacting at home (after I had been discovered as an illicit self-abuser, my parents' gaze became even more suspicious, and my behavior and time still more subject to surveillance and chores). Middle Five One was by far the most complex social and, of course, academic situation I had ever negotiated, and in most respects I quite enjoyed its challenges. Academics were of little interest: there were no teachers of distinction or of obvious talent, although one, Mr. Whitman, a rather fastidious older man who taught Lower Five One, seemed uncommonly interested in classical music and persuaded me (and I then persuaded my parents) to lend him our recording of Strauss's "Dance of the Seven Veils" for the classical music club, of which I was a very occasional member. Aside from that I existed in a state of alert consciousness, my former fears and anxieties lifting like an early-morning fog to reveal a landscape requiring the utmost attention to social and, in a primitive state, political details.

My own class was divided into several cliques and subgroups. A leader was George Kardouche, a small, wiry fellow with formidable athletic skills and a sharp tongue. He was liked by everyone, and, though he, Mostapha Hamdollah, Nabil Abdel Malik, and I were in the same group, Kardouche floated in and out of several smaller cliques by virtue of his quickness and his easy, mature way with older students. He and I sat next to each other in the back row, with Hamdollah and one or two others directly in front of us. A shadow line was crossed in early December when, during one of Mr. Gatley's insufferably monotonous classes, Kardouche accidentally set fire to a small pile of damp papers in his left-hand desk compartment while putting out a cigarette. In a moment, large billowing clouds of ugly gray smoke enveloped him and me, as he tried first with his hands then with his satchel to put out the flames. Droning on in the front, the turgid Gatley seemed all of a sudden to smell something untoward and uncharacteristically lifted his eyes off the book, there to see the amazing spectacle of a smoking desk.

"Kardouche," thundered Gatley in his most intimidating voice, "what is that smoke? Stop it at once, boy!" With great presence of mind, the mightily beset offender, his arms banging away at the smoke and at the same time coughing, gasping, choking, and shielding his eyes, responded: "Smoke, sir? What smoke?" At which the whole class took up the chorus "What smoke? What smoke? We see no smoke!" Intimidated and taken aback, Gatley thought better of pursuing the matter any further and returned to reading aloud with some of the better-behaved boys near the front. Since Kardouche and I sat near the door, we were able to put out the fire, after an enormous amount of loud scuffling (moving desks, piercingly uttered cries of coordination, and the like, all of it deliberately ignored by Gatley) and bringing in sand from outside.

The class also contained a group of francophone boys, many of whom were Jews and were among the most intelligent members of the class: André Shalom, André Salama, Roger Sciutto, Joseph Mani, with whom I shared a great interest in Walter Scott, and Claude Salama, who lived in the Immobilia building in the heart of smart, downtown Cairo. Then there was a group of mainly Arabic-speaking, mostly un-Westernized Egyptians—Malawani, A. A. Zaki, Nabil Ayad, Shukry, Usama Abdul Haq, and a few others. What intrigued and still entrances me about these social groupings is that none was exclusive, or watertight, which produced a dancelike maze of personalities, modes of speech, backgrounds, religions, and nationalities.

For a time an Indian boy, Vashi Pohomool, whose family owned a grand jewelry shop in or near Shepheard's Hotel, was one of us. Then, partway through the year, we were joined by Gilbert Khoury, a Lebanese boy; and the half-American Ali Halim, whose father was of Albanian stock and was King Farouk's cousin; Bulent Mardin, a Turkish boy from Maadi; Arthur Davidson, who had a Canadian father and an Egyptian mother; and Samir Yousef, with a Coptic father and Dutch mother. They made a motley but dazzlingly exciting class, almost totally oblivious to the academic-English side of things, though that was why we were there in the first place.

There were house football teams, but I was a lackluster member of ours; I did better at what was called "athletics"—track and field. There, under Mr. Hinds's uncharitable eye, I developed into a decent, though never brilliant, 100- and 200-meter man. I recall eagerly asking him for assurance that I might do well at the upcoming school games. "I will be surprised if you win the two hundred, but I *won't* be surprised if you win the one hundred," he said. Of course I won neither one. My sorriest moment occurred during the 100-meter race when, a moment after I had left the starting line in my handsome black spikes and my new, too-large white shorts—which my mother insisted were the right size—I felt them slipping down. Pulling at them frantically, my legs churning valiantly if futilely away, I heard Hinds calling out, "Never mind your shorts, Said, just run." And run I did for another yard or two, only to land on my face a second later, the wretched shorts wrapped around my ankles and a jubilant gaggle of Cromer boys jeering rudely at me.

That ended my track career, although I persisted at tennis, and outside school I swam and rode. Neither a winner nor a star, I sensed myself as at the threshold of a breakthrough, particularly in tennis, but routinely found myself held back by the doubts and uncertainties about my body inculcated in me by my father. Could it be, I often wondered to myself after a galling loss at tennis, that self-abuse was in fact undermining my health, and hence my performance? Added to this was the sense of myself as unusual because of my exceptionally complicated background, my (compared to my classmates') large physical size and strength, my secret musical and literary proclivities.

A peculiar example of my odd academic status during that Shubra year occurred during a physics class in the spring of 1950. Because the old Italian school was without labs for science instruction, our class was bused twice a week to the Coptic College in Fagallah, a shabby lower-middle-class area of the city near the Bab-el-Hadid Station. There we first had an hour's chemistry class given by (as I reconstruct my impressions) a semimoronic middle-aged man whose name I have forgotten. He could barely speak English, and made many of his more important points by laying about himself with a long piece of test-tube rubber. Azmi Effendi, our physics teacher, was altogether suave and icily cold and led us systematically and calmly through mechanics, light, gravity, and the like, most of which I found myself absorbing with ease. The class ethos did not permit a manifest submission to the teacher's will— Azmi being considered something of an Englishman in local disguise— so I deliberately held back whenever there was a question to be discussed or answered. On the day he returned our midterm exams,

Azmi prefaced his handing back of the exam books neatly stacked under one of his hands with a scathing attack on the class's miserable performance, overall incompetence, disgraceful inattention. "Only one student has any ideas of the principles of physics, and he produced a perfect exam. A very brilliant performance. Said," he said after a brief pause, "come down here." I recall being nudged by the boy sitting next to me, high up in the raked amphitheater's gallery. "It's you," he said; a moment later I found myself stumbling down the stairs, going up to Azmi, receiving my "brilliant" exam, then trudging back up.

The whole episode seems to have made no impression on my classmates or, for that matter, on me, so accustomed were we all to my status as a member of the troublemakers' set. I am sure that my final physics grade was a respectable but hardly luminous B, and I continued to drift away from any position of intellectual distinction. Whatever cultural ability and knowledge I had were submerged in the complicated business of keeping out of the clutches of masters, prefects, and bullies, avoiding failure, and engineering my way through a murderous supplementary schedule at home and an extremely long day at school. I did enjoy a school performance of *She Stoops to Conquer* in which Michel Shalhoub (who became Omar Sharif) played Mrs. Hardcastle and Gilbert de Botton (later a well-known international financier) played Kate. Through Samir Yousef and Arthur Davidson I became acquainted with Egyptian popular culture and pornography, respectively. But despite the habit of hardened resistance to anything cultural or educational, I remained a fairly timid and sexually deprived adolescent.

Arthur Davidson generally shared with us his pornographic books printed on execrable, lewd-looking paper, written in a nonstyle that suggested haste and an almost total absence of craft, but replete with the utmost in graphic, lurid descriptions. Later someone slipped us coarse, badly processed photographs of men and women copulating: they fairly reeked of illicit, raunchy sex, but since there were no girls on our horizons we embroidered these pitifully inadequate, sadistic writings and representations into what we took to be the talk of streetwise Lotharios. Expressions like "I want white flesh" or "She's wet with desire" drew forth huge claps of laughter and jeers that left at least me with a subsequent feeling of sudden discontent and mortifying frustration. I found it possible as time wore on to write my own pornographic literature; with myself as omniscient and omnipotent narrator, I peopled the episodes with various older women, mostly family friends and even relatives. As if reinforcing my compromised, devalued life at home as someone sexually ill—or so I believed—I hid my writings in places like the woodpile on one of the balconies, or in an unused jacket, with a confused awareness that I might be compromising myself still further than before. My mother's penchant for snooping around—"I saw this letter by mistake" or "While he was cleaning your room Ahmed discovered this paper" were weekly occurrences—strangely did not deter me from hiding the damning pages in different places; some I either forgot about altogether or, helpless to do anything about it, momentarily panicked over during class at school. I suppose I longed to be caught and confronted with my sins, in order to have real adventures in the real world without the parental hobbles that made any movement on that front extremely difficult. Yet the confrontation never occurred, though I dimly remember that on several occasions my parents hinted, or seemed to hint, that they had found me out, had read the incriminating prose. And that made me feel worse, more edgy, more hunted.

There weren't many outlets for my pent-up appetites except the cinema and music-hall and cabaret numbers. It was on a sultry spring night in 1950 that Samir Yousef somehow got us a table at the outdoor Casino Badia, which sat on a little jetty just below what is today the Giza Sheraton Hotel. And for the first time in my life I thrilled to what was the most unmistakably erotic scene I had ever seen: Tahia Carioca, the greatest dancer of the day, performing with a seated male singer, Abdel Aziz Mahmoud, around whom she swirled, undulated, gyrated with perfect, controlled poise, her hips, legs, breasts more eloquent and sensually paradisiacal than anything I had dreamed of or imagined in my crude auto-erotic prose. I could see on Tahia's face a smile of such fundamentally irreducible pleasure, her mouth open slightly with a look of ecstatic bliss tempered by irony and an almost prudish restraint. We were totally transfixed by this fetching contradiction, our legs soft with trembling passion, our hands gripping the chairs paralyzed with tension. She danced for about forty-five minutes, a long unbroken composition of mostly slow turns and passes, the music rising and falling homophonically, and given meaning not by the singer's repetitions and banal lyrics but by her luminous, incredibly sensual performance.

A similar, though less intense, experience of vicarious sex was available in musicals that featured above all Cyd Charisse, less so Vera Ellen, still less Ann Miller—Hollywood dancers inhabiting and emanating from a fantasy world that had no equivalent at all in prosaic Cairo. Many years later, Charisse said in a *New York Times* interview that musicals like *Silk Stockings* used dance as a method for introducing sex that had been forbidden by the censors of the period; that was exactly what I responded to with a violent passion as a sheltered, confused adolescent. My school friends and I spent stolen hours in the cinema watching Rita Hayworth, Jane Russell, and even the by-now fading Betty Grable—longing, without any success, to see a woman's navel, as such inflammatory sights were forbidden by the Hays Code.

No male actors impressed themselves upon our fantasy lives in the way male tennis stars did. Foreign players would appear in Cairo twice a year—Jaroslav Drobny, Eric Sturgess, Budge Patty, the incomparable Baron Gottfried von Cramm, Adrian Quist—and they soon became our class heroes. We imagined their rich, fun-filled lives of luxurious travel. Nicola Pietrangeli, Hoad and Rosewell, and Tony Mottram represented a world of elegance far removed from our everyday reality.

At home our life was in a tiny way less monastic and claustrophic now that all five of us were past the age of infancy, and my parents' social life expanded considerably. A new circle of friends grew around us, and remained in place into the early sixties, when age, politics, and economic upheavals disbanded the little group forever.

Closest to us were the Dirliks, whom we used to see in Lebanon, but who now became intimates of my parents': Renée, the mother, a witty, intelligent woman who was my mother's closest friend, and her husband, Loris, a pharmacist by training who was an excellent rider and cook and a charming companion. Their two oldest children, André, roughly my age, and Claude, his younger sister, we saw less of because they were in French schools and had their own circle of friends. I still recall the Dirliks with extraordinary pleasure, and their visits to us as a treat, a total change from either the dour Palestinian grimness that otherwise existed around us, or the silent bridge-playing pals (like Messrs. Farajallah, Souky, Sabry, among others) whom my father frequented for long bouts of the (to me) increasingly maddening game. Reneé Dirlik, a former student of Auntie Melia's, was the daughter of a Lebanese-Egyptian father and an Armenian mother; Loris was Armenian and Turkish; both were cosmopolitan—fluent in French and English, less so in Arabic—and dinners at their house or at ours, opera outings, occasional evenings at the Kursaal or Estoril restaurants, trips to Alexandria, remain among the pleasantest memories of my youth.

But like us they were marked for extinction in the worldly Cairo environment that was already beginning to be undermined. We were all Shawam, amphibious Levantine creatures whose essential lostness was momentarily stayed by a kind of forgetfulness, a kind of daydream, that included elaborate catered dinner parties, outings to fashionable restaurants, the opera, ballet, and concerts. By the end of the forties we were no longer just Shawam but *khawagat,* the designated and respectful title for foreigners which, as used by Muslim Egyptians, has always carried a tinge of hostility. Despite the fact that I spoke—and I thought looked—like a native Egyptian, something seemed to give me away. I resented the implication that I was somehow a foreigner, even though deep down I knew that to them I was, despite being an Arab. The Dirliks were even less integrated into Cairo society, especially Loris and the children, who were European in demeanor and language, yet seemed to feel no consequent disability as a result. Indeed I envied André his worldliness and savoir faire—very *débrouillard* (resourceful), my mother used to say so as to encourage me to be more enterprising in my life, but that made me feel less so—which took him on long hitchhiking trips through Europe and Asia with very little money in his pocket, but with always something left over when he returned. He seemed to me to accept the *khawaga* designation, whereas I chafed at it, partly because my growing sense of Palestinian identity (thanks to Aunt Nabiha) refused the demeaning label, partly because my emerging consciousness of myself as something altogether more complex and authentic than a colonial mimic simply refused.

Other friends in our circle included Kamal and Elsie Mirshak, he a second-generation Shami Egyptian, she of Palestinian descent, both younger than my father (as were all their circle), both more modern, more "with it" in terms of going out to nightclubs and restaurants. Despite the disparity in our ages, Kamal and I were rather chummy, particularly in that he sensed my sexual deprivation, and when I was seventeen or eighteen—I had already left for the United States but returned regularly for summer and sometimes even Christmas vacation—began to encourage me to consider affairs with married women, a notion that fired me up enormously but then for want of confidence and candidates was never even attempted. Then there were George and Emma (Kamal's cousin) Fahoum. He was a strikingly athletic, swarthy, thin-lipped man of considerable elegance, a dramatically successful businessman in partnership with Emma's father, Elias Mirshak, an unusually wealthy landowner who with George had gone into the import and sale of heavy machinery, mostly agricultural. During his 1930s college days in Beirut, George had been a star runner and field events man, holding records in sprints, middle distances, and long jump that stood into the sixties. He was an avid tennis player whose prowess and cocky assurance provoked my father into challenging him—on my behalf—to numerous matches. To my great humiliation George beat me with ease every time we played, always after a year of playing in school or college in the United States, during which time I told myself that I had improved enough to beat him. I resented my father doing this to me, but I also coveted the challenge and of course felt ashamed of myself after each match, which was always played on Fahoum's home court at the National Club, where in the course of our forty-five-minute encounter he would chat nonchalantly with ball boys and trainers, who always gathered to watch him win.

Emma was then and remains an agreeable, sociable woman who despite her wealth gave herself no airs or phony sophistication. Her sisters, Reine, Yvette, and Odette, were married to Shawam of an altogether more worldly sort and like Emma and George produced large numbers of daughters, with some of whom, like Amira and Linda, I became friendly in a chaste but mildly flirtatious way: both were married young, which at the time left me with an aggravated sense of unfulfilled passion.

A more recent addition to the group were the Ghorras, François and Madeleine, who had difficulty with anything other than French (all the others had been educated at British and American schools); Madeleine was very religious. I must say that I found the Ghorras strangely fascinating because they belonged to no world I had access to—in Madeleine's case that of the Syro-Lebanese high bourgeoisie—but into which I got narrow glimpses when we went to them for visits. I recall meeting de Zogheibs and de Chedids there, recipients of papal titles, which about a decade later, during the high Nasser years, struck me as grotesquely inappropriate for their holders to hold on to from generation to generation. During those earlier days, however, such people represented a kind of Proustian romance for me, especially since none of them ever pretended to have much to do with Egypt or things Egyptian. I had never been to Paris myself, but the Ghorras and their friends gave me the grace of having been there vicariously, although they spoke the heavily accented French of the Levant with its rolled *r*'s, unidiomatic constructions, and interlarded Arabic words and phrases like *"yaᶜni"* or *"yala."*

Outside school our lives were of an inordinate and untoward luxury and peculiarity. The families close to us all had their own staff of drivers, gardeners, maids, washerwomen, and an ironing man, some of whom were familiar to all. "Our" Ahmed, the Dirliks' Hassan, the Fahoums' Mohammed, were almost talismanic in their presence; they turned up in our conversations as staples of our quotidian diet, like the garden or the house, and it felt as if they were our possessions, much like old family retainers in Tolstoy. We were brought up not to be too familiar with the servants, which meant not talking to and joking with them, but I found this was an irresistible rule to break. I remember wrestling with Ahmed, conversing about the deeper meaning of life and religion with Hassan, talking cars and drivers with Aziz, much to my parents' disapproval. I felt that I was like the servants in the controlled energy that had no license to appear during the many hours of service, but talking to them gave me a sense of freedom and release—illusory, of course—that made me happy for the time spent in such encounters.

Our families shopped for food at Groppi's, talking with the plainly Greek or Egyptian employees who staffed the elegant tearoom's delicatessen in jaw-shattering French, when it was perfectly clear that we all could have done better in Arabic. I was proud of my mother for conversing in Arabic, since she alone of the entire social group to which we belonged knew the language well, was literate in it, and seemed to feel no social disadvantage about using it, even though the prevailing atmosphere was such that using French gave one a higher (perhaps even the highest) status. I had picked up spoken French early from GPS and Victoria College, and of course the club, but never felt confident enough to use it as an everyday language, even though I understood it perfectly. So although English had become my main language, French classes at VC being scarcely more edifying than the Arabic ones, I found myself in the odd situation of not having any natural, or national, position from which to use it. The three languages became a pointedly sensitive issue for me at the age of about fourteen. Arabic was forbidden and "wog"; French was always "theirs," not mine; English was authorized, but unacceptable as the language of the hated British.

Ever since then I have been inordinately fascinated by the sheer mechanism of languages, as I automatically shift in my mind among three possibilities. While speaking English, I hear and often articulate the Arabic or French equivalent, and while speaking Arabic I reach out for French and English analogues, strapping them onto my words like luggage on an overhead rack, there but somehow inert and encumbering. Only now that I'm over sixty can I feel more comfortable, not translating but speaking or writing directly in those languages, almost but never quite with the fluency of a native. Only now can I overcome my alienation from Arabic caused by education and exile and take pleasure in it.

Both Victoria College and the Tewfiqya Club, which my father joined late in 1949, expanded my opportunities to use French. Tewfiqya's membership was extraordinarily varied, a bewildering Levantine melange of Greek, French, Italian, Muslim, Armenian, Lebanese, Circassian, and Jewish members, in contrast to the Englishness of the Gezira Club, jammed together in a relatively small place in Embaba, a working-class industrial zone of the city just east and across the river from Zamalek. No polo, no horse racing, football, cricket, bowling greens, or squash, as at Gezira, but about twenty tennis courts, a decent-sized swimming pool, and of course bridge. Several of my VC friends— Claude and André Salama, the Settons, Mohammed Azab, Albert Coronel, Staffy Salem—were members there, and since the only Arabic spoken was to the harassed and overworked servants, I recall an endless babble of expostulation and cliché in French that for years furnished me with a rudimentary arsenal of ready-made phrases for every occasion, salutary and obscene, sometimes mixed with scraps of Arabic and English. *Figure-toi. Fermé ta gueule. Je rentre en ville. Va te faire pendre. Crétin. Je suis esquinté. Je crève.* But I also had the feeling that beneath the

surface of bonhomie and rowdy fun where men and women in short
shorts and very abbreviated bathing suits mixed easily there was an undercurrent of foreign unrest at what Egypt was becoming—a place no
longer hospitable to foreigners, and particularly to privileged enclaves
like Tewfiqya, where an extroverted non-Arab, non-Muslim life that
was not quite European, because tied to Oriental luxury, service, and
sensuality, could take place with relative freedom from outside inter-
ference. The only Arabic I ever heard there was in the form of orders
barked at Nubian *suffragis,* perspiring in their heavy white galabiyas,
bringing pitchers of shandy and orders of *riz financière* (I pleaded with
my mother to let us have that at home, but she refused) to wonderfully
tanned swimmers like Coco Hakim and his friends, who danced and
played Ping-Pong near the crowded *piscine,* as even I began to call it.

Unrest: temporary, short-lived, impermanent, and somehow hostile
to Egypt, a place that had once been the welcoming, open, luxurious,
and voluptuous paradise for foreigners who reveled in its weather,
unparalleled creature comforts, and, most important, the subservience
of its natives. During the middle fifties, while I was at Princeton, the
Times reported on the Israeli plot to blow up Cairo cinemas and
libraries that had American connections, like the Metro and the USIA
center, where our friend Leila Abu Fadil (daughter of Halim, my
father's old tennis partner) worked, a plan designed to sour relations
between Nasser's new government and the Americans. This was the
Lavon Affair, and it was carried out by members of the local Jewish
community, some of whom I remembered from poolside at the Tewfiqya. Perhaps that has influenced my recollections of the time, but I am
certain that the sense of foreboding I had then was real, that the beginning of the end for our community of Shawam, Jews, Armenians, and
the others hung in the heavy but somehow pleasurable air of the Tewfiqya. Slowly, members of this community began to disappear—some
to Israel, to Europe, and a tiny number to the United States. The
lamentable unfolding, or rather dismembering, of Cairo's Levantine
communities began as some left in anticipation of what was to come;
later, others were forced to leave penniless because of the Suez and
1967 wars.

Victoria College and our circle of family friends were totally non-
political. The vocabulary of Arab nationalism, Nasserism, and Marxism

was to come five or six years later, while we still lived deep in the illusions of hedonism, British education, and luxurious culture. Cairo was never more cosmopolitan. In my parents' box at the opera house we took in the Italian opera season, the Ballet des Champs-Elysées, the Comédie Française; Krauss and Furtwängler at the Rivoli; Kempff and Cortot at Ewart Hall. At school, we lived a parallel life to the unreal British syllabus through a regular exchange of Tarzan, Conan Doyle, and Dumas serials. At the same time that Gatley was taking us solemnly through *Micah Clarke,* my friend Hamdollah and I were reveling in the Holmes stories, taking turns at being Mycroft, Lestrade, Moriarty. Later we discovered Wodehouse and Jeeves, but it was the vocabulary of the Tarzan novels that opened up a rich universe for us. "Your skin is as smooth as Histah the snake," one of us would say, to which the other would reply, "Better that than Tantor's bulk." With Arthur Davidson I had many long and learned discussions about the world of Captain Marvel. Would Mary Marvel prove a sexy person to meet or not? No, he said definitively, her pussy would surely be made of iron (*kussaha hadid*); Wonderwoman would be much more enjoyable. We talked about the Marvels, their assorted progeny and kin far more than we ever even mentioned our own families, which I now assume we were all quite happy to escape, wishing they were more like the comic strip. British comics like "Boys Own," "Billy Bunter," "George Formby," and "Sexton Blake" gave us great pleasure. Between Bunter's chaotic and sadistic school and the upright and fearless Australian "cobbers" who dotted "Boys Own" I imagined an idyllic realm far removed from Victoria College.

Every so often I would come up against the school's entrenched authoritarianism in the form of the head boy, Shalhoub. When our class was dragooned into watching a school football game but allowed to wear our own clothes, our bedraggled and scruffy appearance brought forth the scorn of the nattily attired Upper Six boys still in their official school finery. Shalhoub walked by just inside the lines, a sort of monarch inspecting a disappointingly ratty-looking honor guard, his face barely concealing the disgust and indifference that his swaggering gait radiated. With a huge white carnation in his buttonhole, smartly polished black shoes, and glisteningly striped tie, he was the very model of the supercilious head boy. Then Hamdollah crowed rather loudly, "My, what a handsome figure you cut, Captain Shalhoub," at which the outraged Shalhoub stopped and beckoned to Hamdollah and me to step out of the line and follow him. An act of lèse-majesté had been committed.

He marched us to his study off the overheated indoor swimming pool, and after cuffing me twice began to twist poor Hamdollah's arm up behind him. As the pressure and pain increased, the much younger student groaned plaintively, his arm at breaking point. "Why are you doing this, Captain?," to which Shalhoub answered in his impeccably fluent English, "Because, frankly, I enjoy it." Hamdollah's arm didn't break, and Shalhoub got bored with this tiresome pastime. "Back to the football game," he commanded us, "and don't let me hear a word from you."

I do not recall ever seeing him again except at a distance during the last day of school, when, with a small bevy of important British officials, including Roy Chapman-Andrews, a noted Foreign Office type whose evidently high office (and the tremendous deference accorded him) I never fully appreciated, we celebrated the end of term. In such situations it was always supposed that the natives would directly realize that an immensely elevated personage was gracing them with his presence, even though his exact function wasn't given, or was supposed to be irrelevant to said natives. Shalhoub was on the platform to speak a few unctuous and, I thought, rather fawning words of "approbation" for our collective good fortune in having had such a wonderful English education and for Chapman-Andrews's presence; there was a round of hip-hip-hoorays, led by Shalhoub of course (with Bassano, his coeval, standing decorously by him on the platform), and then we all shuffled out. The next I knew about Shalhoub was a decade later when he became Omar Sharif, Faten Hamama's husband, and a movie star whose U.S. debut in 1962 was David Lean's *Lawrence of Arabia*.

My parents seemed always to be agitated, not to say filled with foreboding, about my insouciance in school, my inability to do "well" for long, my carelessness and seat-of-the-pants attitude toward exams and promotions. It seemed funny, I once thought to myself as I played hooky from school in the early spring of 1950, that I had at one time been so anxious about my future that I lay awake unable to sleep.

I began at that time to have a sense that my feelings toward families, my own and others, were not what they were supposed to be. Except for my general dependence on my parents, and my long, frustrated, even exacerbated love and solicitude for my mother, I caught myself by surprise, feeling little of the organic and sustained love and loyalty for my siblings and other members of the extended family—venerated both by my father as "one's family" and also by my sisters, according to what they said—that I saw in others. There was another instance of the detachment and choosiness that I found in myself, which I have never been able to change or humanize. Despite what they said and did to my father, I still liked my cousins because I liked them, not because they were in favor or, when they quarreled with him, out of favor or because "family" dictated some particular set of sentiments. The same was true of my attitude toward my aunt Nabiha, who for a time angered my mother for her disloyalty to her brother Wadie.

I seemed therefore to draw less and less sustenance from the family group; I presumed that I had had it before, but I had somehow lost it, and I never regained it, except in the tortured and yet nourishingly hypnotic dialectic I maintained with my mother and which both of us fed and left unresolved for the longest time. It was while I was at VC that I began to notice the almost absolute separation that existed between my surface life at school and the complicated but mostly inarticulate inner life I cherished and lived through the emotions and sensations I derived from music, books, and memories intertwined with fantasies. It was as if the integration and liberty I needed between my selves would have to be endlessly postponed, although I subliminally retained the belief that one day they would somehow be integrated. With George, Mostapha, Samir, Andy, Billy, Arthur, and Claude I formed a sort of scruffy rat pack, tormenting masters and scorning the curriculum. We hung out together only in school as we lived long distances apart, though we occasionally met at the cinema or at the Tewfiqya Club. We were a generation too early for café life, and hashish was a very infrequent and difficult-to-obtain pleasure, so we settled for the crude humor of *tahshish,* the mostly lewd one-liners supposedly traded by semicomatose habitués of the weed, almost all of these repartees expressing passive acceptance of one's impotence and general stupidity.

So we hung out at school—between classes, near the tuck shop, in the dining refectory, on the sidelines of some match or other. The school provided no moral or intellectual framework—or at least no perceptible one—for us to evaluate our development. I often felt that we had all been judged before we ever got to the place, judged as wanting, or in some fundamental way as debased human material, not English, not really gentlemen, not really teachable. For me this was strangely relaxing, since at last I could be as I was without trying hard to be better, or work harder. Effort was pointless. The result was a curiously weightless life, with no unconscious or moral principle lurking beneath the surface. During my years there I do not recall a single personal conversation with any teacher or older student. My personal life was annulled, except as a Middle Five boy, then as an Upper Five one. The rest was background.

The Dirliks were frequently at our house, and I saw no reason not to be as relaxed as they were about having dinner or tea "out." The Dirliks exuded fun and pleasure, rare in my family life, which remained dour and explicitly formal. André was already an adventurer, his legs scarred with wounds gotten in the Red Sea coral reefs; Loris was always well dressed and elegant (we all remarked how precisely, even surgically, he could strip a bony chicken of all its meat with fork and knife); and Renée was ever ready with a quip or a suggestion for a picnic or the open-air cinema. True, their exuberant lifestyle was compromised by rumors that the handsomely located family pharmacy on Kasr el Nil Street, left to Loris and his brother by their father, was losing money for lack of attention, but this never clouded our time together until the late 1950s, when Loris ended up working for the United Nations in the Congo, having lost the pharmacy to bankruptcy. He died there suddenly and alone in the summer of 1962, to everyone's great sorrow.

In the late spring the long-awaited new school building was completed. Where the money came from I still do not know, but by the bedraggled, cramped, hand-me-down Shubra standards it turned out to be a lavish, superbly appointed new campus at the desert edge of Maadi, still an exclusive, mostly foreign and upper-class suburb, which I knew from both the club there and of course CSAC, nearer to Maadi's placid center and the railway station. All of a sudden I realized that we were at the end of a whole era (not that I knew what exactly *that* meant), when sudden, surprising events could and certainly did occur, and when new requirements were expected of us all. I don't recall thinking of myself very much in individual terms—it still impresses me that our

bonds as a school class, Middle Five One, were based not at all on family or class, which I do recall as positively counting for nothing—but
on a collective, if narrowly defined, set of objects, phrases, words even,
that circulated as if (for me, at least) in a comfortably secure orbit.
There was, to begin with, the dress code—caps, ties, blazers—which
was slowly phased out in Shubra. Then the de rigueur pink-covered
"assignment books," the leather or wooden pencil cases, the various
types of fountain pens (no ballpoints then), including a cheap Parker
lookalike much used and sold on the streets by noisy vendors (it had
"P.Arker" engraved on the clip; Japanese products in those days were
the ultimate in derided, risible brands), VC blue copy books. Then at
least a dozen English textbooks in subjects like physics, history, and
math—books that were as colorless and impersonal as their American
equivalents at CSAC had been chatty and narrativized (e.g., "Morton
gives Shelley $12.23 in change as his share for the class picnic of 18 stu-
dents. What if he thought that there were 15 students, and that each
should pay a share equivalent to . . . ?"), plus two or three literature
books, a Shakespeare play set for that year, a twentieth-century English
novel like C. S. Forester's subliterary *The Commodore,* plus a "classic"
nonfiction prose text (Macaulay's essays), and a selection of what
seemed to be dreary academic poetry (poems by Gray and Cowper).
Much, if not all, of this was packed in a standard brown leather satchel
with two clasps, with the family name (no first names) carefully
scratched in by hand in black or blue capitals on the inside main flap.

More exciting were a whole range of swapping and play objects:
marbles, including the much-prized agates, penknives (prized but outlawed), Ping-Pong racquets, wristbands, Dinky Toys (I still own the red
Humber sedan I won in some preposterously lucky bet over the meaning of "Greenwich Mean Time," often heard on the BBC and little
understood in those days), pocket combs, little vials of locally produced Chabrawichi cologne, rubber bands and key chains, new pencils
with shiny caps and clips over their points, sharpeners and rubbers (the
English word for American "eraser," which my father indefatigably
admonished me to use), slingshots, little round wire- and paper-covered
firework balls (also both prized and outlawed), various pornographic
books, badly printed on the vilest, grimiest, most repellent-looking
paper, written in a sub-English so graphic and vulgar as to actually

GEZIRA PREPARATORY SCHOOL

JUNIOR DEPARTMENT

Name Edward Said   Average Age of Form 6yrs 6mths

Report for term ending March 25th   Form Transition   Position

Subject		
Reading	Fair. Could do better with more effort	K.B.W.
Writing...	Very fair.	W.E.W.
Dictation Spelling...	Very good. Is making satisfactory progress	J.A.S.
English Grammar ...		
Poetry	Good, shown interest	C.B.W.
Scripture	Very good	J.A.S.
Geography	Very good. Shows interest.	J.A.S.
Drawing..	Very fair	W.E.W.
French...	Very fair	L.O.W.
Arithmetic	Too careless and untidy.	W.E.W.
History...	Very good	J.A.S.
Drill – Rhythmics	Should try to hold himself better	W.E.W.
Handwork.		
Nature Study... ...	Good.	W.E.W.

General conduct) Edward has settled down well and
Remarks   is making good progress. He must
try to concentrate more. and be less
fidgety and restless.   K.Wonnell-Jones

K Bullen.
Principal.

Next term begins: April 8th
Next term ends: June 17th

On the swing at ᶜAin al Naᶜas, a park and cafe near Dhour el Shweir, circa 1945–46. Left to right: Rosy, Jean (on swing), Ensaf (the nanny), and me

Outside St. George's Cathedral in Jerusalem at cousin George Said's wedding, April 14, 1947. Front row, left to right: Albert, me, and Robert; back row: Uncle Asaad (Al), cousin Yousif, and Wadie. Al was run over by a truck and died two weeks later

Below: The wedding of Alif Musa, my mother's older brother, in Haifa, 1946. My maternal grandmother, Munira, wearing a turban, is directly behind her son, the groom

With fellow cabin mates and counselor Jim Murray at Camp Maranacook, Maine, 1948. I'm on the left in the back row

Dr. Farid Haddad and Ada at their wedding, c. 1949, Cairo. Haddad was killed in prison in 1959

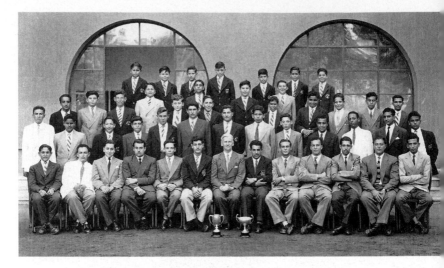

In a Kitchener House photo, 1950, at Victoria College, which I attended
for tenth and eleventh grades. I'm sixth from the left in the second row;
Keith Gatley, the housemaster, sits front row center

A 1951 report card
from Victoria
College stating
"excellent knowledge
and command of
English," signed by
Mr. Griffiths, the
headmaster who
expelled me for two
weeks in February
of that year

VICTORIA COLLEGE
CAIRO

UPPER SCHOOL

Report for SUMMER Term 19 51.   Name E. Said
Form U 5   Av. Age of Form 15·7   Age 15·4

SUBJECT	POSITION IN CLASS			NUMBER OF BOYS	REMARKS
	SET.	TERM	EXAM.		
ENGLISH		A	2	24	Has an excellent knowledge and command of English
HISTORY		B	3	9	Very good.
EGYPT. HISTORY					
GEOGRAPHY		C+	6	20	Good
FRENCH	IV	D+	20	36	Feeble.
ARABIC					
MATHEMATICS		C-	9	12	Fair
PHYSICS		B+	5	31	Satisfactory
CHEMISTRY		C	16	21	als. a
BIOLOGY		A	2	22	V. G.
GENERAL SCIENCE					
DICTION					
DRAWING					
MUSIC					

ABSENT MORNING 20 Times   AFTERNOON   LATE 1 Times

HOUSEMASTER A very keen boy

HEADMASTER Satisfactory progress.

Next Term begins on 3 OCT 1951
Boarders return on the previous day.

In front of Howard Johnson's in Jamaica, New York, March 1951

With my father at graduation from Mount Hermon, June 1953

On the post-graduation trip in New England, with my father and cousins
Charlie (far left) and Abie (far right), my father's nephews with whom
I stayed in Jackson Heights during several Christmases

A family portrait for my parents' twenty-fifth wedding anniversary, Cairo, December 1957. Front row: Joyce, Hilda, Wadie, and Grace; back row: me, Rosy, and Jean

At the keyboard accompanying Afif Bulos at a song recital in Paine Hall, Harvard, 1959

A summer during graduate school at Harvard: at the Acropolis, Athens, 1960

A 1980 view of the summer house rented from 1946 to 1969 in Dhour el Schweir. The rocket hole made during the Lebanese Civil War went through the master bedroom

dampen excitement, though we feigned it loudly and obscenely, and grainy fuzzy photographs of men and women copulating with embarrassed smirks on their faces. "Did you get a couple of servants to do this for you, Davidson?" I recall one of us saying to the enterprising boy who, it turned out later, had bought them from a parking garage attendant.

Our collective intellectual world was not particularly competitive, despite the ceaseless official emphasis on grades and on passing and failing. My own performance was highly unmemorable—wayward, erratic, sometimes excellent, normally passable and little more. Years later, when I had become known as a literary critic, one classmate told another, who relayed the comment to me, "Is that the same Said? He was the way we all were; amazing that he turned out like that." I am still surprised that the actual mental, or intellectual, world we lived in had so little to do with the mind in any serious or academic sense. Like the objects we carried around and traded, our collective language and thought were dominated by a small handful of perceptibly banal systems deriving from comics, film, serial fiction, advertising, and popular lore that was essentially at a street level, by no means influenced by home, religion, or education. The last edifying trace of sensibility and relatively "high" culture in us came, I remember clearly, from two religious films about saintly French women, Bernadette of Lourdes and Joan of Arc, in other words, Jennifer Jones and a crew-cut Ingrid Bergman. I saw the Bernadette film for some reason during its second or third run at the Diana Cinema, which was owned at the time by a Greek family, the Raissys. Its location on the less fashionable end of Emad el Din Street and its generally mediocre appointments made for nothing like the excitement of the Metro Cinema or the Rivoli Cinema, which alone in the Middle East sported the blazingly illuminated theater organ. The Diana's main distinction was that it was both a drab theater where Om Kulthum delivered her interminably long performances and a place where benefits for good causes could be held (my aunt Nabiha, in her unending attempts to raise money for Palestinian refugees, once took it over for a charity screening of *The Little Colonel,* the first and only Shirley Temple film I ever saw and which I have always since detested for its smarmy good-natured faux-naïf wholesomeness and racism), in addition to showing not-quite-glamorous

Hollywood movies. Between them Joan and Bernadette *à l'americaine* imbued me with considerable but very vague enthusiasm for something ungraspable and sent me eagerly to literary and historical sources, mostly to be found on my parents' ecumenical bookshelves. I read Franz Werfel's *Song of Bernadette* and also his *Forty Days of Musa Dagh,* followed by people like Chesterton (or was it Hilaire Belloc?) and Harold Lamb on the Maid of Orleans.

In the fall of 1950, the bus came to pick us up earlier than usual, for Maadi, which lay in the heart of Cairo, was twice as far away as Shubra. Our first distant sight of the new school, still in the process of construction, filled all of us with considerable hope. Three large buildings were complete and ready for us that October. They were Modernist rectangular structures, all of them on struts with, in the case of our class building, two long rows of windows, one above the other. Across the way was a dining hall and gymnasium, with a building for boarders, an infirmary, and masters' quarters at right angles to it; attached to the class building was a square-shaped annex that housed the administration. The grounds were vast, with several playing and track fields, tennis courts, and, because the school abutted on the desert, a well-appointed stable with grooms and a riding ring. All in all it was by far the handsomest school I or it seemed anyone else had been in. We disembarked from the bus feeling that we were at a new beginning.

It took us no more than five minutes to realize that the new school might not be an improvement after all. Beady-eyed, bow-tied, and bald Mr. Griffiths was now both our "additional maths" teacher in trigonometry, calculus, and solid geometry, as well as acting headmaster. He was to be my bête noire whose dogged condemnation stayed with me long after I left VC.

The new place both was grandiose and seemed to be making a pompous, rather disdainful statement as a British institution, and this increased our sense of collective alienation and hostility. There were other changes. Without the catalyzing force of George Kardouche, who had disappeared to the English School in Heliopolis, we tended to dissolve into divisive cliques.

Our new form and English teacher, Mr. Lowe, was a blustering, weak, and incompetent teacher. The new classrooms had a little storeroom behind the blackboard, where he kept his chalk, exercise books, and other supplies. The door, to the blackboard's left, had a lock on it, and just underneath the blackboard a small sliding window gave on to the classroom. It was my idea to trap him inside, inscribe "Take a look, 5 piasters" on the blackboard above the window, and let the students stand by to watch our hapless Englishman in captivity, "in his natural state," I put it as I barked the show. A prefect lured in by Lowe's bellowing and our raised voices quickly put an end to the escapade. I was duly reported to Griffiths, who glowered at me in math class with a distinctly unpleasant gleam in his eye. "A lot of disturbance here yesterday," he said, looking at me but addressing the class as a whole. Weeks later Griffiths was to tell my parents with some regret, not to say bitterness, that my intelligence always inhibited him from sacking me. Ironic that a teacher should feel that a bright student was an impediment to his authority.

The compactness of the Shubra grounds, which kept us in touch with other classes, had been replaced with the vastness of our new grounds. Masters took to patrolling the corridors, something impossible to do in Shubra with its decentralized disorder, and it gradually came to appear to me that the new campus was designed more for controlled surveillance than for utility or education. It took only about a month at the new school for me to feel constantly uneasy: the older boys encroached on us in the corridor, attacking, insulting, pushing. One, an immense tub of flesh weighing at least three hundred pounds, Billy Fawzi, took a great irrational dislike to me, and I spent my time dodging him. But there was no avoiding him completely, as he could block an entire corridor with his great bulk. Once he took hold of my neck in one of his huge hands and said in Arabic, "Said, I've been watching you. Be careful. Don't try to be clever with me. And [in English] don't be cheeky," cleverness and cheekiness being among the most lethal sins with which not only masters but older (and bigger) boys charged us.

Captain Billy was only the worst of the older boys who threatened and tormented me; most of the others were not even names to me, but they were dreaded forces, blotchy-skinned, overweight, and entirely Arabic-speaking. For some reason I was singled out by this group, which had replaced the departed Shalhoub as the school's unofficial disciplinarians, with the masters' obvious complaisance. I was known to be quick-witted, generally in trouble, and a decent student, so during school exams I routinely found myself surrounded by some of these Brobdingnagian creatures, who would then hand me their English papers to write for them while I was frantically trying to do my own. The carrot was "Said, be a decent fellow"; the much more effective cudgel was "Do it or I'll fuck your mother." So I always did their exams. Cowardice and compliance were a way of life in this case.

At Christmas that year it was decided that my mother and I should take the train together to Upper Egypt for a few days' sightseeing in the Valley of the Kings, Karnak, and other sites, whose silence and awful brooding emptiness put me off ancient Egypt forever. Our four or five days were idyllic, a sort of languid respite from the hurly-burly of school and the great city, and it would be the last time I had an extended period of time alone with my mother. We read to each other, suspended without tension or argument in the long winter afternoons and evenings in the salons of the Cataract Hotel without schedules or deadlines or duties to fulfill. She was now beginning to be more aware of her social gifts, and the restful, nourishing, uncomplicated times I enjoyed with her were rather too often vitiated by her impulse to be gregarious, or at least to spend time with American acquaintances staying at the same hotel. I remember my irritation and jealousy but I also cherish the abstraction of those days as furnishing me with a lifetime memory—never equaled nor superseded—of sublime disengagement from the exertions of daily life at VC, which were soon to do me in and drive me away from home literally forever.

Luxor and Aswan: the brief respite before an awful tempest. On a Thursday afternoon early in February Mr. Lowe petitioned us to take out our Shakespeares. We set up a chorus of "Scott instead." He decided to take a stand on Shakespeare and in unwonted aggressive pursuit of his aim he waded into the front row of desks, flailing at his resistant charges, petulantly asserting a will entirely disconnected from his supposed object, which was to get us to read Shakespeare sonnets. Surrounded on all sides by an aroused, insurrectionary class, Lowe was like Samson in the Philistine temple, beset by blows, unable to see whom he was hitting, how (if at all) he was progressing. Suddenly, he lurched forward, encircling the boy nearest him with his oversize arms. Suddenly I found myself trapped in his sweaty embrace, with rivulets of perspiration pouring down his reddened face, and his great obese body pulling me down so that he lay on top of me. "I have you now, Said," he sputtered, "and I'm going to teach you a lesson." He tried to straighten his arms to beat me but he was quickly set upon by three or four students who held on to him shouting frenzied Arab curses. "Stop it," he yelled, "stop it and let go of me this instant." My rescuers drew back, stunned by this astonishing assertion of his flawed authority. As I scrambled free he grabbed me again, marched me firmly to the door, and ejected me from the class, slamming the door shut.

I caught a glimpse of Griffiths staring at me from his office door thirty meters away, but he said and did nothing but look at me expressionlessly. At the start of the break during our math class the next morning, Griffiths told us to remain seated. "Now, Said," he said casually to me in the second row, "I hear that you were misbehaving yesterday afternoon. That's true, isn't it?" Having seen me posted outside the class, he knew it was true. I said nothing. "WHY DON'T YOU ANSWER, BOY?" he suddenly screamed at me, losing control of himself for the first time in our presence. "Yes, sir," I responded noncommittally. "Well, we can't have any of that here. Can't have it." Again noncommittally: "No, sir." To which, very matter-of-factly he said, "You'd better leave then." Not knowing quite what he had in mind I said, "Leave, sir? Now, sir?" "Just leave, Said. I don't care where you go. Just leave. Now."

I proceeded deliberately, with the precision of shocked surprise and shivering uncertainty, to pack my tattered satchel, while everyone sat in a frigid, immobilized silence. I looked sideways at my friend Hamdollah, who lowered his eyes in embarrassment. Isolated, pinpointed, transfixed, I had suddenly stepped outside every circle I had once inhabited. No longer welcome at school, frightened to go home, with no money in my pockets, no prospects for the immediate future except a rail ticket, I somehow managed to walk out of the class feeling strangely invisible, while Griffiths sat impassively at his desk waiting for me to be gone. I do not recollect much of my three-kilometer walk to the railway station, except for crossing the canals with extreme deliberation, idly tossing a pebble or two at their dark algae-colored surface, then moving on to the next canal to do much the same thing all over again. It took me till about one-thirty p.m. to get home, dawdling through Bab el Louk, around Midan Ismailiya, across the Kasr el Nil bridge, down past the Moorish Gardens and the Gezira Club's racecourse, past the little Fish Garden, a five-kilometer trudge from the train station during which I found myself deliberately not thinking of what was about to happen. I experienced a floating, literally utopian sensation of not being there, of being disembodied, relieved of all my customary encumbrances, obligations, restraints. I had never felt quite so dangerously free and undirected as I did then; after years of time-tables, chores, errands, assignments, I was simply walking in the direction of home, with no purpose except that at some point I knew I would have to end up there.

Not having been entrusted with my own set of keys, I had to ring our doorbell. Uncharacteristically, since the task was reserved for servants, my mother opened the door. "Edward," she said in a tone of surprise that quickly gave way to alarm. "What are you doing here? Is something wrong? Are you ill?" Speechless and disoriented, I was ushered in by her to be met by my father, his face glowering with concern and anger. Without my saying a word, he took me into their room for a preliminary whipping with his riding crop.

Not a word passed between us. I went to my room and exploded in tears, my physical pain compounded by a sense of fundamental desolation and abandonment. For two weeks I remained at home like a forlorn shadow, denied books, music, friends, and any kind of pleasure by two mystified and outraged parents who were content to await Griffiths's pleasure before he would consent to see them. When they returned from their appointment it was my mother who did all the talking, most of it essentially endorsing Griffiths's poor opinion of me as a "good-for-nothing," although he seems to have regretfully added the novel complaint that I was "too clever" to be sacked definitively, much as he would have liked to have done so. My mother seems, like Griffiths, to have regarded my intelligence, which was soon becoming my only certainty about myself, resentfully, as a sign of my incorrigibility and inveterately malign or at least unteachable nature. In her eyes, my intelligence got in the way of my being a good student, but it was enough this time to earn me an unenthusiastic reprieve from expulsion. I could return, Griffiths said, but no further misbehavior would be tolerated.

Griffiths had also clearly implied that my future as a student-scholar within the English system was uncertain; he would have to give me an equivocal recommendation should I stay on and get my GCE (the high school diploma awarded to all graduates of British-run schools) and then apply to Oxford or Cambridge (his university). My father was undoubtedly planning my departure for the United States even as I returned to VC in ignorance of this fact. What I was told as the official story was that I would have to leave Egypt because an obscure U.S. immigration law decreed that although I had inherited citizenship from my father, in order to become a citizen I would be required to spend at least five years in the United States before I was twenty-one, as I had not been born there. Since in November 1951 I'd be turning sixteen, the move was imperative.

I suppose he thought that by sending me away to such demanding and all-male institutions as Mount Hermon and later Princeton, he was protecting me not only from self-abuse, but also from the heaving, overabundant emotional luxury represented by my mother with its paralyzing uncertainties and comforts.

Just as I was being shaped by my father's plan for me to go to the United States in the spring of 1951, we suddenly received a postcard from his long-lost younger brother, David, who had been shipped out of Egypt by my father for unregenerate philandering in 1929, exiled to Brazil, and had then vanished. Written in a gigantic, childish scrawl, David's card came from Lourdes and announced, "I am cured. I am coming to see you," followed a week later by a telegram giving his flight number and date of arrival in Cairo. He was a darker, more animated, and more compact Latin-mustachioed version of my father, a sort of cross between Wadie's alter ego and his parody. David's amorous powers were supposed to be irresistible, especially to married women, who were the immediate cause of his original banishment. He spoke a bizarre combination of windswept and tattered old Arabic, with a few dozen American phrases ("Gee Bill, you should see how much money I made one evening in Bahia") and some incomprehensible Portuguese. We were all drawn to his uncomplicated, effusive presence: his brother Wadie and sister Nabiha, their various children, and my mother, at whom he charmingly made a few awkward but gallant passes. Staying at our house, he spent a month in Cairo doing very little except successfully persuading my father to take time off from work so that the three siblings could sit around together and chatter about the old Jerusalem childhood that they had once long ago shared. The Dostoyevskian depths that I intimated in my father (but never saw) were fully in evidence in David—melancholy, volubility, extremes of mood from elation to the darkest depression—and were framed by but never really contained in his relationships with his sober brother and sister.

I never found out what he did exactly. Diamond mines were spoken of, but so too was his skill at being a tour guide, like his father. He gambled and drank, womanized and dashed around the Brazilian countryside. He gave us a leather pouch full of semiprecious stones of small value, but in their gleaming cascading profusion and variety they contained the romance of an entire continent. He and I became great pals: *"ya dini"* ("my religion") he used to call me, unidiomatically. Years later I realized that in his exotic, unbridled, and mysterious personality he was an avatar of Conrad for me—a Kurtz figure, a secret sharer, a Cunningham Graham to my father's British squire. He disappeared again back to Brazil. In September 1967 I saw him for an hour in New York; he was on tour with the Brazilian national soccer team in some mysterious capacity. Just before her death in the spring of 1973, Aunt Nabiha, ravaged by cancer, went to see him, and discovered a "kind of" wife, Adela, and a handicapped teenage child, who may have been adopted. A Virgilian sadness pervaded Nabiha's last days as she negotiated the ruins of her scattered family, her heroic past of no help to her in her disorganized, crumbling life in Amman, where she died in early April on the same day that Kamal Nasir was assassinated by the Israelis in Beirut. In David, Nabiha, and my father I saw a tangle of departures, exiles, and brief returns, and I understood my father's attempt to combine an unpromising mix of hidden, unruly instinct and conscious Victorian determination in his efforts to make a good life for his family. What sustained my father's faith was a simple pedagogical imperative he kept reverting to. "If it's educational," he used to tell me, "then do it." I have been trying to grasp what "it" was ever since, and this book is my record of having tried. Only decades after his death can I see the two sides of his legacy to me bound together irrevocably in an absolute, unarguable paradox, repression and liberation opening on to each other in what is to me still a mystery that I am just beginning now to accept, if not fully to understand.

After the Suez War in 1956, Victoria College was nationalized and was renamed Victory College. I had no further connection with it until 1989, when on a lecturing visit to Egypt with my family I thought it might be fun to show them the school that had once expelled me. We went up to Maadi on a Friday morning in mid-March and drove to the school following the old bus route. I was discontented to discover that what had been a sort of boundary between the school and the desert, beyond which the empty sand stretched for miles, had become a vast expanse of tenements, crowded with people, hanging laundry, cars, buses, and animals. The school itself was closed for the Friday holiday, but I persuaded the gatekeeper to let us in anyway. As we stood in my old classroom, which seemed a good deal smaller than I remembered, I pointed out my desk, the teacher's platform from which Griffiths had expelled me, and the little room where we had imprisoned poor old Mr. Lowe.

At that moment a very angry-looking woman wearing a head covering and Islamic-style dress swept into the room demanding to know what we were doing. I tried to explain the circumstances ("Use your charm," said my daughter, Najla) but to no avail. We were trespassers, and as school director she was demanding that we leave immediately. She refused my extended hand, staring at us with a surfeit of nationalist hostility and unbending zeal as we shuffled out, rather cowed by her evident outrage. The British Eton in Egypt had now become a new kind of privileged Islamic sanctuary from which thirty-eight years later I was once again being expelled.

IX

IN EARLY SEPTEMBER 1991, EXACTLY FORTY YEARS AFTER I left the middle east for the United States, I was in London for a seminar I had convened of Palestinian intellectuals and activists on the eve of the Madrid Peace Conference. After the Gulf War and the Palestinian leadership's fatal stand alongside Saddam Hussein we were in a very weak negotiating position. The idea of the conference was to try to articulate a common set of themes that would enhance the course of our progress toward self-determination as a people. We came from all over the dispersed Palestinian world—the West Bank and Gaza, the Palestinian diaspora in various Arab countries, Europe and North America. What transpired during the seminar was a terrible disappointment: the endless repetition of well-known arguments, our inability to fix on a collective goal, the apparent desire to listen only to ourselves. In short, nothing came of it except an eerie premonition of the Palestinian failure at Oslo.

Midway through the debate, during one of the scheduled breaks, I phoned Mariam, my wife, in New York to ask her if the results of the blood test I had taken for my annual physical had been satisfactory. Cholesterol was what had concerned me, and no, she said, everything was fine on that front, but she added with some hesitation, "Charles Hazzi [our family doctor and friend] would like to speak to you when you get back." Something in her voice suggested to me that all was not well, so I immediately rang Charles at his office. "Nothing to get excited about," he said, "we'll talk in New York." His repeated refusals to tell me what was wrong finally provoked me to impatience. "You must tell me, Charles. I'm not a child, and I have a right to know." With a whole set of demurrals—it's not serious, a hematologist can very easily take care of you, it's chronic after all—he told me that I had chronic lymphocytic leukemia (CLL), although it took me a week to fully absorb the initial impact of the diagnosis. I was asymptomatic but needed the sophisticated diagnostic techniques available at a big New York cancer center to confirm the original finding. It took me another month to understand how thoroughly I was shaken by this "sword of Damocles," as one volubly callous doctor called it, hanging over me, and a further six months to find the extraordinary doctor, Kanti Rai, under whose care I have been since June 1992.

A month after I was diagnosed I discovered myself in the middle of a letter I was writing my mother, who had been dead for a year and a half. Ever since I left Cairo in 1951 it was a habit we had kept up: somehow the urge to communicate with her overcame the factual reality of her death, which in mid-sentence stopped my fanciful urge, leaving me slightly disoriented, even embarrassed. A vague narrative impulse seemed to be stirring inside me, but I was too caught up in the anxieties and nervousness of my life with CLL to pay it much notice. During that period in 1993 I contemplated several changes in my life, which I realized without any perceptible fear would be shorter and more difficult now. I thought about moving to Boston to return to a place I had lived in and enjoyed when I was a student, but I soon admitted to myself that because it was a quiet town, compared to New York, I had been thinking regressively about finding a place to die in. I gave up the idea.

So many returns, attempts to go back to bits of life, or people who were no longer there: these constituted a steady response to the increasing rigors of my illness. In 1992 I went with my wife and children to Palestine, for my first visit in forty-five years; it was their first visit ever. In July 1993 I went on my own to Cairo, making it a point in the middle of a journalistic mission to visit old haunts. All this time I was being monitored, without treatment, by Dr. Rai, who occasionally reminded me that I would at some point require chemotherapy. By the time I began treatment in March 1994 I realized that I had at least entered, if not *the* final phase of my life, then the period—like Adam and Eve leaving the garden—from which there would be no return to my old life. In May 1994 I began work on this book.

These details are important as a way of explaining to myself and to my reader how the time of this book is intimately tied to the time, phases, ups and downs, variations in my illness. As I grew weaker, the number of infections and bouts of side effects increased, the more this book was my way of constructing something in prose while in my physical and emotional life I grappled with anxieties and pains of degeneration. Both tasks resolved themselves into details: to write is to get from word to word, to suffer illness is to go through the infinitesimal steps that take you through from one state to another. And whereas with other sorts of work that I did—essays, lectures, teaching, journalism—I was going across the illness, punctuating it almost forcibly with deadlines and cycles of beginning-middle-and-end, with this memoir I was borne along by the episodes of treatment, hospital stays, physical pain and mental anguish, letting those dictate how and when I could write, for how long and where. Periods of travel were often productive, since I carried my hand-written manuscript with me wherever I went and took advantage of every hotel room or friend's house I stayed in. I was therefore rarely in a hurry to get a section done, though I had a precise idea of what I planned to put in it. Curiously, the writing of this memoir and the phases of my illness share exactly the same time, although most traces of the latter have been effaced in this story of my early life. This record of a life and ongoing course of a disease (for which I have known from the beginning no cure exists) are one and the same, it could be said, the same but deliberately different.

And the more this relationship developed, the more important it became to me, the more also my memory—unaided by anything except concentrated reflection on and archaeological prying into a very distant and essentially irrecoverable past—seemed hospitable and generous to my often importunate forays. Despite the travail of disease and the restrictions imposed on me by my having left the places of my youth, I can say with the poet, "nor in this bower, / This little lime-tree bower, have I not mark'd / Much that has soothed me." There had been a time until the early sixties when I simply could not bear to think about my past, especially Cairo and Jerusalem, which for two sets of different reasons were no longer accessible. The latter had been replaced by Israel; the former, by one of those cruel coincidences, was closed to me for legal reasons. Unable to visit Egypt for the fifteen years between 1960 and 1975, I rationed early memories of my life there (considerably chopped up, full of atmospherics that conveyed a sense of warmth and comfort by contrast with the harsh alienation I felt in my New York life) as a way of falling asleep, an activity that has grown more difficult with time, time that has also dissolved the aura of happiness around my early life and let it emerge as a more complicated and difficult period; to grasp it I realized I would have to be sharply alert, awake, avoiding dreamy somnolence. I've thought in fact that this book in some fundamental way is all about sleeplessness, all about the silence of wakefulness and, in my case, the need for conscious recollection and articulation that have been a substitute for sleep. Not just for sleep but for holidays and relaxation, all that passes for middle- and upper-class "leisure," on which, about ten years ago, I unconsciously turned my back. As one of the main responses to my illness I found in this book a new kind of challenge—not just a new kind of wakefulness but a project about as far from my professional and political life as it was possible for me to go.

The underlying motifs for me have been the emergence of a second self buried for a very long time beneath a surface of often expertly acquired and wielded social characteristics belonging to the self my parents tried to construct, the "Edward" I speak of intermittently, and how an extraordinarily increasing number of departures have unsettled my life from its earliest beginnings. To me, nothing more painful and paradoxically sought after characterizes my life than the many displacements from countries, cities, abodes, languages, environments that have kept me in motion all these years. Thirteen years ago I wrote in *After the Last Sky* that when I travel I always take too much with me, and that even a trip downtown requires the packing of a briefcase stocked with items disproportionately larger in size and number than the actual period of the trip. Analyzing this, I concluded that I had a secret but ineradicable fear of not returning. What I've since discovered is that despite this fear I fabricate occasions for departure, thus giving rise to the fear voluntarily. The two seem absolutely necessary to my rhythm of life and have intensified dramatically during the period I've been ill. I say to myself:

if you don't take this trip, don't prove your mobility and indulge your fear of being lost, don't override the normal rhythms of domestic life now, you certainly will not be able to do it in the near future. I also experience the anxious moodiness of travel (*la mélancolie des paquebots,* as Flaubert calls it, *Bahnhofsstimmung* in German) along with envy for those who stay behind, whom I see on my return, their faces unshadowed by dislocation or what seems to be enforced mobility, happy with their families, draped in a comfortable suit and raincoat, *there* for all to see. Something about the invisibility of the departed, his being missing and perhaps missed, in addition to the intense, repetitious, and predictable sense of banishment that takes you away from all that you know and can take comfort in, makes you feel the need to leave because of some prior but self-created logic, and a sense of rapture. In all cases, though, the great fear is that departure is the state of being abandoned, even though it is you who leave.

In the summer of 1951 I left Egypt and spent two weeks in Lebanon, three weeks in Paris and London, and one week on the *Nieuw Amsterdam* from Southampton to New York, for the rest of my schooling in the United States. This included high school then undergraduate and graduate degrees, a total of eleven years, after which I remained until the present. There is no doubt that what made this whole protracted experience of separation and the return during the summers agonizing was my complicated relationship to my mother, who never ceased to remind me that my leaving her was the most unnatural ("Everyone else has their children next to them") and yet tragically necessary of fates. Each year the late-summer return to the United States opened old wounds afresh and made me reexperience my separation from her as if for the first time—incurably sad, desperately backward-looking, disappointed and unhappy in the present. The only relief was our anguished yet chatty letters. I still find myself reliving aspects of the experience today, the sense that I'd rather be somewhere else—defined as closer to her, authorized by her, enveloped in her special maternal love, infinitely forgiving, sacrificing, giving—because being *here* was not being where I/we had wanted to be, *here* being defined as a place of exile, removal, unwilling dislocation. Yet as always there was something conditional about her wanting me with her, for not only was I to conform to her ideas about me, but I was to be *for* her while she might or might not, depending on her mood, be for me.

After I returned, anticlimactically, to Victoria College for the balance of the 1950–51 school year, I was, as Griffiths was immediately at pains to point out, to be on probation. In effect this seemed to mean that every master was alerted to my threatened status and regularly reminded me just as I was becoming restive that I "had better remember and behave." In this uncomfortable situation I was constantly on tenterhooks, bullied, mocked, or shunned by some of my classmates; only Mostapha Hamdollah, Billy Abdel Malik, and Andy Sharon seemed to behave as before, which limited me to a tight orbit of familiars, isolated and ill at ease. During this period I found myself seeking out my mother even more than before, and she, with that preternatural way she had of sensing and indeed reading my mood, would show me the kind of tenderness and intimacy I desperately needed.

One culminating event at VC that spring brought us closer together. First there were the Furtwängler concerts, which my father, who averred that he only liked "concertos" (not offered by the Berlin Philharmonic), joined us for with restrained enthusiasm. I remember turning to or nudging my mother during a favorite passage in the slow movement of the Beethoven Fifth and later in the bridge to the last movement, feeling again that special blend of intimacy and comprehension that only she could give me, especially while I was in a threatening limbo at school as a semi-outcast. The day after the Sunday concert, during lunch break at school, a few of us gathered on the fringes of the main playing-field area to take turns heaving a shot put, marking off each try, soberly trying to arrive at a ranking of the six classmates taking part. As I reached down to take my turn, three of the senior Lower Six boys led by Gilbert Davidson, as noisy and bullyish as his younger brother Arthur was quiet and understated, demanded that he be allowed to throw the shot. "No," I said firmly, "it's my turn now. Wait till I've thrown it." "You silly fucker, give it to me right away," he replied, his ruddy face quite apoplectic with rage as he lurched at me trying to grab the heavy object in my left hand. Missing it entirely, Davidson's hand locked into the front of my shirt, which in his violent sweeping gesture he ripped open, popping buttons, tearing fabric, and unbalancing me with the sudden angry violence of his intervention. Teetering, I dropped the shot, turning toward him at the moment he took a huge swing at my head and missed me entirely in his by now uncontrollable rage. With what I remember as the coolest deliberation, I put all my strength behind a fist that landed on his nose, producing an alarmingly red stream of blood. Falling on his back, immediately surrounded and propped up by his mates, he threatened to kill me and my mother the moment he could get up. I was hurried away by my classmates, and was saved by the class bell.

Later that afternoon I was required to pay a visit to the infirmary for the purpose of a medical report on the incident written by the elderly Scottish nurse, whose sole comment to me after looking at my hand was "You have a fist like a lump of iron." Davidson in the meantime was taken home, reappearing a week later with all sorts of ugly threats, which in my immense unease I took quite seriously. Griffiths said something disparaging and dismissive to me about being quite hopeless—"There's always trouble where you are, Said, isn't there?" No disciplinary action was taken. But for a month after the incident I confined myself to home and mother, so convinced was I that Davidson would either kill me himself or get some toughs to do it for him.

The memory of my mother's tenderness during those last weeks in Cairo remains exceptionally strong, and was a source of solace during my first years in the United States. Through her I felt encouraged in what our Cairo environment had no conception of, namely books and music that took me way beyond both the inane prescriptions of school and the fluttery triviality of our social life. She had given me a few Russian novels to read and in them during my weeks of seclusion I discovered a turbulent but ultimately self-sufficient world, a bulwark against the anxieties of daily reality. As I read *The Brothers Karamazov* I felt I had found an elaboration of the family dispute between my father, his nephew, and my aunt, now entering its terminal phase of almost daily incidents, recriminations, shouting scenes, and disputes both with and about employees. I also became aware of how despite the cordiality of our friendships with the Shami circle into which we had grown, a gentle but noticeable mockery of my father crept into many of the comments made by them to and about him—his unrelenting use of English (my mother had become fluent in French and chatted up Emma Fahoum and Reine Diab famously in such phrases as *"ma chère,"* *"j'étais etonnée,"* and so forth), his unbending concentration on his business, his penchant for American foods like apple pie and pancakes, which they found too gross for words, his rather sporty dress, including on holidays old shirts and frayed trouser cuffs.

Thinking back to that last period in Cairo, I recall only the sense of comfort and pleasure I derived from my mother's ministrations; she was obviously thinking of my impending departure, trying to make of those last days something very special for both of us, while I, not really imagining the terrible rupture that was to come, enjoyed the time as a liberation from the hectic schedule I had once followed. No more Tewfiq Effendi, no more Fouad Etayim, riding was dropped, piano lessons given up, exercises at Mourad's gymnasium terminated. Coming back from school in the late afternoon I'd often find her sitting on the terrace overlooking the Fish Garden, and, inviting me to sit beside her with a glass of rosewater–flavored lemonade, she would encircle me with her arm and reminisce about the old days, how "Edwardo Bianco" had been such a remarkably precocious boy, and how I was what she lived for. We listened to the Beethoven symphonies, particularly the Ninth, which became the piece that meant the most to us. I remember being confused about the nature of her relationship to my father, but also being pacified that she always referred to him as "Daddy," the two of us using the same name for husband and father. All this may have been her way of trying to win me back from America before I went, her way of reclaiming me from my father's plans, which when he sent me to the United States she always disagreed with and rued. But these afternoons had the effect of creating an image of an inviolate union between us, which would have, on the whole, shattering results for my later life as a man trying to establish a relationship of developing, growing, maturing love with other women. It was not so much that my mother had usurped a place in my life to which she was not entitled, but that she managed to have access to it for the rest of her life and, I often feel, after it.

I am only now aware that those talks before we were to leave for the United States constituted a sort of leave-taking ceremony. "Let's go to Groppi's for tea for the last time," or "Wouldn't you like us to go to the Kursaal for dinner once more before you go?" she would ask. But much of it took place in some complicated labyrinth of her own making, which also involved the arrangements she was making for herself and my four sisters, whom she would be alone with after I left. There was something so terribly giving about her attitude in the last week before we packed the house for the first stage of our trip via Lebanon. As I later realized, she thought of that giving as motivated entirely by unselfish love, whereas of course her sovereign ego played a major part in what she was up to, namely, struggling in a limiting domestic household to find a means of self-expression, self-articulation, self-elaboration. These I think were my mother's deepest needs, though she never managed to say it explicitly. I was her only son, and shared her facility of communication, her passion for music and words, so I became her instrument for self-expression and self-elaboration as she struggled against my father's unbending, mostly silent iron will. Her sudden withdrawal of affection, which I dreaded, were her way of responding to my absences. From 1951 until her death in 1990 my mother and I lived on different continents, yet she never stopped lamenting the fact that, alone of all her friends, she suffered the pangs of separation from her children, most particularly me. I felt guilt at having abandoned her, even though she had finally acquiesced in the first and most decisive of my many departures.

The sheer gravity of my coming to the United States in 1951 amazes me even today. I have only the most shadowy notion of what my life might have been had I not come to America. I do know that I was beginning again in the United States, unlearning to some extent what I had learned before, relearning things from scratch, improvising, self-inventing, trying and failing, experimenting, canceling, and restarting in surprising and frequently painful ways. To this day I still feel that I am away from home, ludicrous as that may sound, and though I believe I have no illusions about the "better" life I might have had, had I remained in the Arab world, or lived and studied in Europe, there is still some measure of regret. This memoir is on some level a reenactment of the experience of departure and separation as I feel the pressure of time hastening and running out. The fact that I live in New York with a sense of provisionality despite thirty-seven years of residence here accentuates the disorientation that has accrued to me, rather than the advantages.

We made our annual removal to Lebanon in late June 1951 and spent two weeks in Dhour. Then, on the fifteenth of July, my parents and I departed from Beirut Airport (Khaldé, as it was called then) by Pan-American Stratocruiser for Paris. From almost the moment we stepped off the plane in Paris until we left for London by night sleeper I was afflicted with a plague of styes in both my eyes, which, apart from two small apertures, effectively closed them. This aggravated the sense of drifting and indeterminacy that followed my withdrawal from all aspects of my familiar world, the sense of not *really* knowing what I was doing or where I was going.

Within hours of arriving in London, where we stayed grandly in an imposingly grandiose suite at the Savoy, my cousin Albert was summoned from Birmingham, where he was doing a degree in chemical engineering, and was installed luxuriously with us at the hotel. He appeared to be unaware of the tensions between my father and his brothers, so jolly and admirably rakish did he seem while with us. I spent many hours eating my first fish and chips with Albert, visiting the new Battersea Fun Fair, and going to an unending number of pubs in search of girls and excitement, all the while trying to learn from him the arts of enjoying oneself without feeling either guilty or lonely. He was the one close relative whom for the first twenty years of my life I found myself hoping to emulate because he was everything I was not. He had an erect posture, was an excellent footballer and runner, seemed to be a successful ladies' man, and was a natural leader as well as a brilliant student. London was certainly the most pleasurable interlude of our trip. The moment he left, his tonic effect dissipated, and I settled back into the anxious gloom of the trip.

From Southampton we boarded the *Nieuw Amsterdam,* a larger, more luxurious version of the *Saturnia.* The six-day crossing to New York was uneventfully crammed with sumptuous dinners and lunches, nightly movies, and my parents' ubiquitous presence. "I hate America and Americans," my mother would say. "What are we doing here, Wadie? Please explain this whole crazy business to me. Must we take the boy there? You know he'll never come back. We're robbing ourselves." My mother was querulous and sad, while my father reveled in his pancakes and coffee, apple pie à la mode, excited about America and his determination, now that I was going to be there, to buy a house. I found myself avoiding, except at dinner, the conflicting moods of my parents with no stable idea of where I was going or for how long.

No sooner did we arrive in a steamy, unpleasantly overcast and dark New York than my mother persuaded my father to let us visit her cousin Eva Malik in Washington. We checked in to the Mayflower for only about an hour: Eva came by in her husband's black ambassadorial limousine almost immediately and, brooking no dissent, pried us and our lordly array of luggage out of the hotel and into the nicely comfortable chancellory. In his capacity as Lebanese minister plenipotentiary in the United States, Charles Malik was away at a U.N. meeting in San Francisco, so we had Aunt Eva to ourselves for a few days of tourism and general relaxation. It was she who also insisted that they would be my guardians while I was at boarding school, an arrangement my mother welcomed, as did I, since I might spend my vacations in the splendors of the Lebanese ambassador's residence, in a style that resembled what I thought I had left behind in Cairo. My father was noncommittal, for reasons that I would only later discover. I could sense, however, that both my parents were soon chafing at our stay, which, they kept reminding Eva—who, being alone and otherwise not engaged or obligated by domestic duties, was obviously enjoying our presence—was already too protracted. They both had this notion that one shouldn't in the Arab sense be "heavy"—in effect, not stay anywhere more than three, at most four, days, all the while taking out our hosts for dinner every night, buying lots of flowers and chocolates, making themselves "lighter" by so doing.

Suddenly we embarked for Madison, Wisconsin, which in a recent *National Geographic* had been described to my father's satisfaction as the "nicest" town in the United States. We spent two days in the pretty town, going around with real estate agents who showed us one imposing house after another, each of which the three of us collectively imagined ourselves living in: "That's your mother's desk" said my father, pointing to an unprepossessing corner filled carelessly with a decrepit bridge table. "Here's where we can put the piano," said my mother with noticeably less enthusiasm as the hours wore on. We gathered great quantities of pamphlets and business cards, all of which my father cavalierly tossed into the hotel wastebasket that evening. There was something disconnected and eerie about our house hunting in Madison, but my mother and I played along with my father, although I never grasped what Madison was a fictional projection of for him, except the opportunity to come to the United States like me and settle here, despite his by now elaborate domestic establishment, prospering business, and very full life in Egypt and Lebanon. He always used to say, and my mother repeated often, that had he been twenty years younger after World War II, he would have come to the United States. When we went to Madison he was already fifty-six, but I know that to some extent his interest in the United States was partly theoretical patriotism, partly the invigoration he felt at being out of his family's grasp, partly the desire to make me feel that I was getting the greatest opportunity ever, and that my clinging moroseness and expectant dread about staying on alone would be dissolved in due course. He had an ideological hatred of sentimentality, represented by the regretted effect of his own mother's importunings to return and my mother's behavior toward me just prior to our trip.

We returned to New York via the Milwaukee Road Railroad and a TWA flight from Midway Airport, and the day after Labor Day finally found ourselves on a train leaving Grand Central Station bound for Mount Hermon. The only part of the long journey on the White River Junction train that I remember was our arrival at the tiny, excessively rural Massachusetts station, where a lone taxicab was waiting to take us the final couple of miles to the school. We barely had an hour together, since my parents were to take the return train to New York. When we had found my room, and my parents had had a brief meeting alone with the headmaster, my mother spent fifteen minutes helping me to unpack and make the bed (my unknown roommate was already neatly installed). Then they rapidly departed, leaving me standing with a lump in my throat at the entrance to my imposing dormitory building, Crossley Hall, as they disappeared from view. The void that suddenly surrounded me and that I knew I had to endure for the one academic year I was to be at Mount Hermon seemed unbearable, but I also knew that I had to return to my room to recover some sense of my mother's recent presence—her smell, a trace of her hands, even perhaps a message.

A blond and blue-eyed youth of my own age was there to greet me. "Hi. I'm your roommate, Bob Salisbury," he said pleasantly, leaving me no opportunity to recuperate some of my mother's disappearing aura as I realized that I had now definitively arrived.

Mount Hermon School, originally founded by the evangelist Dwight L. Moody in the late nineteenth century, was larger than Victoria College. It was the male counterpart of the Northfield Seminary for Young Ladies, and the two establishments occupied several thousand acres on opposite sides of the Connecticut River. A six-mile road and a bridge connected the two quite separate but affiliated schools. Mount Hermon, unlike Northfield, was not in a town or village but was entirely self-enclosed and self-sufficient. Unmarried teachers lived among students in the dorm; married faculty with children had little houses scattered over the campus. Although it was in the traditional picture-book sense a beautiful, leafy, hilly, and perfectly maintained New England site, I found it altogether alienating and desolate. The beauties of nature spoke little to me, and at Mount Hermon I found them particularly unseen and repressed.

Crossley Hall was the largest building on campus, a long, glowering redbrick Victorian building that could have been a factory. Salisbury and I were on the second floor; the toilets and showers, which stood in an open row, each exposed to its neighbor, were in the basement. Each student was required to do manual work for ten to twelve hours a week, according to Moody, whose quotations were an early analogue of Chairman Mao's little red book, inculcating in us "the dignity of manual labor." My task with four other boys was to pick the eyes out of potatoes. For the amount that was required each night the job took us a solid one hour and forty-five minutes, during which time we worked nonstop, singing, cracking jokes, but otherwise totally focused on our work, which began right after breakfast, at seven-fifteen, and ended at nine, just before our first class. Our supervisor was a short, stocky middle-aged man—Eddie Benny—a former army sergeant who treated us as recalcitrant, not to say unfit, recruits who had to be ridden constantly.

The daily routine was not only rigorous, it was also long, repetitive, and unrelieved by any of the urban amusements I had grown accustomed to in Cairo. Mount Hermon had a post office and a store, which was open only a few hours a day, where you could buy toothpaste, postcards and stamps, candy bars, and a tiny selection of books. Classes ran until noon. All meals included grace, and lunch was followed by announcements about sports and club meetings. At one we broke for two hours of sports.

Afternoon classes resumed from four till six. Dinner was immediately followed by a short break period for activities. Then we were confined ("locked in" would be a better phrase) in our rooms between eight and ten-fifteen for a two-and-a-quarter-hour study period, policed by floor officers. These were students elevated to this position not because of seniority or academic accomplishment but for mysterious reasons having to do with "leadership," a word I heard for the first time at Mount Hermon. Talking during study hall was forbidden. At ten-fifteen we were allowed a fifteen-minute bathroom and tooth-brushing seance, then lights out and silence.

Each student was allowed two Saturday afternoons per semester to go to Greenfield, a miserable little place about ten miles away. Other than that, except for sport team trips, we were imprisoned in Mount Hermon's stifling, claustrophobic regimen for three months. Phones were both scarce and rare. My parents called me once from New York before they returned to Cairo to break the news that "Dr. Rubendall and we thought that you should repeat your junior year, even though technically you passed Upper Five." My father came on the line. "If you graduate next spring you'll only be sixteen. That's too young to go to university. So you'll be at that school"—he often forgot the school's name—"for two years. You're a lucky fellow!" he said cheerily, and without irony. "I wish I had had your chances." I knew he meant this, although I realized that as someone who had struggled hard earlier in his life he also slightly resented the privileged life he was giving me. I remembered the shock I had felt a few weeks earlier in London, when, having put us and Albert in rooms and suites at the Savoy with no expense spared, and having taken us to fancy restaurants, theaters, or concerts every night (including the most memorable musical comedy I ever saw, *Kiss Me Kate* with Alfred Drake and Patricia Morison, and a super *H.M.S. Pinafore* with Martyn Green at the Savoy Theatre), he rounded on me angrily for spending sixpence to buy a theater program. "Do you think you're the son of a rich man, throwing money away like that?" he said harshly. When I turned to my mother for help and comfort, she explained, "He had to work so hard," leaving me speechless and shamed, unable to point out the disparity between the rage over sixpence and the vast expenses being disbursed in luxury hotels and restaurants.

"Goodbye, sweetheart. When you feel blue," my mother ended the call impetuously, "try not to be alone. Find someone and sit with them." Her voice started to quiver disturbingly. "And think of me and how much I miss you." The void around me increased. "Daddy says we must go. I love you, darling." Then, nothing. Why, I remember asking myself in the silence, had I been sent so far away to this dreadful, godforsaken place? But these thoughts were blown away by the dry New England voice of Mr. Fred McVeigh, the French teacher, in whose tiny Crossley apartment I had just received my parents' call. "Okay?" he asked me laconically as if to say, if you're done, please return to your room. Which I did, with the dawning realization that here were no lingering, suggestive communications but only cut-and-dry, mean-what-you-say exchanges, which in their own way, I discovered, were just as coded and complex as the ones I had supposedly left behind.

A day later I wandered over to see Mr. Edmund Alexander, the tennis coach and English teacher. Aside from Dr. Rubendall, "Ned" Alexander was the only other Cairo connection at Hermon. I had been told about him by Freddie Maalouf, a close family friend who had been a classmate of Ned's. Small, dark, and wiry, wearing a white wool tennis sweater, Alexander was not at all welcoming. We stood facing each other across a tan station wagon parked in the driveway of his large white clapboard house. "Yes?" he asked curtly. "I'm from Cairo," I said enthusiastically. "Freddie Maalouf urged me to look you up and say hello." Not a line softened in his hard, leathery expression. "Oh, yes, Freddie Maalouf," was all he said, without a single additional comment. Undaunted I switched into Arabic, thinking that his and my native language might open up a more generous avenue of interaction. It had exactly the opposite effect. Stopping me in midsentence, Alexander held up his right hand, "No brother"—a very Arab locution, I thought, even though uttered in English—"no Arabic here. I left all that behind. Here we are Americans"—another Arabic turn of phrase, instead of "We're in America now"—"and we should talk and act like Americans."

It was worse than I thought. All I wanted was some friendly contact emanating from home, something to make an opening in the immense fabric of loneliness and separation that I felt surrounding me. Alexander revealed himself as not only unfriendly but something of an antagonist. He immediately placed me on the varsity–junior varsity tennis ladder, which meant weeks of challenge matches that protected the varsity from newcomers, and when those ended with the first onset of snow in early November I was established (unfairly I thought) on the JV list. Then for a year I had nothing more to do with Alexander, whom I would see with his wife, the senior Mount Hermon farmer's daughter, tooling around on campus in their station wagon, being as American as could be. I became a charge of the British JV coach and American history teacher, Hugh Silk, to whose "coaching" I brought all my residual anti-British sentiment. Even though I had won the top spot, he kept me at number 2 because, he once told me admonishingly, I wasn't fit to be number 1. Too many gestures, too many complaints, too many temperamental outbursts proved that I wasn't, he said, "equable enough."

Alexander's behavior proved the sagacity of my father's minatory observation that in the United States one should stay away from the Arabs. "They'll never do anything for you and will always pull you down." He illustrated this by putting out his hands flat and bringing them down to two feet from the floor. "They'll always be a hindrance. They neither keep what's good about Arab culture, nor show any solidarity with each other." He never gave examples, but the graphic figure he made with his hands and the definitive way he said it suggested no exception or qualification to the *aperçu*. Both Alexander's reaction to my banal overture and Silk's disciplinary iron fist–velvet glove approach turned out to be a more subtle form of moral pressure than what I had encountered in years of often brutal confrontations with British authority in my Egyptian or Palestinian schools. There, at least you knew that *they* were your enemies. At Hermon, the going currency was "common or shared values," care and concern for the student, interest in such intangibles as leadership and good citizenship, words of encouragement, admonishment, praise administered with a kind of fastidiousness I never dreamed of in VC, where war was a constant feature of daily life, with no palliatives either offered by the authorities or accepted by us, the students. Judgment in the Unites States was constant but concealed under a teasing fabric of softly rolling words and phrases, all of them in the end borne up by the unassailable moral authority of the teachers.

I also soon learned that you could never really find out why or on what basis you were judged, as I was, inadequate for a role or status that relatively objective indicators like grades, scores, or match victories entitled you to. While I was at Mount Hermon I was never appointed a floor officer, a table head, a member of the student council, or valedictorian (officially designated as number 1 in the class) and salutatorian (officially number 2) although I had the qualifications. And I never knew why. But I soon discovered that I would have to be on my guard against authority and that I needed to develop some mechanism or drive not to be discouraged by what I took to be efforts to silence or deflect me from being who I was rather than becoming who they wanted me to be. In the process I began a lifelong struggle and attempt to demystify the capriciousness and hypocrisy of a power whose authority depended absolutely on its ideological self-image as a moral agent, acting in good faith and with unimpeachable intentions. Its unfairness, in my opinion, depended principally on its prerogative for changing its bases of judgment. You could be perfect one day, but morally delinquent the next, even though your behavior was the same. For example, Silk and Alexander taught us not to say things like "Good shot!" to our tennis opponents. Never give them anything or concede anything; make your opponent work extra hard. But I recall that once during a close match against Williston Academy I was taken aside and reprimanded for having made my opponent pick up a ball that *may* have been closer to me. "Take the extra step," I was told, and was made silently furious at the shifting grounds for judgment. But what developed in my encounters with the largely hypocritical authority at Mount Hermon was a newfound will that had nothing to do with the "Edward" of the past but relied on the slowly forming identity of another self beneath the surface.

It soon became clear to me in my homesick disorientation that except for the words of advice in my weekly letter from my mother I had to deal with the daily routine at Hermon entirely on my own. Academically, the going was relatively easy and sometimes actually enjoyable. Whereas in VC we had only the dry material itself to deal with, none of it prettified or packaged, at Mount Hermon much that was required of us was prepared for by elaborate, simplifying instructions. Thus, our forceful and articulate English teacher (also the golf coach), Mr. Jack Baldwin, took us through one month of reading and analyzing *Macbeth* by minute studies of character, motivation, diction, figural language, plot pattern, all of the topics broken down into subgroups, steps, progressions that led cumulatively to a notebookful of short essays capped by a summary paragraph or two on the meaning of the play. Altogether more rational and thoughtful than in previous schools, this system invigorated and challenged me, particularly by comparison with the Anglo-Egyptian style of studying literary texts where all we were required to do was to articulate the very narrowly defined "correct" answers.

During the first weeks Baldwin assigned us an essay topic of a very unpromising sort: "On Lighting a Match." I dutifully went to the library and proceeded through encyclopedias, histories of industry, chemical manuals in search of what matches were; I then more or less systematically summarized and transcribed what I found and, rather proud of what I had compiled, turned it in. Baldwin almost immediately asked me to come and see him during his office hours, which was an entirely novel concept, since VC's teachers never had offices, let alone office hours. Baldwin's office was a cheery little place with postcard-covered walls, and as we sat next to each other on two easy chairs he complimented me on my research. "But is that the most interesting way to examine what happens when someone lights a match? What if he's trying to set fire to a forest, or light a candle in a cave, or, metaphorically, illuminate the obscurity of a mystery like gravity, the way Newton did?" For literally the first time in my life a subject was opened up for me by a teacher in a way that I immediately and excitedly responded to. What had previously been repressed and stifled in academic study—repressed in order that thorough and correct answers be given to satisfy a standardized syllabus and a routinized exam designed essentially to show off powers of retention, not critical or imaginative faculties—was awakened, and the complicated process of intellectual discovery (and self-discovery) has never stopped since. The fact that I was never at home or at least at Mount Hermon, out of place in nearly every way, gave me the incentive to find my territory, not socially but intellectually.

The Browsing Room in the library basement provided me an escape from the often insufferable daily routine. It housed a record player (33 rpm records had just been introduced) and several bookshelves of novels, essays, and translations. I listened to a heavy three-record album of *The Marriage of Figaro* conducted by von Karajan, with Erich Kunz,

Elisabeth Schwartzkopf, George London, and Irmgaard Seefried, over and over again; I read some of the many sets of American literary classics (Cooper's *The Leatherstocking Tales,* Twain's travels and novels, Hawthorne and Poe stories) with considerable excitement, since they revealed a complete, parallel world to the Anglo-Egyptian one in which I had been immersed in Cairo.

But the major breakthrough for me was in music, which, along with religion, played a substantial role in the school's programs. I tried out for and made the chapel choir, as well as the entirely secular glee club. We were all required to go to chapel services four times a week (including Sunday), where the organist, one Carleton L'Hommedieu, played a robust prelude and postlude, generally by Bach, but occasionally by second-rate American composers such as John Knowles Paine and George Chadwick. During one of these early services I found myself impulsively driven to go to speak to L'Hommy, as everyone called him behind his back, about piano lessons. My wasteful years at VC had taken the life out of my piano career, but listening to records and L'Hommy's playing inspired me to begin again.

L'Hommy was about five feet eight inches and cadaverously thin, given to plaid bow ties and striped shirts, always very well put together (no one ever saw him tieless or in shorts). He had a disconcertingly mincing walk, with his two exceptionally fine and slender hands often held out (like a rabbit's) as he tripped along, but at the keyboard he cut a very confident, even authoritative figure. I owe him the fact that he took me seriously and was never impatient with me as a pianist. Still, L'Hommy typified the cautious, often pedantic kind of teacher who would constantly try to hold the student back. His teaching style notwithstanding, his superb playing and music history teaching filled me with enthusiasm. Soon music was an all-consuming knowledge as well as experience: I listened, played, read, and read about it systematically (in the library's *Grove's Dictionary of Music and Musicians*) for the first time in my life, and I have never stopped. But there had to be, I now realize, a L'Hommedieu figure for me to react against, someone whose competence gave him the right to an on-the-whole "measured" (not wildly enthusiastic) judgment. We rarely saw eye to eye, but at least I had a hard taskmaster's ear to prod me on my way, *against* his, always held in check, as, for example, by his excessively polite "Oh yes,

Ed! That was very nice. But don't you think that the insecurities of the opening could be fixed up," etc., after my playing the gavotte of the Bach G-minor English Suite for him, and toned down a bit. I remember one steamy Sunday afternoon practicing the gavotte with the windows open, and after working meticulously on the little things that my teacher had caught me with, I decided to let out all stops, playing the piece through passionately, the way I felt it. At that moment L'Hommy and Mr. Mirtz, an elderly English teacher, walked by the very window and obviously heard and saw me. "Hey, that's great Ed," was Mirtz's unbuttoned expostulation. "Uh-uh," was L'Hommy's own rather disapproving response. I played on, giving myself even more steam. I remember that on the next meeting we switched abruptly from the Bach to (in my view) a dinky, tinkly C-major Haydn Sonata: "Solomon, the very fine British pianist, played it in his last recital." So there it was, his Solomon versus my Rubenstein.

The abrasive rough and tumble of my daily life in the six-hundred-student boarding school was nonetheless unpleasant and sometimes intolerable. There was no cultural background for friendship of the kind I had experienced at VC. I roomed with Bob Salisbury (who was one class below me) for two years, but we were never close in any but superficial ways. I felt that there was no depth, no ease, to the Americans, only the surface jokiness and anecdotal high spirits of teammates, which never satisfied me. There was always the feeling that what I missed with my American contemporaries was other languages, Arabic mainly, in which I lived and thought and felt along with English. They seemed less emotional, with little interest in articulating their attitudes and reactions. This was the extraordinary homogenizing power of American life, in which the same TV, clothes, ideological uniformity, in films, newspapers, comics, etc., seemed to limit the complex intercourse of daily life to an unreflective minimum in which memory has no role. I felt myself to be encumberingly full of memories, and the best friends I made at Mount Hermon were recent immigrants like Gottfried Brieger, an extremely ironic German student, and the socially awkward but intellectually curious Neil Sheehan.

The mythology of D. L. Moody dominated the school and made it the not-quite-first-rate place it was. There was the "dignity of manual labor" part, which seemed to me totally silly. There seemed to be unquestioned assent to the man's incredible importance: it was my first encounter with enthusiastic mass hypnosis by a charlatan, because except for two of us, not one teacher or student expressed the slightest doubt that Moody was worthy of the highest admiration. The only other dissenter was Jeff Brieger, who cornered me in the Browsing Room and said, *"Mais c'est dégoûtant,"* pointing at one of the many hagiographical studies we were meant to read.

And so it was with religion—the Sunday service, the Wednesday evening chapel, the Thursday noon sermon—dreadful, pietistic, non-denominational (I disliked that form of vacillation in particular) full of homilies, advice, how-to-live. Ordinary observations were encoded into Moodyesque sturdy Christianity in which words like "service" and "labor" acquired magical (but finally unspecifiable) meaning, to be repeated and intoned as what gave our lives "moral purpose." There had been nothing of that at V.C.; now it was a full load of the stuff. And no beatings, or bullying prefects. We were all Hermon boys, six hundred of us marching on after Moody and Ira Sankey, his faithful sidekick.

Clothes were a problem for me. Everyone wore corduroys, jeans, lumber jackets, boots. While in London my father had taken me to a Dickensian establishment next door to the Savoy called Thirty Shilling Tailors and bought me a very dark gray suit. I also had the VC assortment of gray slacks, a blazer, and a few dress shirts, all of them packed into two gigantic beige leather suitcases, along with a stamp collection, two albums of family photos, and a mounting pile of my mother's letters, each of which I preserved carefully. I had to write my parents to get permission to buy a more appropriate wardrobe and by October I was almost but not quite like everyone else. It took me another month to master the academic system completely, and by late November I was (to my surprise) astonishing my classmates with my intellectual performances. Why or how I did well I do not really know to this day, since following my mother's injunction not to be blue or alone I was both, and alienated from the extended stag sessions in the Blue Cloud (the smoking and pool room), or the little cliques that formed in Crossley, or around the various athletic teams. I longed to be back in Cairo; I kept calculating the time difference of seven hours (leaving my bedside alarm set on Cairo time), missing our family's Cairo food during school meals, an unappetizing regime that began with chicken à la king on Monday and ended with cold cuts and potato salad on Sunday night— and above all missing my mother, each of whose letters deepened the wound of abandonment and separation I felt. Sometimes I would pull out one of my massive suitcases from under the bed, leaf through the albums or letters and begin gently to cry, quickly reminding myself of my father's "Buck up boy; don't be a sissy. Pull your back up. Back, back."

I experienced the changing of seasons from fall to winter with dread, as something unfamiliar, having come from a basically warm and dry climate. I have never gotten over my feelings of revulsion for snow, which I first saw on my sixteenth birthday, November 1, 1951. Since that time, try as I might, I have found little to enjoy or admire about snow. For me snow signified a kind of death. But what I suffered from was the social vacancy of Mount Hermon's setting. I had spent all my life in two rich, teeming, historically dense metropolises, Jerusalem and Cairo, and now I was totally bereft of anything except the pristine woods, apple orchards, and the Connecticut River valley and hills stripped of their history. The nearest town of Greenfield has long symbolized for me the enforced desolation of middle America.

On the other hand, a small number of teachers and students, as well as subjects like literature and music, gave me moments of great pleasure, normally somewhat tinged with guilt. "Don't forget how much I miss and love you; your absence has made everything seem so empty," my mother would repeat down the years, making me feel that I couldn't, mustn't feel all right unless she was with me, and that it was a serious betrayal for me to do something that I liked doing if she wasn't present. This gave my American days a sense of impermanence, and even though I spent three quarters of the year in the United States, it was always Cairo to which I accorded stability.

The authorized school social life was with the Northfield Seminary for Young Ladies, six miles across the river. One could have football, movie, or dance dates on Saturdays only, but being an incredibly shy sexually inexperienced newcomer I could only look wistfully at the others holding hands, petting, kissing, and generally feeling each other up. This was like China to me, since Cairo had never provided anything like this practically sanctioned adultery (as my feverishly repressed mind represented the practice of necking to me), and without any acquaintance at Northfield I was the weekly wallflower, along with Brieger and one or two other forlorn souls. When I was eventually introduced to one or two girls, a second date rarely followed. It was only in my second and final year that I had any kind of limited success with girls.

To my increasing sadness, by early December 1951 I had become Americanized as "Ed Said" to everyone except Brieger, whose unbridled irony and polyglot wit seemed more precious to me every day, as more and more of my past seemed to slip away, worn away slowly but ineluctably by the American modalities of our routinized days and evenings. Even Tony Glockler, an early acquaintance who had grown up in Beirut, had gone through the changing machine. We used to speak Arabic and French to each other, but that soon stopped and we drifted apart. With no close friends, I battled my way through, trying more and more successfully to hold on to and develop the sensibility that resisted the American leveling and ideological herding that seemed to work so effectively on so many of my classmates.

It wasn't nostalgia for Cairo that kept me going, since I remembered all too acutely the dissonance I had always felt there as the non-Arab, the non-American American, the English-speaking and -reading warrior against the English, or the buffeted and cosseted son. Instead it was the beginning of a new independent strength that I sensed as I swam fifty laps during swimming practice, feeling my arms were going to fall off with leaden fatigue, my breath coming harder and harder, my legs dragging heavier still as I pumped them desperately, a germ that helped me think about how I was going to make a radio script out of "The Cask of Amontillado" for Baldwin's class, with me regulating the voices, volume, music (third movement of *Eine Kleine Nachtmusik,* where I wanted my audience to hear the courtly dance rhythm against the poor immured hero's weakening voice). Independent strength or nascent will: it marked the beginning of my refusal to be the passive "Ed Said" who went from one assignment or deadline to the next with scarcely a demurral.

Most of the school went home for Thanksgiving, a holiday that still means very little to me, even though my father had imposed a turkey dinner on us in Cairo for what he called "traditional reasons." For the three-week Christmas break, my father contacted his oldest brother's sons Abie and Charlie in New York, who together with their widowed mother, Emily, and sister, Dorothy, had moved to Queens shortly after Asaad's death in 1947. No Washington vacations after all.

Abie was fair-haired, gregarious, an open, kind man about ten years my senior; my mother thought that he most resembled my father in generosity, loyalty, and transparency. There was what was considered a problematic strain in my uncle Al's family that came through Emily— she was a Saidah from Jaffa—and only Abie seemed to have been spared that much-remarked hereditary defect, which was a certain deviousness allied with a somewhat cretinous cackle that emerged disconcertingly for no particular reason.

Their apartment in Jackson Heights, 72-42 Fifty-first Drive, was on the second floor of a house in a row of identical townhouse lookalikes with which those streets were lined for mile upon mile on end. The space in the Said apartment became extremely cramped after I arrived with my gigantic suitcases (I could have left them over at school but neurotically and categorically refused to go anywhere without *all* my belongings). It must have been hell for my aunt and her children to have me there, but to their undying credit none made me feel unwelcome or in the way.

Abie and Charlie by now had regular jobs at a bank and insurance agency, respectively, and went to New York University night school in business. Dorothy still worked as a secretary at Reuben Donnelley, the enormous printing firm responsible for producing the phone book. The three of them were gone by about seven-thirty a.m. and did not return until eight or nine at night. Emily would prowl the apartment most of the morning, talking constantly to herself in Arabic punctuated by peals of mysterious laughter, making beds (but not mine, which I made up soon as I could), picking up clothes, puttering in the kitchen-cum-dining room with lots of clattering, breaking, slamming, all of it without pattern or obvious system. She seemed quite deaf to the sounds around her, so even though she turned on the radio to some dreadful talk and music show, I was usually able to keep switching it to WQXR, even though that snooty station—its nine-thirty "Piano Personalities" show being my favorite—was, I thought, too often insanely submerged in Barney's and Rogers Peet commercials. These sometimes caught the attention of Emily, who would then sing along and, later, gratuitously sing alone, "You save at Barney's, you save at Barney's," certainly unaware of what she was saying. At around ten she would ask me if I'd like something to eat: I never ventured to the fridge or breadbox on my own, partly because even if she was making beds or messing about in the bathroom, she'd suddenly interrupt herself and shoot back to the kitchen like a bull to its *querencia*. I quickly understood that she not only cared for the kitchen but also guarded it, as if it contained some sort of primitive treasure hoard.

At about noon she usually announced that she was going out and I was made to understand that if she left I couldn't remain at home unattended or alone. I usually took the Woodside bus to the Jackson Heights subway station, then flew into Times Square, where I had my daily lunch of a Nedick's hot dog and orange drink and began to walk around, mainly among newsreels and third-run films plus an occasional foray into Ripley's Believe-it-or-Not. Museums, libraries, places of profit and education seemed not to be part of my perspective, but from Dorothy I discovered that quiz shows gave away tickets to their live audiences, so I did frequent those at Rockefeller Center for a while, then moved on to more films and newsreels (continuous in those days) before heading for Jackson Heights in the late afternoon. On Christmas Day there'd be a short phone call from Cairo but with my cousins and Emily requested by my parents for a formulaic salutation, I had the briefest but satisfying feeling from my mother's incredibly warm "Happy Christmas, darling," and then it was over.

Abie and I usually did companionable things on the weekend evenings that he wasn't busy with his Masonic lodge. My cousins belonged to an Arabic-Protestant church in Bay Ridge, Brooklyn (two hours and several changes away by subway), which provided the "Syrian" community, as the Arab-Americans were known in those days, with a social center, at which *haflés* (dinner and dancing) made it possible for everyone to mix together over kibbeh and hummus. Abie and I ended up by going together without the others, I quite reluctantly, since I found the elderly Arab-Americans lost in a world of commerce—rug selling, groceries, furniture. They were strange, almost Swiftlike creatures, with Poconos summer homes, fragmentary 1920s Arabic, and studiously patriotic Americanism: the phrase "Uncle Sam" appeared regularly in their speech, although they spoke more about the "Communist threat" than (to the disappointed ears of a Palestinian teenager) about Israel. The women were dowdy and unhappy at being separated from their villages, marooned in Brooklyn, their daughters overdressed, gum-chewing, squeaky-voiced bobby-soxers.

Or Abie and I would go to the weekly Arabic film showing on Atlantic Avenue, Saturdays at midnight, which got us back to Queens at four a.m., totally exhausted. But the effort was leavened for me by seeing sultry actresses like Naeema Akif, Samia Gamal, or Tahia Carioca dance and Ismail Yassin shoot off his moronic yet endearingly toothy one-liners. It was the Cairo lilt in their dialogue that made us nostalgic as we rode back in the empty clattering train, but after about three such excursions we were too worn out for more.

Once during the vacation I went to Bay Ridge by myself as a guest of Aunt Salimeh and Uncle Amin Badr. She was a lively, witty, pretty, and unmistakably lusty woman in her forties, and he—Faris Badr's younger brother, who had been resident in the United States for at least fifty years—was an incredibly precise, very carefully put together man (never had I seen such razor-sharp trouser creases and so fastidiously pressed shirts) in his middle seventies, a retired sheet and towel salesman. Salimeh's volubility and irreverence, which she exaggerated to further dramatize the age difference between her and Amin, amused me enormously, a vivid contrast to my life at Queens; besides, Salimeh's connection by marriage to my mother's family I treated subliminally as an antidote to the Saidian dourness of my father's far less colorful family.

I would meet Salimeh at her Fourth Avenue store, Mrs. Beder's Bra and Corset Shop, where with two assistants she labored from early morning to evening. My mother was a customer, I knew, as was Eva Malik, though both found Salimeh's tiresome complaints against her plainly exploited underlings both comic and unseemly. "They keep asking me for more money and an eight-hour day. Do you think I only work eight hours? *Hawdy*"—mountain Lebanese for "those"—"are communistic ideas," she would say, but never so solemnly as not to let me in fact stand up for the girls. "You're too soft," she'd say with a smile. "You need more of your father's guts." What particularly endeared me to her was not only her wonderful abundant cooking for dinner that night, nor the comfortable bed in a room of my own, nor even the gay banter between herself and the "old guy," as she called him, but her ingenuity for promoting her trade. There, right in her shop window, she had installed a headless, legless manikin whose ample bosom was clad in one of her shocking-pink bras. Underneath the two breasts was a taunting sign that read: UNITED WE STAND, DIVIDED WE FALL. "Doncha think I know what I'm doing here? Your uncle Amin is scandalized by the model, but doncha think I'll ever pay attention to him. He won't come near the place, but wait until I put up my corset display!"

The next morning as we set off, she to work, me to Jackson Heights, she stuffed my overnight bag with a jar of pickles, a container of green olives, and a large bag of spinach cakes that she had baked. "Give my regards to your people," she said, "especially Abie. He'd make a good husband." It wasn't until some years later that I started to see her as a kind of Wife of Bath figure, elemental and irrepressible, hopelessly out of place among the solemn Syrian denizens of Bay Ridge, borne along by a rare energy and humor that created a bond between us that has lasted till now, retired as she is, and mostly amnesiac, in Florida.

THE UTTER LONELINESS AT MOUNT HERMON SEEMED heightened three weeks after I returned to school in early January. We were entombed, I felt, in the aftermath of another huge ravaging blizzard, trees bent over in snowdrifts of ten feet nearly everywhere, temperatures near zero, a bright sun lighting up the unyielding whiteness almost luridly. Hatless I went from dorm to class, to gym, to dining hall, busily cursing the sense of confinement and impediment I felt all around me, totally unprepared for the message delivered to me as I left my late-afternoon chemistry class with the diminutive, bespectacled Dr. Paul Bowman. A student helper from the headmaster's office was standing at the door waiting for me; he said, "Dr. Rubendall would like to see you now." As we trudged off together I wondered almost absentmindedly what new infraction I had committed, even though my general behavior at Mount Hermon had been, I thought, unimpeachable. There were no gangs, no hated masters, no volatile political situations. Rubendall was the one urbane and totally agreeable man in the school, partly because of his fond memories of his days as basketball coach in Cairo, partly, I speculated, because at six foot four, with a massive yet graceful bearing and great charm, he exuded a kind of confidence that had little to do with the Moody legacy that seemed to weigh down the others. I couldn't imagine him having much to do with the dour Ned Alexander, though both had Cairo in their background. But I was always glad when Rubendall picked me out of the crowd—"Ed," he would say using my new Americanized name, "how are things going? I hope you're enjoying Hermon. My best to your parents and to Cairo. Drop up to the house some evening," which I of course didn't, but the man's genuine welcome and friendliness carried me a long way past the daily gloom of the school, even though during my two years there this was the only time I entered his house.

Rubendall greeted me warmly. "I've just heard from Cairo, Ed. Your family's fine. The news, or what we have of it, is pretty alarming, but everyone's safe." Not knowing what exactly he was referring to, but alarmed nevertheless, I asked for more details. "There have been riots, much of the city has been burned, no one knows who is behind it. Come up to the house at seven and we'll see what the TV has." Of course I did, but the reception was extremely poor: images of large crowds and burning buildings alternated with unclear pictures of officials, generals, and politicians presided over by a smudgy photograph of King Farouk taken well before he had become a 350-pound caricature. It was a Monday evening: the fire had taken place two days earlier, and somehow my father had gotten through to Rubendall on the phone.

I was truly frightened as much for what might have happened to my parents, my father especially, in this unprecedented maelstrom, as for the possibility that I would have nothing to return to. I knew that something had irrevocably changed. The stunning scenes of destruction that lasted for about twenty seconds on the Rubendall family TV—he and his wife stood protectively next to me as I sat squarely in front of the large brown console—originated somewhere else and from somebody I had never imagined as being lodged in the familiar Cairo of my early days: "impersonal forces"? enraged people? foreign spies? I could not imagine nor articulate the causes of what I saw before me. The next day, reading the Tuesday *Boston Globe* in the Crossley lounge, I was stunned to see my father's name in a three-page report that detailed the enormous damage done on Black Saturday.

It was the first time that our existence had taken so objective and, to me, so vulnerably assertive a form. "The Standard Stationery," ran the passage, "owned by an American citizen, William A. Said, was totally gutted by the mob as it moved down Malika Farida Street, destroying the British Turf Club, a noted British Cairo institution . . ." Other familiar places mentioned were Papazian's Music shop, where I had bought music books and records, Kodak, Salon Vert, Gattegno. All of them up-market, obviously foreign, right in the heart of the modern colonial city. The mob was stopped by a valiant police captain (who for his pains was later fired) at the head of a handful of his men just at the beginning of the Kasr el Nil bridge, which led across the Nile to Zamalek, our residence. And there but for that captain . . . I couldn't possibly take in everything that had happened, although my mother's letter about ten days later filled in some of the blanks. The important thing is that both our main places of business (B Branch was destroyed too) had been reduced to rubble; a month later they sent me pictures of the damage, the only recognizable objects being some Sebel tables and chairs twisted into surrealistic shapes beneath which were fragments of typewriters, Ellams duplicators, and one large but apparently un-harmed Chubb safe (an image later to be used by my father in his sales material) and huge amounts of charred paper. My mother sadly com-mented on how at that time my cousins and aunt expressed to my father their desire to separate themselves from the firm, so summoning all his financial reserves (I never really understood from where) he bought them out, leaving himself alone in charge of a completely ruined estab-lishment. "All right, Lampas" he was quoted by my mother as telling his old manager, "let's roll up our sleeves"—the phrase has stuck in my head for over forty-six years—"and begin again." And so they did: clearing up the debris with a few faithful helpers, announcing that busi-ness as usual would be conducted from his unharmed office across the road, getting all the requisite bank loans, plus small compensation for damages from a hastily convened government commission, beginning reconstruction on an altogether grander and more luxurious scale. By the time I arrived home in June for the summer vacation the last re-maining effects on his business of the January 26, 1952, fire—apparently set by the Muslim Brothers—were a string of photographs showing the ruins that he had had framed and hung behind the cashier's desk and in his office.

I still marvel at his almost superhuman recovery. I never heard him speak regretfully about the prefire days or about how much he lost or about what a catastrophe it had been for him. And the twice-monthly typed letters kept arriving on precisely the same day, as if nothing had changed, except news of arriving "goods" as he called them, supplied to SSCo with emergency speed by his European and American suppliers. Trying perhaps to penetrate the mystery of his overwhelming strength, I wrote my mother complaining that his formal, typed, obviously dictated letters signed "Yours truly, W. A. Said" were perplexing and that "I couldn't understand" why he never wrote me a truly personal letter. I was concerned about the pressures on him and wanted some human indication of his continued and assured presence in my life. "Dear Edward," ran a one-page letter that arrived two weeks later, written in his untidy scrawl, "Your mother tells me that you don't like my typed letters to you, but I am very busy as you can imagine. Anyway, here is a hand-written letter for you. Yours truly, W. A. Said." I kept the letter for at least twenty years, since it seemed to symbolize perfectly my father and his attitude to me. It was as if he believed that expression and feeling could never be equal or inter-changeable, and that if they were there was something clearly wrong with either or both. So he kept his council, reserving his efforts for what he did, which he protected with the silence or lapidary style that so maddened me.

All his life my father was deliberately circumspect about what property or wealth he possessed, and now that he had to rebuild a business with a large load of debt he became uncharacteristically voluble on the subject of his obligations. "Can't you see," he would say exasperatedly to us dozens and dozens of times "how heavily I am in debts?" using the plural "s" as an emphatic reminder that this was no ordinary amount of debt. "Debts" in fact plagued us (as a family) for three or four years, until once, while I was in his office, taking over for him during a summer afternoon, I started idly leafing through his accountant's report for the recently concluded fiscal year. I was astounded at the many many thousands of pounds he was making on a quarterly basis. When I raised this with him, he looked at me with great contempt. "Stop talking nonsense, Edward. Perhaps one day you'll learn to read a balance sheet. In the meantime concentrate on your studies, and let me take care of the business." But it was difficult not to notice that during the mid-fifties my parents had more frequent and larger parties, acquired handsome objects, and had moved out of the Sharia Aziz Osman apartment and into a larger and luxuriously appointed one in a building next door that housed embassy residences. Nonetheless, his protests about being "in debts" never stopped.

By the early spring of 1952 I had suspended my feelings of paralyzed solitude—missing my mother, my room, the familiar sounds and objects that embodied Cairo's grace—and allowed another less sentimental, less incapacitated self to take over. Forty years later a similar process occurred, when I had been diagnosed with leukemia and discovered myself for a while almost completely gripped by the grimmest thoughts of imminent suffering and death. My principal concern was how terrible it was to have to separate from my family and indeed from the whole edifice of my life, which in thinking about it I realized I loved very much. Only when I saw that this dire scenario constituted a paralyzing block at the center of my consciousness could I begin to see its outlines, which helped me first to divine and then make out its limits. Soon I became conscious of being able to move this debilitating block off center, and then to focus, sometimes only very briefly, on other, much more concrete things, including enjoyment of an accomplishment, music, or a particular encounter with a friend. I have not lost the acute sense of vulnerability to illness and death I felt on discovering my condition, but it has become possible—as with my early exile—to regard all the day's hours and activities (including my obsession with my illness) as altogether provisional. Within that perspective I can evaluate which activities to hold on to, perform, and enjoy. I never lost my sense of dislike and discomfort at Mount Hermon, but I did learn to minimize its effect on me, and in a kind of self-forgetting way I plunged into the things I found it possible to enjoy.

Most, if not all, were intellectual. During my first year we were all required to take a simple-minded class (doubtless an idea of Dr. Moody's) designed to make us pious. This not only repeated the material I had already gone through for my confirmation, but went further in literalistic and, I must say, fundamentalist Old Testament interpretation than I would have thought was humanly possible. Amos and Hosea, Isaiah and Micah, stick in my mind: we not only read over the texts, student by student, but no less relentlessly paraphrased what they said, literally, unimaginatively, repetitiously. Were it not that my record was so good I'd have had the same Bible teacher (Chester something) in senior year, with the New Testament as our text, but instead I was allowed to take the alternate Bible IV given by the school chaplain and co-swimming coach Reverend Whyte, known to all as Friar Tuck for his portliness, red hair, and all-around good humor. I was seventeen, but thanks to his openness and total absence of dogmatism we had a superb reading course in classical philosophy, from Plato and Aristotle, through the Enlightenment to Kierkegaard.

Try as I could, I didn't much thrive as a sportsman. I made the swimming and tennis teams and won events and matches, but the actual competition often made me physically ill. At lunch in the spring of my first year a senior boy (the student council president and soccer captain Dale Conley) was going from table to table slipping small bits of paper underneath each plate. Mine read simply, "14 out of 157"; it was my class ranking, a much higher one than I had imagined possible. During the senior year my rank was to alternate between 1 and 2, yet at the end of the summer I spent the night before I was due to return in a hastily installed bed in my parents' Dhour el Shweir bedroom begging not to be sent back. The inevitable departure took place at dawn, and we drove to Beirut in total silence. Once back I was given the odious job of pressing shirts in the laundry, but after a fuss and partly due to my academic success, I was mercifully moved to a sinecure in the library.

By the middle of that second year, with college applications on our minds, I had consciously grasped that there would be no imminent return to Cairo. I envied my sisters at Cairo's English School, the comfort of being together and at home, the solidity, as I imagined it, of well-furnished certainty, all of which were going to be denied me except during brief returns for the summer. The Free Officers' Revolution had occurred in July 1952, but with the avuncular, pipe-smoking General Mohammed Naguib in charge—the king having been sent off to Italy—I had the impression, as did my parents and their friends, that this new situation wasn't so different from the old, except that now there would be younger, more serious men in charge, and corruption would end. Little more than that. Our little community—Dirliks, Ghorras, Mirshaks, Fahoums—Shawam all, making money handsomely, living incredibly well, continued their lives as if nothing had happened. And after a few weeks in Cairo during June and the first half of July, we moved off as usual for the long dreary period in Dhour. I experienced the Egyptian part of my life in an unreflecting, almost sham, way during the summer, slipping into it the moment I arrived in Cairo, whereas my American life was acquiring a more durable, more independent reality, unrelated to Cairo, my family, and the familiar old habits and creature comforts that my mother kept in readiness for me.

It was on a bright spring afternoon in 1953 during tennis practice that Bob Salisbury, passing the courts on his way back to Crossley from the post office, shouted to me that he had heard college acceptances were in. Rushing quickly to the post office, I discovered that both Princeton and Harvard had accepted me, though I had never visited the latter and had little idea what it represented other than the smoothly genteel impression made on me by Skiddy von Stade, the visiting Harvard admissions gentleman, whom L'Hommy had identified further as a "Long Island polo player." When I returned to the court with my letters, the coach, Ned Alexander, said, "Good. Now you'll play on the freshman team at Harvard," but for the strangest and, as I look back on them now, the flimsiest of reasons I quickly made up my mind to go to Princeton, which I had visited once with my parents the summer before entering Mount Hermon. We had gone there from New York to visit relatives of Dhour el Shweir neighbors of ours, and their presence there, although I had never returned to see them again, the leafy pleasant afternoon of tabbouleh and stuffed grape leaves in their house, drew me to Princeton for entirely fictitious reasons. In my serene and superficial fantasy it seemed to be Mount Hermon's opposite: non–New England, comfortable, unaustere, idyll–like, a projection of Cairo life in the United States.

A month later I learned that my father was going to come from Cairo, at enormous expense, for my graduation, and that afterward he and I and my cousins Abie and Charlie would go on a tour of New England in their 1951 Ford. This trip was a graduation present for me.

During my last weeks at Hermon I reflected that though in all my activities I had distinguished myself I remained a kind of *lusus naturae,* a peculiar odd boy out. I had won letters and important matches both in swimming and tennis, I had done brilliantly in my academic work, I had become a pianist of distinction, yet I seemed incapable of achieving the moral stature—I can think of no other phrase to describe it— that the school's general approval could bestow on one. I was known as someone with a powerful brain and an unusual past, but I was not fully a part of the school's corporate life. Something was missing. Something, I was to discover, that was called "the right attitude."

There were students like Dale Conley or, in my class, Gordie Robb and Fred Fisher (unlike, say, Brieger and me) who seemed to have no rough edges: they offended no one, they were well liked, they had a remarkable capacity never to say anything that might be wrong or offensive, and they gave me the impression of fitting in perfectly. In short, they were natural choices for various honorific jobs and titles— captains, student council members, floor officers, or table heads (in the dining room). All of this had nothing to do either with their evident intelligence or with academic performance, which though above average was not distinguished. Still, there was a certain chosenness about them, an aura, that I clearly lacked. Yet one couldn't describe these students as being teacher's favorites nor ascribe their status to something resembling hereditary nobility or wealth, as might have been the case in the world I came from.

Just a week before graduation, a knock on the door announced Fred Fisher, a student council member, fellow swim-team member, floor officer in Crossley, and one of the most visibly successful boys in the school. Salisbury and I were, I recall, finishing our term papers. Although I was about to graduate, I was still imprisoned in my room for our nightly penance, but Fisher as floor officer could roam the dormitory at will. "Hey woz," he said, using a friendly appellation much in use then, "haven't you been first or second in the class? Academically, I mean."

I replied, "Yes, it's alternated between Ray Byrne and myself. He's first now I think, but I'm not absolutely sure. Why?"

Here Fisher, seated on my bed, seemed plainly uncomfortable. "I've never been higher than six or seven, but they've just told me I'm going to be salutatorian and Byrne's valedictorian. I can't figure it out. What happened?" Fisher's puzzlement at his unexpected elevation was genuine, but I was thunderstruck. I could make no reply to the just anointed Fred, who left our room a moment later with what seemed to me a troubled, even mystified, look on his face. I felt I was entitled to such a graduation honor and had been denied it, but in some strange yet peculiarly fitting way I knew I should *not* have been given it. So I was hurt, unable to accept the injustice, or to contest or understand what may after all have been a justified decision against me. Unlike Fisher, I was not a leader, nor a good citizen, nor pious, nor just all-round acceptable. I realized I was to remain the outsider, no matter what I did.

It was also at this point that I felt that coming from a part of the world that seemed to be in a state of chaotic transformation became the symbol of what was out of place about me. Mount Hermon School was primarily white: there were a handful of black students, mostly gifted athletes and one rather brilliant musician and intellect, Randy Peyton, but the faculty was entirely white (or white-masked, as in Alexander's case). Until the Fisher-graduation episode I felt myself to be colorless, but that forced me to see myself as marginal, non-American, alienated, marked, just when the politics of the Arab world began to play a greater and greater role in American life. I sat through the tedious graduation ceremonies in my cap and gown with an indifference that bordered on hostility: this was *their* event, not mine, even though I was unexpectedly given a biology prize for, I firmly believe, consolation. My father, having come from Cairo for what I thought would be a disappointment, was both elated and jocular. Without my mother (who had to stay home with my sisters) he was unusually talkative and engaging; far from needing her social expertise, he seemed to thrive without it, spending some amusing moments with the very German Brieger père, a Hahneman Medical School professor.

The key to my father's mood seemed to be his cheery satisfaction with a school that had at last turned me into a citizen with a cap on my head. At the postgraduation garden party he carried a large, circular package wrapped in brown paper. He was especially effusive with Rubendall, whose extraordinary charm carried everything before it. Towering over my father, he beamed at us both. "How wonderful of you to come all the way from Cairo. I'm so sorry that Mrs. Said couldn't make it. Isn't it great how Ed has done?" At this point my father gave me his fruit punch cup to hold and in his characteristically impetuous and untidy way started to tear at the wrapping paper to reveal an immense embossed silver plate, the kind that he and my mother must have commissioned from a Cairo bazaar silversmith. In his best presentational style he handed it rather pompously to the overjoyed Rubendall. "My wife and I wanted to give you this in grateful gratitude for what you've done for Edward." Pause. "In grateful gratitude." I was embarrassed at how lavish and eccentric both his gift and accompanying words were, especially considering how unfit I must have seemed to Rubendall and his colleagues for the position of either class valedictorian or salutatorian.

For a week my father and I, with Abie and Charlie (who did most of the driving) went to places like Keene, New Hampshire, and Boston, my father footing the bill for everything, his way of paying the two young men for their time and effort. I was anxious to get back to Cairo and home. I had had my fill of motels and dormitories, and even after two more weeks in New York at the well-appointed Stanhope Hotel, the desire to return to the Cairo I had left two years ago was overwhelmingly powerful.

X

RETURNING TO CAIRO IN THE SUMMER ALSO MEANT GOING back to Dhour. And, by the time I had become a Princeton under-graduate, Dhour had come pretty exclusively to mean Eva Emad, whose presence there I could count on. Given what happened to Lebanon a few years later—the 1958 civil war, the Palestinian decades of the seventies and eighties, the catastrophic seventeen-year civil war that erupted in 1975, the Israeli invasion of 1982—it was as if our unin-terrupted summers in Dhour prior to the upheavals were a kind of prolonged daydream whose center after I met Eva became the infini-tesimally slow growth of our romance. Nothing else I did then seemed to interdict or interrupt my concentration on seeing and being with her for most of the day, Sundays excepted.

We were drawn imperceptibly to each other: always playing doubles together, sitting next to each other, partnering each other in games of trump, a primitive genre of bridge, sharing small confidences. As a young woman from a conservative Arab family, Eva was reserved and correct, as women her age were supposed to be in the mid-1950s. Her education had ended after secondary school, and, although I did not realize it at the time, she was waiting for marriage, with no other career offered or contemplated. While I knew that I was more attracted and attached to her than I had been to any woman before, our future had

no place at all in my reflections or daydreams. Over three or four summers I found myself increasingly attracted to her, unable to do or say
more than what one said in informal, daily banter.

There was an illicit thrill in being close to her without anything
physically or even verbally overt passing between us. I felt I had to see
her every day, and spent every moment in her company searching for
some sign, however faint, that she cared for me as I did for her. But if
our attachment to each other remained unspoken, it became evident to
others, if only in the most casual way. "Have Eva and Edward already
played their doubles?" Nelly might ask; "You and Eva will sit there,"
someone might say at the movies; "Has Eva seen your new racquet?"
Neither of our parents had any knowledge of our friendship. Although
we would be apart for nine months of the year—she in Tanta while I
was in Princeton—when we were in Dhour our relationship resumed
as if we had seen each other the day before. We wrote, infrequently,
cordial and correct letters, and I carried hers in one of my pockets for
weeks on end, imagining myself to be closer to her by doing so.

It was inevitable that my mother would hear about Eva. I can
remember my father mentioning Eva's age—"When you're in your
prime she'll be a sixty-year-old woman. Do you know what that will
be like?"—and then adding one of those prepackaged phrases that
served the purpose of a minatory adage: "If you're single everyone will
invite you, but once you get married no one will look at you." At least
I knew where I stood with him, unlike with my mother. At first her
behavior was quite circumspect, suggesting little more than a sort of
neutral curiosity about Eva and my attitude toward her. Gradually her
tone hardened, becoming faintly challenging as she'd ask, "And I suppose Eva was there too?" Then Eva seemed to her to have overstepped
certain limits of propriety and decency as she remarked, "What do her
parents think that she is up to, spending all her time with young people
like you. Don't they realize that she's compromising her chances to find
a husband?"

By the time Eva and I had settled on each other in our glacierlike
progress, over about three years, I was subliminally aware that talking
to my mother about Eva, responding (however laconically) to her un-
solicited observations was to be avoided. Eva's age, her different, largely
idle, style of life, her religion (Greek Orthodox), and her francophony

clearly made my mother fearful, but I didn't suspect that she was determinedly set against my continuing liaison.

In the summer of 1956, when I was twenty and Eva was almost twenty-seven, the Tabbarah Club embarked on a group beach outing to Beirut. This was very different from our family excursions the decade before—there were no parents and no hours to be carefully observed. Our group destinations that year had been the Eden Roc pool, a California-style kidney-shaped basin attached to a restaurant-nightclub on a cliff overlooking the sea, and "Pigeon Rock" next to it; and Sporting Club, a new beach club just below Eden Roc, built on the rocks with a spirited café, numerous sunbathing areas, and a bar. "Sporting," as it was known, had several inlets into which the sea flowed, and where when the water was not too rough, one could hire a rowboat and go out toward Pigeon Rock and the cool caverns just beyond. I suggested to Eva that we do just that, the sea being wonderfully placid, the sunlight piercingly luminous, the whole scene suffused with a sense of marvelous, calming stillness. She sat on the seat facing me as I rowed out of the Sporting's precincts and then diagonally back into the huge rocks whose shelter from inquisitive eyes we both seemed to want.

In her one-piece bathing suit, Eva had never looked more desirable. She had smooth brown skin, perfectly rounded shoulders, elegantly shaped legs, and a face that, while not conventionally beautiful, had a lively responsiveness that I found irresistible. Beneath a craggy promontory we embraced for the first time. The embrace released all my suppressed emotion: we declared our love and, in the manner of suddenly illuminated narrators, retold the story to each other of our years of distance and unspoken longings. I was stunned by the strength of my passion. We returned to Dhour that afternoon and in the evening, with the rest of the group, met at the City Cinema, where sitting next to each other in the dark we whispered, passionately declaring our love for each other again and again.

Outside the cinema, aware that everyone was looking at us, we said good-bye rather casually and Eva went off with Nelly. The next day I would be gone, and would not see her again for nine months. As I got into the car with my sister Rosy I was seized with terrible stomach pain. When our doctor examined me the following day he found my stomach tender but with no other symptoms. A certificate was produced for

Princeton explaining that as a result of illness I would be returning a
week later. Whether love was responsible I don't know, but I certainly
didn't want to be separated from Eva so soon.

After dropping off Eva on my real last evening with her, I found my
mother waiting up for me in the living room. The room's former
bleakness was mitigated now by a few decent armchairs, Persian rugs on
the floor, and landscapes of Lebanon that she had purchased from a
Beirut art dealer. She claimed that she was worried about my being on
Dhour's deserted and poorly lit streets, and concerned that I was so late
when I had to get up early the next day for my twenty-hour journey
to New York. There was an unexpectedly unsympathetic edge to her
voice as she quizzed me about where I had been. Normally more than
happy to share my comings and goings with her, I found myself responding grudgingly, monosyllabically, trying to protect both myself
and Eva. My old vulnerability returned as if from another unwelcome
life. "And I suppose you kissed her also?" she demanded, turning
excitement at first love to guilt and discomfort.

She spoke with distaste in a tone I'd noticed whenever the subject
of sex or sexuality came up in conversation. Reacting angrily to her
question I said that it was none of her business while trying to ignore
the nagging feeling that somehow it was. My mother's tightly coiled
ambivalence was unleashed. Her love for me meant that she saw any
other emotional attachment as a diminishment of her hold over me.
And yet she was also highly conventional in her belief that people *should*
marry despite her abhorrence of sex.

I remained in love with Eva for two more years, all the while refusing in an almost childlike way to acknowledge that for her marriage was
the logical outcome of our liaison. When I graduated from Princeton
in 1957, at least two of her friends tried to persuade me to think seriously about marriage. I was to spend the next year (1957–58) in Egypt
before going to Harvard for graduate study. Eva lived in Alexandria
with a recently widowed sister, and I went there, ostensibly on my
father's business, to see her. Our physical relationship remained passionate but unconsummated because we both had the notion that once
we had crossed that line we would to all intents be a married couple;
and out of what I have always considered to be her profound sensitiv-
ity and love, Eva deterred me, saying that she did not want me to bear

the responsibility. As our passion and our discreet meetings in Alexandria continued, my admiration for Eva's strength, her intelligence, and her physical attractiveness grew. She was not intellectual but showed a wonderful patience and interest in listening to me talk about what I was reading and discovering. Eva was my new interlocutor, replacing my mother, who had already sensed the diversion of my attention and closeness from her to this other woman.

Separated by enormous distances, differences in the kinds of life we were each leading, I as a graduate student at Harvard the next year, she as her family's last unmarried daughter in Tanta or Alexandria, we saw each other less and less. My happiness diminished the more I realized how seriously Eva's life would be affected if we did not marry. Her family was making her life intolerable, only very grudgingly allowing her some months' respite in Rome, where she studied art history and Italian. On one of her trips back to Egypt, Eva told me, she had finally if rather desperately resolved to go to see my mother in Cairo and get her approval. This, Eva believed, was the only way to cure my irresolution on the question of marriage. I was away at Harvard when Eva arrived; she was cordially greeted by my mother, but from what Eva, my mother, and one of my sisters later told me, I was able to appreciate, not to say marvel at, my mother's virtuosity.

Averring her love for me, Eva opened by saying that she wished to know what the objections to her might be. An understated, typically modest Eva put her case in credible and convincing terms. My mother listened patiently and, in her view, she later told me, sympathetically. Then she proceeded to respond: "Let me be perfectly honest with you. You're a wonderful person with a great deal to offer. The problem isn't you, it's Edward. You're much better than he is: he barely has a university degree, he's very uncertain about what he's going to do, and given his inclination to go in either for years of further study or simple dilly-dallying he has no way of supporting himself, much less a wife and family." Eva quickly interjected that she had more than enough money for us both, but my mother chose to ignore this point. "You're a mature, extremely accomplished woman with a very full life ahead of you. Edward is of course my son, whom I love a great deal, but I am also objective about him. I know him extremely well. He is unformed, and given his record of inattentiveness and lack of concentration I must say that I am very concerned and even worried what will become of him. I can't in good conscience advise you to put much hope in him, although naturally I think he has great potential. Why throw away your future on someone as unstable as he? Take my advice, Eva, you can do much better than that."

When I reproached my mother for all this I could scarcely sort out which of her observations had injured, relieved, or upset me the most. Tactically, my mother had taken the wind out of Eva's sails, who, having come to defend herself, found instead that she was trying to convince my mother of her own son's virtues. My mother's maddening insistence that because she loved me, she alone knew what I was, what I had been, and would always remain infuriated me. "I know my own son," she would say sanctimoniously, pinning me down with her disapproval and insistence that she knew what I would always be—a disappointment in the long run. Any attempts to dislodge her sense of deterministic certitude about me was impossible. It was not so much her clemency I wanted, but for her to admit that I might have changed, and to modify her views held with such a dispiriting combination of serene confidence and unassailable cheerfulness, as if her son were fixed forever in his inventory of vices and virtues of whom she had been the first, and certainly the most authoritative, chronicler.

And at the same time I also felt a niggling and barely perceptible sense of relief that she had deflected Eva's marriage plans. My mother's unstated achievement was to have nudged me back into her orbit, to allow me to bask in her love, however peculiar and unsatisfying, and at the same time to get me to see my relationship with Eva in a new, unflattering light. Why should I assume the responsibilities of a family now (marriage being portrayed by my mother as essentially a sober, funless activity expected to endure "forever") and why couldn't Eva and I maintain a relationship as friends? Hidden in my mother's warnings to Eva was an implied endorsement of irresponsible liaisons for me that did not have the awful seriousness of marriage and that would allow *her* relationship with me to remain predominant.

A few years later in Dhour, my mother handed me an item from *al-Ahram,* the Egyptian daily, announcing Eva's engagement to her cousin. It struck me that Eva had probably heard that I too was with someone else and was planning to marry her—which I did during the

very week that I read about Eva's engagement. That my own first marriage was a short-lived and unhappy one only added to the depressing
feeling that I was unworthy of Eva, whom I have not seen again in the
nearly forty years that have ensued.

Eva and I had stopped seeing each other by the summer of 1961,
when in mid-July my father had to have a small operation to remove
an oozing mole just above his ankle. Over several years he had shown
it to various doctors in Egypt, the United States, and Lebanon, but only
Farid Haddad cautioned him about it early on, urging him at least twice
to have it excised. Loath to do anything at all, my father kept seeing
other doctors, until the wound became festering and quite painful,
and he went to Beirut to have it taken out at the American University
Hospital. I was twenty-five at the time, late in my career as a Harvard
graduate student. Later in the week of his little operation, my father received news from the dermatologist that the biopsy had revealed a
malignant melanoma already in a state of advanced metastatic transformation. The following week Sami Ebeid, a young but well-known
general surgeon whose parents we knew from Dhour, performed a
massive excision on his leg, carving out a deep trough that was to give
my father a permanent limp, as well as removing a great chunk of infil-
trated lymph nodes farther up on his body.

Munir Nassar was a resident in cardiology at the time, and one late
afternoon, just after the local excision for biopsy and before the operation, he and I stood together next to our Dhour house, to one side
of the blossoming cherry tree, as he solemnly explained the nature of
melanoma and the likely sequence of events. I wanted confirmation
of the diagnosis, which I was duly given, but I also wanted to know
from Munir whether this was going to be my father's end. I was then
deep in the study of Conrad, Vico, and Heidegger, among other
gloomy and severe writers who have since remained a strong presence
in my intellectual work, but I found myself astonishingly vulnerable to
the dire news of my father's operation, radiation treatment, and the
possible complications of all this. Propelled by the same morbid curiosity that I felt had its beginnings in the long hours spent as a ten-year-
old peering into the glass cases at Cairo's Agricultural Museum that
showed detailed wax reproductions of disfiguring diseases like elephan-
tiasis, bilharzia, and yaws, I finally asked Munir whether after all this my

father had a chance of survival. He didn't answer. "But will he die?" I persisted, to which, his voice lowered and his face obscured by the quickly descending darkness, Munir answered very slowly, "Probably."

In 1942 and 1948 I had been disquieted by but mercifully only half aware of the gravity of my father's illnesses. I had no comprehension of the facts of death, nor even of prolonged, debilitating physical illness then. During both those earlier incidents I recalled watching my father as if from a protected distance, apprehensive but detached. Now I was able in a series of imagined flashes to see his body being taken over by a dreadful, creeping invasion of malignant cells, his organs slowly devoured, his brain, eyes, ears, and throat torn asunder by this dreadful, almost miasmic, affliction. It was as if the carefully constructed supports maintaining and nourishing my life were being suddenly knocked away, leaving me standing in a very dark void. What I felt more than anything else was that my direct physical connection to my father was in danger of complete rupture, leaving me unprotected and vulnerable, despite my dislike of the demanding and hectoring presence he so often embodied. What would happen to me without him? What would replace that amalgam of confident power and indestructible will to which I had become irrevocably attached, and on which I realized I had unconsciously been drawing?

Why at this moment, when it might have been possible to glimpse the potential for liberation, why did I see my father's death as so terrible, so undesired a calamity? "But there is a chance that he will survive the operation and live for some time, isn't there?" I nearly pleaded with Munir. After a considerable pause he said something like "I see what you mean: live past the operation for some time. Yes of course. But melanoma is very treacherous, the worst of cancers, so the long-term prognosis has to be"—he paused again—"has to be poor." I quickly turned away from him and slowly mounted the stairs to our dark, deserted house, hoping that someone would soon turn up to alleviate my solitary despondency.

Later I realized that the cancer invasion was the first irreversible intervention in what I had thought, despite the hard time I had had in its midst, was my family's inviolable privacy. My three older sisters responded similarly. "It's the creeping horror of the disease," Rosy once said to me with great anguish. On hearing, when she arrived at the airport, that our father's life was in danger, Joyce collapsed in a fit of shattering anxiety. Jean was the only one of us who seemed able to steel herself: during our father's three months in hospital she stayed constantly by his side, showing an extraordinary strength, which I simply did not have.

His subsequent operation for the removal of lymph nodes and the rest of the melanoma was overshadowed in drama and suffering by what happened afterward. My father recovered from the operation slowly enough, and for a week seemed a little stronger each day. The bellwether of his progress was a cheery little barber who would show up at around ten each morning. If my father was doing well he would allow himself to be shaved; if not, the barber would bounce away without a word. As is the custom in the Arab world, when someone is in hospital members of the family are there from morning till night. The constant stream of visitors would come to show solidarity with the family, rarely to visit the patient, in return for which they would get a chocolate or biscuits. We were living in Dhour but would arrive at the hospital in Beirut at about nine every morning and stay till evening. Because his condition was so grave, my father required twenty-four-hour nursing care, all of it delivered by elderly Armenian spinsters, one of whom, Miss Arevian, became a close family friend until my father's death ten years later.

During the summer of 1961 he seemed to have died about half a dozen times. On those occasions we would leave him at about eight at night and be awakened in Dhour by a phone call at three the next morning: "Come immediately," a voice would say, "he's very near the end." We would bundle ourselves in a taxi and arrive at the hospital near dawn to find him in shock or in a coma. He seemed to have attracted every complication imaginable. First it was a murderous urinary tract infection; then he would miraculously recover, only to fall to a massive stomach hemorrhage. Then two days later he'd be sitting up being shaved by the little barber, and chatting away. On these occasions an enormous sense of freedom would allow me to go off to the beach, or even a movie, before saying good night to him and returning to Dhour. Two days later, another four o'clock phone call, and this time when I arrived I'd hear a doctor say that for four minutes my father had been clinically dead—his heart had simply stopped beating. A young intern, Alex Zacharia, happened to be near his room, rushed in, and quickly revived him, but the damage to his system had been grave; for a week he lingered between extinction and a restless, half-conscious state.

Two days more of this and once again he'd be being shaved as if nothing had happened. His autocratic manner returned. "You must go to that lunch given by Wadia Makdisi," he said sharply to me one day. "You'll be my representative," he added by way of justification. I didn't go, and having found out about my absence from my mother, he cold-shouldered me for a day from his bed: for at least two weeks he kept returning to the subject, dwelling on my infraction as if I had misbe-haved or defied him, me a twenty-five-year-old child, he a stern par-ent. He had developed an insistent way of coming back repeatedly to a subject, reiterating exactly the same questions and comments, until, a mysterious limit having been reached, he stopped as if satisfied that he (or the situation) had persisted as long as was necessary. *"Khalas,"* that's it; it's over, he would say, convinced that he had taken care of the prob-lem to his satisfaction. Later during his illness when one of my sisters developed symptoms of acute psychological depression, he kept asking, "But why does she do this? Haven't we been good parents to her?" He would rephrase such questions over and over for five years as she went through one crisis after another, one institution after another, with little improvement. My father's chronic—and by now legendary—difficulty with unfamiliar words ("feeta beta" for Phi Beta Kappa, "Rutjers" for Rutgers, etc.) foundered spectacularly on the word "psychiatrist," which emerged as "psypsy" or "psspss" or "qiatrist" or "something-trist," but his questions suddenly stopped when he considered her case settled and she seemed to be better: *"Khalas,"* he said to me, *"irtahna,"* we were able to rest.

The complications of his illness continued through August. More stomach problems, more urinary tract infections, more consternation on the floor, more postmidnight calls, more shock, more hanging on by our collective fingernails. A date with my draft board for a physical examination had been postponed three times since the Berlin Wall cri-sis of 1960, and they now became unexpectedly obdurate, granting me no more extensions. So I dutifully prepared to leave at the end of August. Miraculously, my father seemed clear of most of his problems, though still weak from his ordeals of the past eight weeks. I remember returning to Dhour on the evening before my very early morning departure, packing my bags, collecting a few items of dried fruit and nuts from the town, and going to bed at around eleven, after an evening spent with the Nassars. Dr. Faiz, the Colonel, was there, and when I said something about being assured enough of my father's stable condition to travel, he said touchingly, with a tremor in his very halting voice, "When he was all alone, in shock, last week, I went into his room for a moment, prostrated myself on the floor like this"—he lifted his arms very slowly above his head and then brought them down slowly—"praying to the Almighty to save Wadie. I think my prayers were answered," he concluded, sinking back into the glacial silence of his last years.

At three on the morning of my departure, having once again been woken by a call summoning us to the hospital, we rushed to Beirut. I remember standing in front of my open suitcase, stupefied and exhausted by the ups and downs of my father's illness, unable to do more than stare at the bag on the floor, uncertain whether to leave or stay. Leila, Munir Nassar's wife and a trained nurse, came to my rescue, prodding me into finishing my preparations for travel, helping me load my books and suitcase into the car, urging me to stop by the hospital only as a brief interim visit on my way to the airport. It was an exceptionally brilliant, cool night, the sky ablaze with thousands of distant pinpricks of light, the dark Dhour setting indifferent to our problems and quandaries. We all experienced a sort of anesthetized silence; there seemed no end to this appalling series of crises assaulting us and rendering us impotent except to rush to and from the hospital, in whose dreaded "Tapline" unit (named for the Trans Arabia Pipeline company that had endowed and air-conditioned that small number of rooms) my father fought, succumbed for a time, then fought back again. He was semicomatose and did not recognize me when I entered. Several of his doctors—he had become a celebrated case for the sheer, bewildering number of his rarely encountered complications—had been by to see him: "Your father will certainly make the literature," one of them told me with esteem.

Numbly I left for the airport: my only contribution to the slough of busy despond was to convince my mother to summon a distinguished

British surgeon, Sir Rodney Maingott, from London for emergency consultation. There was some resistance to the idea from a couple of the more hubristic local physicians ("He'll come in a couple of days, your father as usual would have recovered, and once again the White Man will be credited over the native"), but my mother and I were unyielding. Later that morning, while I was flying over Europe, Maingott agreed to fly out; his fee was a flat one thousand guineas in cash plus all expenses. Just as had been expected, by the time he got to Beirut thirty-six hours later, my father had already recovered, and the great physician enjoyed a sunny weekend basking in the luxury of the fabled Hotel St. Georges. From Cambridge I followed my father's almost total healing with an increasing fear that I too was infected with malignancies and that I too would suffer as he had. Various dermal excrescences and lumps were self-diagnosed symptoms that the Harvard Health Service doctors routinely dismissed with marked exasperation. The overpowering depth of the link I felt to my father mystified me.

Weakened, his limbs (especially his legs) extremely thin, his face somewhat shrunken, his balance quite shaky, my father decided that having battled through traumas he was not expected to survive, he would return to smoking cigarettes, cigars, and pipes, play even more bridge, and enjoy luxurious travel. I was eager for him to be well again so that we could return to the familiar terrain of dominance and subterranean resistance where "Edward" would be hectored and bullied, while my other diffuse and generally hidden self bided its time and sought avenues of its own over which my father's commanding presence could cast no great shadow. Yet I also knew that, however unpleasant, his force and sheer presence had provided me with an internalized framework in a world of volatile change and turbulent upheaval, and that I could no longer rely directly on him for that sort of support. The gravity of his illness acted as an early announcement of my father's and my own mortality and at the same time signaled to me that the Middle Eastern domain he had carved out for us as a home, a shelter, an abode of sorts, with its main points tied to Cairo, Dhour, and Palestine, was similarly threatened with discontinuity and evanescence. Twenty years after his death, when I found myself in the course of a psychoanalytic session concentrating on my complaints about my father's attitude toward me, I experienced a kind of epiphany. I found myself shedding tears of sorrow and regret for both of us, and for the years of smoldering conflict in which his domineering truculence and inability to articulate any feeling at all combined with my self-pity and defensiveness kept us so far apart. I was overcome with emotion because I could suddenly see how all those years he had struggled to express himself in a way that both by temperament and background he was not equipped to do. Perhaps, for oedipal reasons, I had blocked him, and perhaps my mother with her skill at manipulating ambivalence had undermined him. But whether this was true or not, the gap between my father and me was sealed with a longstanding silence, and it was this in my therapist's office that I confronted with tears, allowing me a redemptive view of him for all his awkwardness and the rough but perceptible care that he had shown his only son.

My father's long decline over the last ten years of his life marked the end of a period in our Lebanese experience as the seismic shifts rocking the Middle East began to register on our microcosm in Dhour, irrevocably altering the world we lived in. During the early period of the Egyptian revolution (July 1952) we were still resident in Cairo, but except for my father, who bided his time, we were all infected with the spirit and rhetoric of what Gamal Abdel Nasser said he was doing for his people. My mother especially became an ardent supporter of his nationalism; yet it was in Dhour, amid the humdrumly conventional visits she courted and paid, that she gave vent to her enthusiasm, with a flamboyance and fervor that alarmed her listeners. Unbeknownst to us, the political alignments in Lebanon—sectarian, byzantine, and often invisible—were beginning to respond to Nasser's stature as Arab superperson, and although we did not realize it, to our little Christian circle in Dhour, he began to seem like an emanation from not Cairo but Mecca, a pan-Islamist with evil designs not only on Israeli Jews but on Christian Lebanese.

In the summer of 1958 a small civil war erupted in Lebanon between partisans of Camille Chamoun, the incumbent Maronite president, who wished (unconstitutionally) to renew his term, and those of the largely Muslim Arabist parties, who quickly gathered the extremely strident support of Cairo's "Voice of the Arabs" radio station. That was the only summer after 1943 that we did not go to Dhour as usual. The hills just before the town were full of American troops sent there by

John Foster Dulles to bolster the "pro-Western" forces of Chamoun's supporters, whose opponents, it was alleged in the overwrought rhetoric of the day, were reported to be Moscow's Marxist-Leninist agents. During prior summers my parents and I had easily determined that despite blood ties with our Lebanese relatives, the Badrs, we felt neither the Muslim-Christian animosities that haunted them, nor the Arab-versus-Lebanese conflict that made them so defensive. In addition, and to make the issues even more convoluted, there was the (to them) abrasive fact that we too were Christian, but our pan-Arabism and absence of prejudice constituted at least disloyalty if not betrayal.

In this unstable and often uncomfortable set of currents my mother soon acquired the status of a true, believing Nasserite, a mirror image of her no less doctrinaire cousins and friends in the ultraright Christian factions. She would occasionally irritate even me with her often preachy disquisitions on Nasser's socialist pan-Arabism, and to make matters worse I saw one of her cousins in an unguarded moment giving her a look of dismissive contempt. I think that for her it was partly social, this carrying on a heated conversation while insulated from politics in a life of ease, but her stance also revealed a fairness of mind and an ability to think beyond "our" minority interests: "We don't count for very much," she would always say. "It's the porter, the driver, the worker for whom Nasser's reforms have changed their lives and given them dignity." It took courage to go against her upbringing and family. After 1958 Dhour felt even more alien, our friends less secure, the fault lines clearer, and our strangeness more evident. By 1962 and partly because of my father's slow recovery my parents and sisters had taken a furnished flat in Beirut, leaving Cairo to recede along with the slowly disappearing world of our childhood.

The polarizing, charismatic figure of Charles Malik also emerged during this period. He was not just the former ambassador to the United States from Lebanon, nor just the husband of my mother's first cousin Eva, but also foreign minister under Chamoun, a position that involved him directly in the decision to call on Dulles for U.S. troops for the country. Not very big in size, he conveyed an impression of extraordinary gravity and massiveness that he exploited during his years as teacher, diplomat, and politician. He had a booming voice, an unmistakable confidence, an assertive bearing, and an extraordinarily overpowering personality, which I found attractive initially but later increasingly saw as troubling. By the 1970s he had turned himself—with the support of my mother's (and his wife's) Dhour relatives and friends—into the symbol and the outspoken intellectual figurehead of everything most prejudicial, conflicted, and incompatible with the Arab and largely Islamic Middle East. He began his public career during the late 1940s as an Arab spokesman for Palestine at the U.N., but concluded it as the anti-Palestinian architect of the Christian alliance with Israel during the Lebanese Civil War. Looking back at Malik's intellectual and political trajectory, with all that it involved for me as his youthful admirer and companion, relative, and frequenter of the same circles, I see it as the great negative intellectual lesson of my life, an example which for the last three decades I have found myself grappling with, living through, analyzing, over and over and over with regret, mystification, and bottomless disappointment.

I first became aware of Malik in wartime Cairo where his widowed mother lived. He was then a professor of philosophy at the American University of Beirut, and was married to Eva, my mother's cousin. He was quite attached to my parents; my father, Malik once told me, gave him his first typewriter. Eva, who had spent her vacations in Nazareth at my mother's house, was an affectionate, handsome woman of considerable personality with whom I quickly made a close friendship, despite the great disparity in our ages. There was something ingenuous and rough-hewn about the couple then, he with his strong north Lebanese village (Kura) accent affixed to a sonorously European English redolent of his rich and for me transfixing educational experience. A student of Heidegger's at Fribourg and Whitehead's at Harvard during the thirties, Malik had already acquired the sobriquet "the divine Charles," as much for his brilliance as for his religious penchant. Greek Orthodox by birth, he was Roman Catholic (and by association Maronite) by predilection; Eva, the granddaughter of a staunchly Protestant pastor, converted to Catholicism during her marriage to Charles, as did her younger sister Lily, my mother's closest friend among her relatives.

After becoming Lebanon's U.N. ambassador at Lake Success, Malik assumed the additional role of Lebanese minister plenipotentiary in Washington, and later ambassador. When Eva's father, Habib, and some of his children started summering in Dhour, the Maliks also found a house there and came for a few weeks from Washington. I was very attracted to their presence. In the unforgiving sparseness of Dhour, their home, Charles's conversation, and my aunt's evident liking for me further provoked my thirst for ideas, for the great issues of faith, morality, and human destiny, and for a whole gamut of authors. "During the summer of 1930-something," Malik once said to me, "I used to sit by the banks of the Nile and I read through all of Hardy and Meredith. But I also read Aristotle's *Metaphysics* and Aquinas's *Summa*." No one else I knew then spoke of such things. When I was twelve I remember finding Malik sitting on his veranda overlooking the misty Shweir valley with a large tome in his hands. "John of Chrysostom," he said, holding the book up for inspection, "a marvelous, subtle thinker, not unlike Duns Scotus." It was at about that time that I felt the curiously teasing quality of his remarks on books and ideas. He had a tendency (then welcomed by me) to drop names and titles, which I would later ferret out and go into, but also to resort to one-liners, rankings, and reductive questions. "Kierkegaard was very great, but did he really believe in God?"; "Dostoyevsky was a great novelist because he was a great Christian"; "To understand Freud you must visit the Forty-second Street pornography shops"; "Princeton is a country club where Harvard sophomores spend their weekends." Perhaps he felt I was too callow, too unprepared for the bracing arguments he had alluded to in dealing with Heidegger and Whitehead at their universities, but I also sensed some condescension mixed in with the teacher's vocation to guide and instruct.

During the early Nasser years Malik encouraged me to tell him about my enthusiasm for the popular leader's reforms. He listened to everything I had to say, and then he said deflatingly, "What you've said is interesting. Egypt's per capita income is now eighty dollars per annum: Lebanon's is nine hundred. If all the reforms work, if every resource is marshaled, then Egypt's per capita will be doubled. That's all." From Uncle Charles, as we all called him, I learned the attractions of dogma, of the search for unquestioning truth, of irrefutable authority. From him I also learned about the clash of civilizations, the war between East and West, communism and freedom, Christianity and all the other, lesser religions. In addition to telling us about it in Dhour, he played a central role in formulating all this for the world stage. Along with Eleanor Roosevelt he worked on the Universal Declaration of Human Rights; names like Gromyko, Dulles, Trygve Lie, Rockefeller, and Eisenhower were the common currency of his conversation, but so too were Kant, Fichte, Russell, Plotinus, and Jesus Christ. He had a dazzling command of languages—English, Arabic, German, Greek, and French were all excellent working instruments, though of the first three he had a mastery that was positively remarkable. With his huge shock of black hair, piercing eyes, aquiline nose, substantial width, and great hiking feet he commanded the room without a trace of hesitation or crippling self-consciousness. During the forties and early fifties Malik's comforting moral certainty and granitic power, his inextinguishable faith in the Eternal, gave us hope and reminded me of Gorky's remark that he slept better knowing that Tolstoy was alive in the same world.

Malik rose and rose in the public world of nations, but he and Eva always returned to Dhour: the village was like the *Heimat,* homeland, of which Heidegger spoke, but for Malik the place also embodied an earthy Lebanese simplicity. He always retained what seemed to be an enduring admiration and affection for my father: "No one I've ever known," he once told me with a certain amount of amazement and condescension, "no one is so purely a businessman as he. He has the business instinct to an astonishing degree." I later thought that he had meant to suggest that my father was really an excellent businessman but wasn't much else; perhaps I got it wrong. I enjoyed, however, a memorable exchange between Charles and my father on our Dhour balcony one scintillatingly bright night. "How can they [presumably scientists] determine the distance of those stars from earth?" my father wondered out loud. "Charles, do you know?" "Oh," the philosopher said, "it's quite easily done. You take a fixed point on earth, deduce the angle, then calculate the distance" was the prompt, somewhat off-putting reply. Child's play. My father was not satisfied, his phenomenal gifts for calculation—or at least the principles behind the calculations—stirred into excited demurral. "No, no: I meant exactly. Which angle? Where? Surely there must be more to it." Everyone else present quieted down: it seemed like an unaccustomed challenge to authority that my father had launched. I saw confusion on Malik's face, and an unattractive impatience, as if he were trying to gather what the little businessman was all about. But clearly he couldn't produce the answer that my father's genuinely puzzled interest had provoked. Bluster was no good. Better to change the subject to Berdayev. On the morning of my father's funeral fifteen years later he came to our Beirut house to pay his respects but not to attend the actual service. "I have a very important lunch with the papal nuncio," he said to me by way of explanation.

But it was his spiritual force, which had once moved people to conversion, that as he became more political deviated into prejudice and resentment against those who could neither accept the idea (it could only be an idea, since Lebanon was multiconfessional) of a Christian Lebanon nor of Lebanon as an Arab country entirely within the American camp. He must have been a superb teacher and lecturer in his early days at the university. Lily, his sister-in-law, once told me how after he returned from Harvard to Beirut he singlehandedly elevated the discourse into discussions of truth, the ideal, beauty, and the good. One of his students in the forties was my first cousin George, who, destined at first for a business career, a full decade later quit everything to convert to Catholicism and move to Fribourg, Switzerland, with a few like-minded Malik disciples, there to found a colony of devout men and women who would ready themselves to return to the Muslim world in order to convert people to Christ. All of these people, who remain in Switzerland to this day, their grandiose mission sadly unfilled, are testimony to the depth of Malik's influence as an intellectual whose goals were, in the Bible's sense, not of this world. And I, too, felt that influence, not only in the perspectives and ideas he introduced me to but in the dignity of the kind of moral-philosophical inquiry he had engaged in, which was so lacking either in my formal education or in my environment. Malik's informal quasi-familial presence in Dhour made me realize that I had never before had a teacher of intellectual distinction. When did that invigoration end, to be replaced instead by an antithetical force so exactly the opposite of what had once been openness, courage, originality of thought?

I have sometimes speculated that Dhour, with its insidious but ultimately false embodiment of bucolic authenticity, had corrupted us all into believing that its unfertile sparseness, policed simplicity of life, enforced Christian unanimity, played some role in its own and Malik's later political extremism. But at the same time I think the sleepy withdrawal from the world that it promised for the summer months was also a negation of its own Arab context. Well past the colonial period, we collectively thought of ourselves as being able to lead an ersatz life, modeled on European summer resorts, oblivious to what was going on around us. My parents tried to reproduce our Cairo cocoon in the Lebanese mountains: who could blame them for that, given our peculiarly fractured status as Palestinian-Arab-Christian-American shards disassembled by history, only partially held together by my father's business successes, which allowed us a semifantastic, comfortable, but vulnerable marginality. And when the disturbances of postmonarchical Egypt led the country to fall in pieces about us we carried their effects wherever we went, including Dhour. There Malik represented our first symbol of resistance, the refusal of Christian Lebanon to go along with Arab nationalism, the decision to join the Cold War on the United States's side, to fight and turn intransigent rather than to enthuse about and accommodate Nasser's rousing exhortations.

I all too uncomfortably remember the shock of the total Arab defeat of 1967, and how in late December of that fateful year I drove up to Uncle Charles and Aunt Eva's imposingly large, monolithic house in Rabiyé, a hillside suburb northeast of Beirut. In this house they had finally been able to deposit the books, furniture, and papers accumulated during years spent in rented houses, embassies, and temporary quarters, including their various Dhour residences. Fresh snow lay on the road, the sky was dark, the wind sharp, and the whole atmosphere glowering and inhospitable. I was not too sure what my errand was, except in some vague way to ask Charles to come out, so to speak, and help guide the Arabs out of their incredible defeat. A stupid idea perhaps, but at the time it seemed plausibly worth pursuing. What I was not prepared for was his uncharacteristically passive answer: that this was not his time, that he did not feel he had a role to play anymore, and that a new situation would have to arrive for him to reenter politics. I was stunned by this, astonished that what I had assumed was a common need to resist and rebuild was not shared by a man whose views and commitments I still had faith in. During the Lebanese Civil War, Malik became an intellectual leader of the Christian Right, and long after his death in 1988 I still feel profound regret at the ideological gulf that came to separate us, and at the enormous, complicated maelstrom of Arab politics that ultimately divided us, leaving us both with very little positive history and experience to show for it.

It is difficult now not to read back into our Dhour years elements of the wasteful desolation of the Lebanese Civil War, which began in 1975 and officially ended about seventeen years later. Insulated from the depth of the antithetical communal and political currents that had riven Lebanon for decades, we lived a pseudoidyllic life that teetered on the edge of a very deep precipice. Stranger yet was the sense my father had that Dhour was a refuge from the growing travails of business life in Nasser's Egypt. In early 1971 when he was near death he told us that he wished to be buried in Dhour, but that was never possible, since no resident was willing to sell us land for a little plot on which to grant his wish. Even after his years of devotion to it, his many material contributions to its communal life, his love for its people and locale, he was still considered too much of a stranger in death to be allowed in. The idealized pastoral existence we thought we were enjoying had no real status in the town's collective memory.

One of the enduring images of that eerily out-of-touch life we passed through for those twenty-seven years was of Emile Nassar sitting alone at night, writing at a table in the middle of his deserted living room. No matter how late his bridge game, no matter how many guests they had had for dinner, he indefatigably brought out his large, leather-covered notebooks and a stack of newspapers and proceeded to write. What he wrote exactly we did not know until my father once asked him directly whether he was writing his memoirs. "In a way, yes. What I do is to copy out passages from the day's journalism, and thus keep a record of what happened," replied Mr. Nassar. "But you add comments too, don't you?" my father rejoindered. "Absolutely not. Just a faithful record of what happened." With a slight note of exasperation inflecting his voice, ever the efficient manager, my father said: "But why don't you just cut out the articles and paste them in your notebooks, instead of going through all that trouble?" Nassar seemed momentarily taken aback by the question, but quickly responded by saying that he was doing all that work for his sons' sake, so they would have a lasting record of the times by him after his death. Not to be deterred, my father turned to Alfred, the middle boy, reclining on a nearby sofa. "Are you going to read these books after your father's death?"—to which, without the slightest hesitation Alfred responded, "No. No chance."

I have retained this curious scene in my memory for all these years as a symbol of the triviality and impermanence of what so many of us lived out in Dhour, the unrepaid, unrequited attempt to belong to and somehow retain a place that in the end was set on its own course as part of a country more volatile, more fragmented, more bitterly divided than any of us suspected. We were out-of-touch strangers to the contests and feuds that gave Dhour its peculiar identity. Our house is still there, uninhabited, dotted with bullet scars and gaping holes in the walls where mortars and Katyusha rockets entered. In 1997, twenty-seven years after our last summer there, I went to Dhour to see what was left. Still a Syrian army stronghold with soldiers and officers billeted there, it is one of the few popular summer places that has not been rebuilt and filled with new residents flocking there after the civil war to escape Beirut's noisy, frantic, and unzoned building boom. Most of Dhour's houses from our time are still in ruins, the cafés and shops mostly closed or shrunk in size. My sister Jean and her husband and sons have bought and refurbished a house in Shweir, next door to where, forty-three years ago, I had my geography tutorials with Aziz Nasr. Their garden and carefully planned interiors with every modern convenience have nothing in common with the rough barrenness of our accommodation years ago. As I lay down for a brief rest in the afternoon, that juxtaposition filled me with melancholic recollections of the summer's final days as we readied ourselves for the return trip to Cairo, with Dhour's sunny harshness yielding to the cooling mists of approaching autumn.

I remembered the end-of-season days with considerable pleasure: most of the other summer residents had packed and got out before us, the town's shopkeepers dressed in their shabby suit jackets, slowed down by a reduced clientele and the need, I suppose, to calculate their profits and plan for the next year's. A routine subject of conversation around the *saha* was whether it had been a good season; I once overheard Mr. Affeish, the large lethargic pharmacist, and Bou Faris, the man who ran the bicycle rental service, discussing the past summer rather mournfully in terms of the number of houses that went unrented. "God willing, it'll be more crowded next year," they said simultaneously to each other. Only Farfar of the taxi battalion remained in the *saha* through September, his battered Ford and raucous voice filling the still air with their lively cacophonous sound; his colleagues had left Dhour to ply their trade on Beirut's streets. And on the final day at dawn, our bags packed, the breakfast things put away for the last time, we stood in the cold morning air as the drivers loaded the two oversize taxis and we coasted languidly to Beirut, and from there to Jerusalem and Cairo. After 1948 it was airplanes from Beirut.

XI

WHEN I ARRIVED IN CAIRO AFTER GRADUATION, I SOON saw that my memory of it during my exile in the United States as a place of stability was no longer accurate. There was a new uncertainty: the placid paradise for foreigners was beginning to lose its durability. In a few months Gamal Abdel Nasser was to replace General Mohammed Naguib as head of the government, and what had been "our" environment became "theirs," "they" being Egyptians to whom politically we had paid less attention than to our inert stage set. I recognized this in the poetry of Cavafy some years later—the same indifference, the world taken for granted as privileged foreigners like us pursued our concerns and worried about our businesses without much consideration for the vast majority of the population. Ironically, during the fifties, separated from his nephews and former partners (who had gone into a variety of businesses, from building washing machines to exporting casings for sausages to dressmaking), my father's fortunes soared and his influence as a businessman grew. In 1955–56 he opened an ill-fated branch in Beirut, which he kept pouring money into without any return at all. During the school and college summer holidays I was increasingly drawn into our Egyptian business, pressed into service as his deputy during the afternoons, without specific duties or responsibilities. It was his way of inviting me in, then shutting the door in my face by showing me that there was no functional place for me. Putting me in a similar double bind, he and my mother kept insisting that as the man of the family I was responsible for my sisters, even though my four siblings were my equals in every respect. They gave me the duty without the privilege; on the contrary, I felt that my sisters were shown far greater consideration and I neither accepted the burden of responsibility nor agreed with it in principle. I felt that my father often favored my sisters over me as an act of chivalry, somehow of a piece with his amazing reconciliation with his nephews and sister after their protracted hostility toward him. Once on their own, they returned to being my father's nephews in earnest, so much so that one of them later told me how remorseful he felt about what he had said to and done against my father during their business feud.

When I was a Princeton sophomore and my oldest sister came to attend college in the United States, I felt the difficulty of communicating and of relating to her acutely. But by then I had already realized that both my family and what used to be my native environments in Cairo and Lebanon were no longer available to me. My years in the United States were slowly weaning me away from Cairo habits—of thought, behavior, speech, and relationships. My accent and dress were slowly altering; my terms of reference in school and, later, college were different; my speaking and thinking were undergoing a radical change that took me far beyond the comfortable certainties of Cairo life. I regarded my sisters' existence at the English School, for example, as utterly remote and alien.

After Mount Hermon I moved to Princeton in the autumn of 1953 entirely on my own. I was much more independent and resourceful than I had been only two years earlier and was surprised to find that I managed in a short time and unfamiliar place to purchase furniture, books, and clothes, and to install myself with three ill-assorted roommates in a shared room, which I deserted for a single one at Christmas. My first quintessential Princeton experience occurred on my second day there, when, while looking for the dining room in Holder (a sophomore redoubt), I was waylaid by a large, slightly tipsy young man in an orange and black polo shirt, pink bermuda shorts, straw hat, and blue tennis shoes carrying an immense moose head. "Hey," he said to me in very exuberant tones, "I really hate to part with Sam here, but he'll look magnificent in your room." I said something about it not fitting—with its great head of horns it was the size of a Volkswagen—but he persisted. "You give me only twenty dollars for Sam and I'll get him into your room, even if I have to use a crane to pull him through your window." I finally managed to convince him that Sam and I couldn't live together, but it was my first encounter with a Princeton humor barely distinguishable from that of boarding school, except for the admixture at Princeton of beer and secular learning. Otherwise, the two institutions resembled each other.

Princeton in the fifties was entirely male. Cars were forbidden, as were women, except for Saturdays until six p.m.; the great collective achievement of my class during its years there (1953–57) was that "sex after seven" on Saturdays was allowed as a result of student agitation. To see or date girls they either had to be invited down for weekends from places like Smith and Vassar, or one went to those places in hopes of finding a date that way. I was woefully unsuccessful at this for my first two years, during which my summer romance with Eva made up for what Princeton didn't give me. I could neither persuade a girl to come down, nor make the requisite trip with even the slenderest possibility of meeting someone. The student population around me was largely homogeneous. There wasn't a single black, and most of the foreign students were graduate students, among them a handful of Arabs whom I occasionally spent time with.

My classmates either were or tried to be cut from the same cloth. As at Mount Hermon, nearly everyone wore the same clothes (white bucks, chinos, button-down shirts, and tweed jackets), talked in much the same way, and did the same thing socially. We were all trapped in a hideous eating club system, so that after sophomore year we all had to become club members through an appalling system called Bicker or, in effect, we would perish. Socially, Bicker meant that for two weeks in the February of your second year you were shut up in your room for entire evenings awaiting delegations from each of the clubs. Gradually their number decreased as more and more candidates were weeded out (Jews, non-prep-school boys, badly dressed people), whereas in the case of athletes (jocks), St. Paul's and Exeter graduates, or the children of famous parents (Batista, Firestone, DuPont) the visits of the now importuning clubs intensified. There was a hierarchy among the seventeen functioning clubs: a big five (Ivy, Cottage, Cannon, Cap and Gown, Colonial), a middle group (Quadrangle, Tower, Campus, Dial, Elm, etc.), and finally a bottom group stocked essentially with members who today would be called nerds and outcasts but were in fact largely Jewish.

Terrible things happened during Bicker, all of them condoned and even encouraged by the administration. In 1955, my Bicker year, for example, the club presidents and the men who ran the university decided that every sophomore, no matter how socially unacceptable, would get a bid. Inevitably a group of twenty to thirty would be left unchosen at the end, and public meetings would be held apportioning the "100 percenters"—the students no one wanted, most of them Jews—among the various magnanimous heads of the clubs. The whole grotesque exercise was reported in juicy detail in the student newspaper. Equally gruesome was the sight of those students who knew that by virtue of race, background, or manner, they could not make the club of their choice as they set out to transform themselves into WASP paragons, usually with pathetic results. This was symbolized by the junior and senior vogue for blue button-down shirts with frayed collars; I remember watching in astonishment as two classmates in an adjoining suite applied sandpaper to a pair of new blue button-down shirts, trying in a matter of minutes to produce the effect of the worn-out aristocratic shirt that might get them into a better club.

I was surprised how obligingly our teachers took the fact that for those two Bicker weeks no one did any reading. But I could see from the first knock on the door that I was a puzzling anomaly to the wandering delegates, since the prep school I went to was hardly fashionable, my dress and accent barely traceable to any known source, and my name totally unplaceable to most of Princeton's sophisticated upperclassmen from Darien and Shaker Heights. Because my parents had by chance befriended an elderly retired couple from Boca Raton and St. Croix over dinner and bridge on the *Andrea Doria,* the gentleman, an alumnus of Cap and Gown, got a delegation from that club to visit me a few times, but we were clearly not meant for each other. My then roommate, a gifted but, alas, socially undeveloped musician, drove nearly all the committees off, though three of the middle-level clubs kept coming back to see me; they would encircle me at one end of our tiny living room and leave him sitting sadly alone at the other end. Finally, on the night when the entire class descended on Prospect Street to go to the clubs to pick up their bids, I was given three bids, my poor roommate none.

Then one of the clubs, through its spokesman, a fat young man who was also a champion golfer, offered to strike an unappealing bargain with me: join here and, as an extra inducement, he said, we'll take your roommate too. As I was about to reject this offer and walk out of the place, I heard a heart-rending wail: "Oh Ed, please don't leave me. Please accept. What'll happen to me?" And so I accepted membership but I never enjoyed the club. I felt alienated and wronged by a publicly sanctioned university ritual that humiliated people in this way. From that moment on Princeton ceased to matter to me except as a place of study. I have lectured there several times, but a new faculty, the de-emphasis of the wretched clubs, and of course the presence of women and minorities have transformed it from the provincial, small-minded college I attended between 1953 and 1957 into a genuine university.

Apart from the company of a few unusually brilliant and gifted fellow students, like the composer John Eaton, Arthur Gold, Bob Miles, and a few others, my immersion in reading and writing was the only antidote to Princeton's poisonous social atmosphere. I became a major not in literature but in the humanities, an honors program that allowed me to take as many courses in music, philosophy, and French as in English; all were systematically chronological, crammed with information, tremendously exciting to me, so far as the reading was concerned. There were two professors of distinction there (only one of whom I actually knew and studied with) who have made a lasting impression on me. One was R. P. Blackmur, the literary critic and (despite the fact that he didn't have a doctorate or even a high school diploma) English professor, a lonely, difficult-to-follow writer and lecturer, whose sheer genius in uncovering layer after layer of meaning in modern poetry and fiction (despite his gnarled and frequently incomprehensible language) I found utterly challenging. His example for me opened the secret delight of interpretation as something more than paraphrase or expla-nation. I never took a course with him or met him, but apart from reading him avidly I intermittently used to go to his lectures on poet-ics and modern fiction. He was one of the two readers of my senior thesis on André Gide and Graham Greene—a tortured affair, alas—who in his written comments praised my "great powers of analysis." He died in 1965.

The other figure of distinction was (and indeed still is) Professor of Philosophy Arthur Szathmary, a spritely, energetic little figure who was everyone's gadfly, whether student, colleague, or great writer. For a number of disaffected outsiders, Szathmary came to represent, and even embody, the intellectual life. He was intensely skeptical, asked irreverent questions, and generally made one feel that the accurate articulation of objections and flaws were activities of the highest order. There was nothing of the Princeton "tweedy" ethos about him or anything that suggested careerism and worldly success. No one could place his vaguely European accent. Later he admitted to us that he was a Massachusetts boy who had never left the country, although during the war he had been an interrogator of Japanese prisoners of war. His brother was the writer and comedian Bill Dana, whose celebrated TV character was José Jimenez.

My humanities courses were unreflectingly historical in organization, taught by men of the utmost competence and philological rigor. My readings in the history of music, of literature, and of philosophy formed the foundation of everything I have done as a scholar and teacher. The sedate comprehensiveness of the Princeton curriculum gave me the opportunity to let my mind investigate whole fields of learning, with at that time a minimum of self-consciousness. Only when that learning came into contact with the energizing criticism of Szathmary or the visionary empowerment of Blackmur did I find myself digging deeper, beyond the level of formal academic accomplishment, and beginning somehow to fashion for myself a coherent and independent attitude of mind. I was conscious during the first few weeks of my second year of further developing an early fascination with complexity and unpredictability—especially, and lastingly, in the multiple complexities and ambiguities of writing and speech. Paradoxically, this was stimulated by some of the more conventional professors in approach and temperament, including Coindreau in French, or Oates in classics, and Thompson, Landa, Bentley, Johnson, in English. In music, I forced myself through the obstacle course of harmony and counterpoint, then on to rigorously historical and positivistic seminars on Beethoven and Wagner in particular, where Elliot Forbes and Ed Cone were models of musicianly and scholarly pedagogy.

I was very aware of myself as intellectually underdone, especially in comparison to someone like Arthur Gold, the most brilliant student in my class, who possessed a superb talent for reading as well as writing literature. To survive as he did intellectually, and to a lesser extent as I did, in the Princeton atmosphere of those days was almost miraculous. We both contemplated transferring to Harvard in our junior year, and were both at odds with the casual, pipe-smoking, tweedy anti-intellectualism of many teachers and students alike. During my last two years at Princeton, hating my club—where one had to go for meals, since no other facility except expensive restaurants existed—and feeling no connection with the weekend social life of house parties, raccoon-skin coats, and endless drinking, I became quite isolated, though exhilarated intellectually. Princeton had set in motion a series of deep currents, most of which were in conflict with each other, pulling me in different, radically irreconcilable directions. I could not give up the idea of returning to Cairo, nor of taking over my father's business, yet I wanted to be a scholar and academic. I was going more and more seriously into music, even to the point of doing nothing else despite my years of unsatisfactory piano lessons.

Princeton in the fifties was unpolitical, self-satisfied, and oblivious. There was no collective Princeton in any political sense aside from football games, rallies, and parties. The closest thing to it was when my classmate Ralph Schoenman (later Bertrand Russell's secretary and spokesman) organized a campus visit for Alger Hiss; that brought out a crowd of curious undergraduates and some picketing protesters. Until the Suez invasion in the fall of 1956 (like the Cairo fire, an event I experienced at a distance with great emotional stress since my family was there) whatever politics came up was restricted to my conversations with Arab graduate student friends, Ibrahim Abu-Lughod—a recent Palestinian refugee, then a doctoral candidate in Oriental, i.e., Middle Eastern, studies at Princeton—principal among them. And yet except for these private exchanges my growing concern with what was taking place in Nasser's Egypt had no outlet at all. During the Suez Crisis, however, I discovered what for two years I hadn't known—that one of my roommates, Tom Farer, who has remained a friend, was Jewish but gave no support for Israel or what Israel was doing. I remember a rather heated conversation with Arthur Gold in which we screamed at each other about the injustice (my word) of Israel to us (as Palestinians), he taking a viewpoint totally opposed to mine—but that was an isolated event which was totally disconnected from anything else I was doing at Princeton at the time. Over the years our views, however, became more reconciled. McCarthy was treated at Princeton as a bagatelle and no Princeton professor was known to us as having been persecuted for his Communist views. In fact there was no left presence of any sort at Princeton. Marx was barely read or assigned, and for most of us Gordon Craig's big final lecture on Hitler (complete with blood-curdling imitation) in History I was the closest we came to contemporary history.

A very strange incident took place in Dodge Hall, which housed studios, a tailor shop (run by the freshman tennis coach), a cafeteria, a small theater, and several offices for students of various religions—the Catholics, the Jews, etc. I was on my way to the cafeteria and suddenly came face-to-face with the rabbi of the Hillel Foundation; he was walking down the stairs from his office, and our eyes met. "You're from Egypt," he said to me with a slight edge to his voice. I admitted to that bit of intelligence, taken aback that he not only knew me but knew where I lived. "What do you plan to do when you finish here?" he asked peremptorily. I said something vague about graduate or even medical school (for at least half of my Princeton career I had been a premed, though I was a humanities major), but was impatiently stopped short by him. "No, no. I mean after you finish all your education." Then, without waiting for an answer, he preached on. "You should go back. Your people need you. They need doctors, engineers, teachers. There is so much misery and ignorance and illness among the Arabs that people like you are a crucial asset." Then he marched out of Dodge without waiting for my response.

This happened before the Suez invasion, when I volunteered to write a column about the war from the Arab point of view for the university newspaper. The article was published without provoking the kind of response that it might have had if it had appeared after 1967. It was my first piece of political writing, but so quiescent were political passions and so muted were Zionist opinions—this was, after all, when

Eisenhower in effect compelled Israel to withdraw from Sinai—that I was able to publish it quite easily. Even so, I was aware of Cold War tensions and of problematic patterns in the Arab world by virtue of time spent with the Maliks in Washington.

While at Princeton I first approached the political currents and issues not only of the period but which in one way or another were to influence my outlook intellectually and politically for the rest of my life. It was then that I heard from Malik about ideology, communism, and the great battle between East and West. He was already close to John Foster Dulles and was beginning to make a mark on American life of the time: universities showered him with honorary degrees, he gave lectures, and was much in demand socially. He had an amused contempt for Princeton and me, but he was willing to talk to me at quite some length (conversation, except for an occasional question from me, wasn't really possible). Later I understood that Nasser's approach to the Soviet Union coupled with his Islamic faith were the real problem for Malik; hidden beneath the discourse of statistics and demographic trends were Communism and Islam. Yet I was unable finally to sustain any kind of counterargument: Malik's manner kept reminding me that I was only a sophomore, whereas he lived in the real world, dealt with great people, was so much more elevated in vision, etc.

Malik's attitude really troubled me in its mixture of politics with family, his and my sense of community and genuine relationship coming up against alien forces that he felt (and, I realized, most of my Lebanese relatives also felt) threatened "us." I couldn't feel that, somehow, couldn't feel either that social change and the majority culture had to be opposed as a way of preserving our status as Christians, or that we had a separate status at all. It was in those Washington discussions that the inherent irreconcilability between intellectual belief and passionate loyalty to tribe, sect, and country first opened up in me, and have remained open. I have never felt the need to close the gap but have kept them apart as opposites, and have always felt the priority of intellectual, rather than national or tribal, consciousness, no matter how solitary that made one. But such an idea during my undergraduate years was difficult for me to formulate, although I certainly began to feel it keenly. I had neither the vocabulary nor the conceptual tools, and I was too often overcome by emotions and desires—basically unsatisfied in the Princeton social wilderness—to make those distinctions clear that would later become so central to my life and work.

What remained from the relentless daily pressure of my Cairo years was an equally intense feeling of drivenness at Princeton: a lot of my unfulfilled emotional energy went into intense activity. I kept up with sports by playing tennis and, through my sophomore year, being on the swimming team. Choir and glee club, where I was both singer and accompanist, took up time, and piano playing. I had won a generous prize given by the Friends of Music at Princeton to study with an eminent New York (usually Julliard) teacher; following the sudden death of Erich Itor Kahn, my first teacher, there was the redoubtable and abrasive Edward Steuerman, the amiable Beveridge Webster, the awkward Frank Sheridan, none of whom in their unimaginative conformity proved as useful a teacher as Louise Strunsky, a local Princeton woman of great insight and musicality with whom I studied for some months.

During the last part of my time at Princeton, the sense of myself as unaccomplished, floundering, split in different parts (Arab, musician, young intellectual, solitary eccentric, dutiful student, political misfit) was dramatically revealed to me by a college classmate of my oldest sister, Rosy, whom I happened to meet in Philadelphia when she asked herself along to join the two of us for a performance of *Death of a Salesman* with Mickey Shaughnessey as Willie Loman. Both of them were Bryn Mawr sophomores, my sister barely getting over her crippling homesickness but not her dislike of the place, her friend a blue-blooded Social Registered campus leader whose devastating personableness and charm overcame, indeed obliterated, any reservations one might have had about her unusual but modest good looks. She was very tall, but carried herself with astonishing grace. She cried liberally during the performance, borrowing and promising later to return (this pleased me) my handkerchief. There was something wrong with her front teeth which she tried to hide when we spoke face-to-face.

The next time I saw her a couple of weeks later she had had them fixed. And then I realized that I had been gripped by her with such intensity and passion that I felt I wanted to be with her constantly, a desire that fed itself just as constantly on the fact that I could not be. Princeton's regulations, the distance to Bryn Mawr, complicated academic schedules abridged the frequency of our encounters. But this was also the time of my involvement with Eva, which developed and took place only during summers in Dhour el Shweir. Thus for my final year at Princeton I would chase after—with results only once every six weeks or so, and then most frustratingly—my Bryn Mawr love, as in a sense a part of my American life, while Eva in the Middle East was integral to *that* life. Both relationships, counterpointed and plotted with fiendish regularity, were chaste, unconsummated, unfulfilled. As an older friend of hers told me ten years later, this stunning American woman was a Diana figure, infinitely attractive to me and at the same time infinitely unattainable.

After my relationship with Eva lapsed in the late fifties I continued fitfully with this enigmatic, strangely passionate, and yet increasingly elusive American woman. I made an unhappy marriage with someone else, and when after a short time it ended, I returned once again to my Bryn Mawr friend. We lived together, were genuine companions for almost two years after twelve or thirteen years of intermittent relationship touched by, not to say drenched in, sexual desire constantly heightened and just as constantly and bizarrely dampened. She was neither an intellectual nor someone with very clearly outlined goals for her life. We were at Harvard together for the first year, 1958–59, she in education, I in literature. Once during that fall she confided in me about the difficulties of a relationship she was having with someone else (this hurt and puzzled me, but I managed to keep calm, and offer a friendly ear and counsel), but by the middle of the year we were seeing each other regularly again. She left for New York to work as a private school teacher for a while, then went to Africa to teach for two or three years. She was always interested in theater and film, but because her degree was in education she ended up teaching, though my impression was that despite her fantastic gifts for dealing with young people, this was expedient for her, rather than a vocation.

It is difficult to describe the tremendous power of her attraction, the romance of her body, which was for a time just beyond sexual reach, the overwhelming pleasure of intimacy with her, the utter unpredictability of her wanting and rejecting me, the irreducible joy of seeing her after an absence. These were what tied me to her for so many years. At times, she represented that aspect of an ideal America that I could never gain admission to, but which held me enthralled at the gate. She had a moralistic "don't-say-bad-things" side to her, which sometimes made me feel even more alien, and put me resentfully on my best behavior. There was also (and later centrally) her family, which was represented to me as blue-blooded, and more or less impecunious because her dashing lawyer-father quixotically took on gigantic opponents like the defense department for purely idealistic reasons, bankrupting himself in the process. But there was taste and breeding, elegance, and a sort of literary refinement about her family, whom I was not to meet for a considerable time, that sometimes induced in me an almost subservient attitude. Her closest attachment in life was to her eldest brother, a famous athlete and exact contemporary of mine, though he was at Harvard. I think I saw them together only twice, but in what she said about him over the years I sensed a more-than-usual combination of love, awe, respect, and, yes, passion that for years I dimly felt prevented us from the fulfillment I quite desperately wanted and which seemed impossible. In this, it now seems to me, I must have been complaisant.

It is difficult now to reconstruct the feelings of terrifying abandonment she induced when she was about to, as she so often did, leave me. "I love you," she would say, "but I am not *in love* with you," as she announced her decision never to see me again. This happened in the late spring of 1959, on the eve of my departure for Cairo and the long summer vacation. I was at Harvard graduate school, and still dependent on my father's business, which by now was hemmed in by Nasser's socialist laws, nationalizations, and the illegality of foreign accounts, on which our business was built. Entering the city from the airport I felt a direct sense of being threatened, an insecurity so profound that it could only come, I thought, from the sense of our being torn up by the roots, such roots as we had in Egypt. Where would our family go?

A few days later the city's eternal rhythms—the people, the river, my Gezira Club acquaintances, even the traffic, certainly the Pyramids, which I could see from my bedroom window—had calmed my spirit. This was the East, I remember a friend of my parents saying, and things happen slowly. No abrupt changes. No surprises, although there were, ironically enough, new "Arab socialist" laws being promulgated daily. Contradictions and anxieties notwithstanding, I was lulled into the routine of going to my father's business every day, still, as ever, with very little actual work to do there. Then a postcard arrived from Chartres. It was from her, and two weeks later she asked if she could visit me in Cairo. It was bliss for me but after a week the Diana impulse asserted itself. "I must leave," she said, and would not be deterred. A few weeks later we were together again, and then we weren't, and so it continued.

When she went to Africa some months later, she had to come rushing back almost immediately because her brother had been taken ill. Three weeks later he was to die in her arms—of leukemia, a disease for which there was no effective therapy thirty years ago. It was the worst blow of her life, and although she returned to Africa for two more years I was not able to gauge accurately the profound extent and depth of her loss. Later we drifted apart, as I finished my graduate career, started work at Columbia, and married my first wife. When my marriage began to fall apart I returned to her, but my feelings for her had changed. All the years of waiting for my Diana had suddenly come to an end. She had been so intimate a part of my life, so necessary to my starved and repressed hidden self, that life without her, I had felt, was unimaginable. She seemed to speak directly to that underground part of my identity I had long held for myself, not the "Ed" or "Edward" I had been assigned, but the other self I was always aware of but was unable easily or immediately to reach. She seemed to have access to that part of me when I was with her, and then suddenly (actually, over a period of a few restful weeks in Lebanon) my becalmed spirit recognized that she and I could no longer go on. Our time was over. And so we did not continue.

I graduated from Princeton in June of 1957 with a pronounced case of German measles. My parents were there to watch the Phi Beta Kappa ceremony, and later to meet with some of my professors. Though I had done very well, my father persisted in asking my teachers whether in fact I had done my best, with a tone suggesting that I hadn't. My mother tried unsuccessfully to reassure me later how proud he was of my achievement (among them a fat fellowship to Harvard, which I deferred for a year). Most of the professors (as is their lamentable wont) mumbled something polite, whereas only Szathmary literally assaulted my nonplussed parents with a short diatribe on the philosophical nonsense contained in the logical (or rather illogical) form of the question "Did he do his best?" What a champion of critical thought he was, I thought glowingly, and how I wished I would be able to be one too.

So torn was I by differing impulses that I finally decided with my parents that I should have a year off to return to and sample the Cairo life I would lead if—there was always an "if" in my life then—I decided to take over the business. But the year (1957–58) turned out to end with a number of closed doors. No, I *could* not work in something my father owned and had created: it was his terrain and the dependency I felt was hateful to me. Money and property were two things I knew instinctively I could not win from him in a contest. During my Princeton and even graduate years at Harvard when he was still generously providing me with money, a disagreeable ordeal for me was the day of my return home. He would act agitated and uncomfortable around me until, to end his restlessness, he would say, "Edward, could we have our little talk?" For at least ten years "our talk" took the same form, duplicated exactly year after year. He would pull a piece of paper out of his pocket and read a figure, a sum in dollars, from it. "This year I sent you $4,356. How much do you have left?" Since I knew that I would have to answer the question once I got home, and since also I never kept records of what I spent, I would employ several anxious hours during the long plane journey back to the Middle East trying to make a list of my expenses, among which were tuition, room rent, and board. This sum always fell very far short of the total, so when I faced him I was left with a terrible sense of culpability and guilt, and felt relatively speechless, or silly. "You say you spent fifty dollars on haircuts. That still leaves fifteen hundred you haven't accounted for. Do you realize how hard I have to work to earn that money? How much do you have left in the bank?" he would then say, as if giving me an opportunity to redeem myself. Before leaving for the summer I had drawn out all but about ten dollars. He remonstrated irritatingly. And again and again until I was in my mid-twenties.

I could never reconcile this with his extraordinary generosity— paying for expensive piano lessons in Boston, letting me buy a car in Italy for a long European summer tour in 1958, including weeks spent at Bayreuth, Salzburg, Lucerne, and on and on. I felt that only by asking my mother to intercede could I get him to say yes, since his rapid-fire answer to any request I made was invariably negative; besides, I should confess that most of the time I was too timid, intimidated, embarrassed, to ask him myself. The fact is that he financed my education and my extracurricular undertakings and still I couldn't talk to him about money, nor did he like me to have too much of it.

It must also be said that my father clearly possessed an owner's sense, something I never acquired nor in a subtle, silent way, I believe, was ever allowed to acquire. Until the fall of Palestine he and his cousin Boulos's family (Boulos had died in 1939 or 1940) co-owned the businesses in Egypt and Palestine. During that time none of us, least of all my father, ever took anything from the showroom, not even a pencil, without signing for it. He was scrupulous about protecting *their* interests. Along with that scrupulosity went an unbridled anger at any sign of extravagance or heedless expenditure in us. For years and years— during which time his profits were based on enormous machine and furniture sales to the Egyptian government, the British army, and large corporations like Shell and Mobil Oil—he would fire at us, saying, "Do you realize how many pencils I have to sell before I can make the fifty piasters you squandered on cakes at the club?" I really believed this amazing fiction until I was about twenty-one; I clearly remember challenging him with "What pencils are you talking about? You don't sell pencils; you sell Monroe calculators and make thousands of pounds in one sale." That stopped him, although the sly smile on his face suggested to me that in spite of himself he enjoyed being bested that once.

Because he literally made the business and came to be its exclusive owner, my father was, and in every sense acted the part of, the sole proprietor. As a result, nothing escaped his scrutiny, no detail was too small for him to know about, no corner of his office, showrooms, factories, workshops was exempt from critical examination. Business started at eight a.m., ended for lunch at one, reopened at four (in summer, in winter at three-thirty) and shut at seven-thirty; Saturday was half-day, and Sunday the weekly holiday. My father always appeared at nine-thirty, never in the afternoon. On feast days he always had the American flag hoisted, a habit that infuriated a visiting American Orientalist whom I knew from Princeton, who lectured me (I don't think he was ever able to get past the various obstacles to actually see, much less meet, my father) on how inappropriate this was: "This is Egypt," he said tautologically. "Flying that flag is an insult to Egyptians." To his many Egyptian employees, however, my father seemed like a natural presence. He knew all his clients and in a pinch would appear and take over from a flagging salesman. But it was his powerfully impressive frame standing anywhere on the premises on Sharia Abdel Khalek Sarwat, or in his offices at Sharia Sherif, that communicated something I never ever possessed, a sense of deep, unchallengeable ownership.

I was the outsider, the passing stranger. Of course, all the staff, even the most senior, referred to me as "Mister Edward," but I always found the title both ludicrous and embarrassing. I could not refer to the SSCo with proprietary adjectives like "us" and "our," and I was never given any specific thing to do there. I felt that my father wanted me to work with him as his son, but it is extraordinary that during that entire year I would drive my car alone to the place at eight, spend the whole day in the shop and office, be there alone in the afternoon, and do all this without any specific assignment to fill, no job to get done, no department or service to be responsible for. I'd ask him for something to do on a regular basis and he would always say, "It's enough for me that you're there." Even my mother would once in a while remonstrate with this extraordinarily vague, even in a sense dismissive, idea of a mission—after all I *did* already have a Princeton B.A. and was a member of Phi Beta Kappa—but to no avail. "It's enough for me that you're there!"

By Christmas I started coming in to "work" in the morning later and later. I would spend my afternoons alone in his office while he was playing bridge at the club; I would either read—I remember I spent a week reading all through Auden, another leafing through the Pléiade edition of Alain, still another puzzling through Kierkegaard and Nietzsche, yet another reading Freud—or I would write poetry (some of which I published in Beirut), music criticism, or letters to various friends. By late January I started to stay home to practice the piano. My father, however, remained serenely unperturbed. I was far too uncertain to challenge him, and for reasons I still have not fully come to terms with, I didn't feel like the oldest, indeed the only, son, actually entitled to property from him. SSCo was never mine. He paid me what was then the considerable monthly salary of two hundred Egyptian pounds during that year and insisted that on the last day of each month I should stand in line with the other employees, sign the book (for tax purposes I was called "Edward Wadie"), and get my salary in cash. Invariably when I came home he would very courteously ask me for the money back, saying that it was a matter of "cash flow," and that I could have whatever money I needed. "Just ask," he said. And of course I dutifully did, ever in bondage to him.

It was his money, after all, his business, his work. Those facts made such an impression on me that I could only feel like a useless appendage to him, "the son," as I imagined his employees to be calling me. What came in and out of the business had nothing to do with me at all: I just happened to be there when I was, but the commerce continued as it had all along, without me. I was useful to him on occasion, most notably in the summer of 1960 when Nasser's "Arab socialism" meant that foreign hard-currency transactions and the imports that they were intended for were forbidden, and my father had to resort to complicated triple or quadruple barter export agreements, involving, say, Egyptian peanuts sold to Rumania, which in turn bought locomotives from France, which in turn allowed the additional export of franking machines to my father in Egypt. I tried to follow these arrangements, but could not: my father could do all the figuring in his head (plus conversion rates, commissions, fluctuating dollar prices) while his favorite middleman, Albert Daniel, would sit across from him with a pocket calculator. They would make the deal, and I would just watch, wondering how legal all this was, since it was clearly designed to circumvent the inconvenience and obstacles placed in the way of importers like my father. He had already made the switch to locally produced steel office furniture, for instance, but still needed to get hold of the raw material from abroad: for this, even more complicated machinations were necessary, but he was up to the task, and the materials were soon to be had.

I recall that he seemed to revel in the complexity of what he was doing, but his evident pleasure induced despondency and a considerable sense of inadequacy in me. I never had anything useful to add, since my father and Daniel were much too fast, too certain and deft in what they traded back and forth. Yet, one weekday afternoon my father made a rare call from the club; I was sitting in his office, reading a magazine, I think. "You're going to get some papers—a contract—delivered to you this afternoon. I want you to sign them and send them back to Daniel with the messenger." He explained that he had made me the principal because, he said, "After all, you're an executive too." It didn't seem like anything of great interest to me: here was I "just being there" for him, only occasionally performing what appeared to be a useful task or two. The contracts he had told me about were duly signed an hour later; I recall clearly not giving the transaction any further thought. Yet for the next fifteen years I was unable to return to Egypt because that particular contract, and I as its unsuspecting signatory, were ruled to be in contravention of the exchange-control law. My father told me that police officers came to his offices looking for me, one of them once threatening to have me brought back in handcuffs from abroad. But there, too, I did not for a very long time feel that my father was to blame for this surprising lapse by which he put his son up to do something basically illegal. I always assumed that the Egyptian police were to blame, and that it was their zeal, not my father's ostensible indifference to my fate, that had led to my being banned for fifteen years from the one city in the world in which I felt more or less at home.

Thus, our Cairo world started to close menacingly in on us, actually to come apart, as the Nasserite assault not only on the privileged classes but also on left dissidents like Farid Haddad opened up in earnest. I realized by my second year of graduate school (1959–60) after Farid's death and George Fahoum's trial for "business corruption," that our days as alien residents in Egypt were finally drawing to a close. A palpable air of anxiety and depression pervaded my family's circle of friends, most of whom were making plans to leave (which most of them did) for Lebanon or Europe.

MY FIVE YEARS (1958–63) AS A HARVARD GRADUATE STU-dent in literature were an intellectual continuation of Princeton so far as formal instruction was concerned. Conventional history and a wan formalism ruled the literary faculty, so in fulfilling my degree requirements there was no possibility of doing much beyond marching from period to period until the twentieth century. I recall hours, days, weeks, of voracious reading with no significant extension of that reading in what professors lectured on or what they expected from a largely passive student clientele. There was scarcely a ripple on the surface of student placidity, perhaps because, with no sense of intellectual example to animate our exertions, all of us were out of place, or uncomfortable in the institution. My own intellectual discoveries were made outside what the regimen required, alongside those of gifted originals who were also at Harvard, like Arthur Gold, Michael Fried, and Tom Carnicelli. The most momentous events for me, as the Middle East drifted further and further from my consciousness (after all, I did no reading in Arabic then, nor did I know any Arabs, except Ralph Nader, who was, unlike me, an American-born law student at Harvard, who helped me resist and finally evade the Selective Service draft at the time of the Berlin crisis in 1961), were such things as Vico's *New Science,* Lukacs's *History and Class Consciousness,* Sartre, Heidegger, Merleau-Ponty, all of whom shaped my dissertation on Conrad, written under the benign supervision of Monroe Engel and Harry Levin. Twice I tried to study under the aging I. A. Richards, the most avant-garde figure then at Harvard, and twice he defected from his courses just after the midpoint, when his secretary would enter and say that the course had been unilaterally dissolved. He was a comic miniaturization of the once-adventurous thinker—vague, vain, rambling—and as I read it, his major work struck me as thin and unaccomplished, as unprovocative as Blackmur's was stimulating and, despite its gnarled syntax, suggestive. There was occasional excitement from visitors, very few in those days, but I was stirred by Kenneth Burke's lectures on "logology," as he called it.

The most important musical influence on my life, even while I was at Harvard, was Ignace Tiegerman, a minuscule (four foot ten) Polish pianist, conservatory director, and teacher resident in Cairo since the mid-1930s. Very few musicians to my knowledge have had his gifts as pianist, teacher, and musician. A student of Lechetitzky and Ignaz Friedman, he came to Egypt on a cruise, loved it, and simply stayed, perfectly aware what the advent of Nazism would mean to Jews like him in Poland. He was endemically lazy, and when I knew him he had already stopped practicing and giving concerts. But he had the whole of the piano literature from mid-Beethoven to early Prokofiev in his head and fingers, and could play pieces like *Gaspard de la nuit* or the Chopin études in thirds and sixths fabulously well and with the utmost polish. As for late Brahms pieces, or Chopin nocturnes, mazurkas, and above all the Fourth Ballade and the Impromptus and Polonaise Fantaisie, no one I have ever heard played them as Tiegerman did, with

such perfection of tone and phrase, unfailingly "right" tempo, anago-
gies and all. He encouraged me more than I can adequately say, less by
what he said directly to me than by what he did on the second piano,
and by showing what in my playing (which he could mime perfectly)
might be modified. Above all he was a musical companion—not a hectoring or admonishing authority—for whom music was literally a part
of life in the sense that during our long conversations on hot Sunday
evenings in Cairo, or later in his little summer dacha in Kitzbühl, we
would drift naturally, meander, between periods of talk and periods at
the piano.

When it came to music, my interest in a professional career diminished as I found myself intellectually unsatisfied by the physical requirement of daily practice and very occasional performance. And, it must
be said, I realized that my gifts, such as they were, could never be adequate to the kind of professional trajectory I imagined for myself. Paradoxically, it was Tiegerman's example, living and acting inside me, that
finally discouraged me from making of the piano anything more than
sensuous pleasure, indulged in at a decent level of competence for the
rest of my life; I felt that there was a shadow line of raw ability I could
not cross separating the good amateur from the truly gifted executant,
someone like Tiegerman or Glenn Gould, whose Boston recitals I
attended between 1959 and 1962 with rapt admiration, for whom the
ability to transpose or read at sight, a perfect memory, and the total
coordination of hand and ear were effortless, whereas for me all that was
truly difficult, requiring much effort and in the end only a precarious,
uncertain achievement. Yet with my flamboyant friend, Afif (Alvarez)
Bulos, a former Jerusalemite about fifteen years older than I who was
studying for a degree in linguistics and who was, for those days, an
unusually colorful and almost parodistically mannered gay, I gave concerts, he with his good baritone, I on the piano. He was one of the rare
contemporaries from my Harvard days whom I continued to see in
Beirut, where he taught until his appallingly lurid death by stabbing in
the spring of 1982. It was a ghastly sign and premonition of the Israeli
invasion three months later, and of the Lebanese civil war raging furi-
ously all around where Afif lived in Ras Beirut.

In Cambridge, Afif and I used to practice where I lived, in the house
at the end of Francis Avenue of my gentle landlady Thais Carter, whose

daughter had been a Bryn Mawr classmate of Rosy's. Thais was a divorced, middle-aged woman who lived alone, except during the summer months, when her Florida-based father, Mr. Atwood, would come up to stay with her. She rented out two rooms on the top floor, one of which I lived in for three years, and where thanks to her understated wit, hospitality, and capacity for friendship, I was genuinely contented. Roughly my mother's age, Thais was patient where my mother was impetuous, methodical where my mother delighted in surprising and upsetting any method, quietly worldly where my mother was a unique combination of naïvete and busy sophistication. She and my mother became good friends, although a more contrasting pair of opposites could not be imagined. Thais easily tolerated and had an amused affection for Afif's flamboyant homosexuality, whereas Afif made my mother uncomfortable. I remember in 1959 telling her that Afif was homosexual and, to my astonishment, discovering that she had no idea what that meant, except that, like all mentions of sexuality, it made her shudder with apparent revulsion.

I still regarded her as my point of reference, mostly in ways that I neither fully apprehended nor concretely understood. In the summer of 1958, while driving in Switzerland, I had a horrendously bloody, head-on collision with a motorcyclist; he was killed and I was badly hurt. I can still recall with a jolt that awesomely loud and terrifyingly all-encompassing sound of the actual collision, which knocked me unconscious, and the very moment I awakened on the grass with a priest bending over me trying to administer the last rites. A moment later, after pushing away the intrusive cleric, with infallible instinct I knew I had to call my mother, who at that very moment was in Lebanon with the rest of my family. She was the first person to whom I needed to tell my story, which I did the moment the ambulance delivered me to the Fribourg hospital. That feeling I had of both beginning and ending with my mother, of her sustaining presence and, I imagined, infinite capacity for cherishing me, softly, imperceptibly, underwrote my life for years and years. At a time when I was myself going through radical change—intellectual, emotional, political—I felt that my mother's idealized person, her voice, her enveloping maternal care and attention, were what I truly could depend on. When I divorced my first wife, the terrible confusion I felt was, I believed, best sorted out by my mother, despite her extraordinary ambivalence, which I either overlooked or overrode: "If things are so bad between you, then, yes, by all means you should divorce." This was followed immediately by "On the other hand, for us [Christians] marriage is permanent, a sacrament, holy. Our church will never recognize divorce." These were statements that often paralyzed me completely.

Yet I managed for years to get past her irresolution, and reach the sustenance she gave me, especially after I lost Cairo, behind which I began to realize more and more was the continuing loss of Palestine in our lives and those of other relatives'. And 1967 brought more dislocations, whereas for me it seemed to embody *the* dislocation that subsumed all the other losses, the disappeared worlds of my youth and upbringing, the unpolitical years of my education, the assumption of disengaged teaching and scholarship at Columbia, and so on. I was no longer the same person after 1967; the shock of that war drove me back to where it had all started, the struggle over Palestine. I subsequently entered the newly transformed Middle Eastern landscape as a part of the Palestinian movement that emerged in Amman and then in Beirut in the late sixties through the seventies. This was an experience that drew on the agitated, largely hidden side of my prior life—the anti-authoritarianism, the need to break through an imposed and enforced silence, above all the need to draw back to a sort of original state of what was irreconcilable, thereby shattering and dispelling an unjust Establishment order. Some of my mother's frenetic restlessness was a reaction to my father's loss, and to the many bewildering changes around her as the PLO grew in size and importance in Beirut along with the Lebanese civil war. She lived through the Israeli invasion of 1982, for instance, with admirable good humor and fortitude, taking care of a house in which my youngest sister, Grace, lived, plus two homeless friends, Ibrahim Abu-Lughod and Sohail Meari, whose apartment had been gutted by an Israeli rocket early in the war. It was an amazing display of bravery under fire. Yet when I tried to talk to her about politics, *my* dissenting politics in particular, or the complex political realities that caused the daily problems of her life since her marriage, she would upbraid me: go back to being a literary man; politics in the Arab world destroy honest and good people like you, and so on.

It took years after the end of my formal education for me to realize how much she had, whether by design or instinct I shall never know, insinuated herself not just into our affairs as four sisters and a brother, but also between us. My sisters and I still live with the consequences of her redoubtable skills, all of them resulting in prickly barriers between us, fed, to be sure, by other sources as well, but first erected by her. Some of those barriers are immovable, which I regret. Perhaps they exist in all families. But I also realize now that our odd family cocoon back then was no model for future lives, nor was the world we lived in. I think my father must have sensed that, when at inordinate expense he did the totally unheard-of thing and sent four of us to the United States (my sisters for college only) for our education; the more I think about it, the more I believe he thought the only hope for me as a man was in fact to be cut off from my family. My search for freedom, for the self beneath or obscured by "Edward," could only have begun because of that rupture, so I have come to think of it as fortunate, despite the loneliness and unhappiness I experienced for so long. Now it does not seem important or even desirable to be "right" and in place (right at home, for instance). Better to wander out of place, not to own a house, and not ever to feel too much at home anywhere, especially in a city like New York, where I shall be until I die.

During the last few months of my mother's life, she would tell me plaintively and frequently about the misery of trying to fall asleep. She was in Washington, I in New York; we would speak constantly, see each other about once a month. Her cancer was spreading, I knew. She refused to have chemotherapy: *"Ma biddee at^cadthab,"* she would say, "I don't want the torture of it." Years later I was to have four wasting years of it with no success, but she never buckled, never gave in even to her doctor's importunings, never had chemotherapy. But she could not sleep at night. Sedatives, sleeping pills, soothing drinks, the counsel of friends and relatives, reading, praying: none, she said, did any good. "Help me to sleep, Edward," she once said to me with a piteous trembling in her voice that I can still hear as I write. But then the disease spread into her brain, and for the last six weeks she slept all the time. Waiting by her bed for her to awaken, with my sister Grace, was for me the most anguished and paradoxical of my experiences with her.

Now I have divined that my own inability to sleep may be her last legacy to me, a counter to her struggle *for* sleep. For me sleep is something to be gotten over as quickly as possible. I can only go to bed very late, but I am up literally at dawn. Like her I don't possess the secret of long sleep, though unlike her I have reached the point where I do not want it. For me, sleep is death, as is any diminishment in awareness. During my last treatment—a twelve-week ordeal—I was most upset by the drugs I was given to ward off fever and shaking chills, and manifestly upset by the induced somnolence, the sense of being infantilized, the helplessness that many years ago I had conceded as that of a child to my mother and, differently, to my father. I fought the medical soporifics bitterly, as if my identity depended on that resistance even to my doctor's advice.

Sleeplessness for me is a cherished state to be desired at almost any cost; there is nothing for me as invigorating as immediately shedding the shadowy half-consciousness of a night's loss, than the early morning, reacquainting myself with or resuming what I might have lost completely a few hours earlier. I occasionally experience myself as a cluster of flowing currents. I prefer this to the idea of a solid self, the identity to which so many attach so much significance. These currents, like the themes of one's life, flow along during the waking hours, and at their best, they require no reconciling, no harmonizing. They are "off" and may be out of place, but at least they are always in motion, in time, in place, in the form of all kinds of strange combinations moving about, not necessarily forward, sometimes against each other, contrapuntally yet without one central theme. A form of freedom, I'd like to think, even if I am far from being totally convinced that it is. That skepticism too is one of the themes I particularly want to hold on to. With so many dissonances in my life I have learned actually to prefer being not quite right and out of place.

A NOTE ABOUT THE AUTHOR

Edward W. Said is University Professor of English and Comparative Literature at Columbia University. He is the author of seventeen books, including *Orientalism*, which was nominated for the National Book Critics Circle Award, *Culture and Imperialism, Representations of the Intellectual*, and *The Politics of Dispossession*.